Dreams in Group Psychotherapy

INTERNATIONAL LIBRARY OF GROUP ANALYSIS 18

Dreams in Group Psychotherapy
Theory and Technique

*Edited by Claudio Neri, Malcolm Pines
and Robi Friedman*

*Forewords by Sabar Rustomjee and
Walter N. Stone*

Jessica Kingsley Publishers
London and Philadelphia

First published in the United Kingdom in 2002
by Jessica Kingsley Publishers Ltd
116 Pentonville Road
London N1 9JB, England
and
325 Chestnut Street
Philadelphia, PA 19106, USA

www.jkp.com

Copyright © 2002 Jessica Kingsley Publishers

Library of Congress Cataloging in Publication Data
A CIP catalog record for this book is available from the Library of Congress

British Library Cataloguing in Publication Data
A CIP catalogue record for this book is available from the British Library

ISBN 1 85302 923 8

Printed and Bound in Great Britain by
Athenaeum Press, Gateshead, Tyne and Wear

Contents

Foreword

This book edited by three eminent group psychotherapists – Robi Friedman, Claudio Neri and Malcolm Pines – is the most integrated text on 'dreams' that has, as yet, been published. Its depth and richness lies in the diverse frameworks in which dreams are conceptualised by eighteen authors coming from seven different countries.

A dream being a transient encounter by the dreamer of his or her repressed wishes, fears, hopes, inhibitions and conflicts provides a fertile soil for exploring not only the unconscious of the dreamer, but also the 'here and now' setting in which the dream is presented.

How the group, along with its conductor, is able to recognise, hold, contain and respond to the raw emotions expressed in a dream, along with the transference of the dreamer to the group, is an art in its own right. Such work is actualised only after years of experience and a very sound underlying theoretical framework.

This book, in providing innumerable examples of this, has reached far beyond the primary aim described by its very modest title 'Dreams in Group Psychotherapy: Theory and Technique'.

Dr Sabar Rustomjee
President, International Association of Group Psychotherapists

Foreword

Dreams! What do we dream about? Who do we dream about? What influences our dreams? Certainly our minds do not stop when we close our eyes and fall asleep. As group clinicians our task is to find ways of making the best therapeutic use of members' or participants' dreams. Dreams became a focus for scientific study with Freud's landmark study *The Interpretation of Dreams*, published at the turn of the twentieth century. Now, more than a hundred years later, comes a monograph focused on dreams reported in group settings.

The primary focus of this book is the examination of dreams in a spectrum of group settings. Dreams are seen not only from the perspective of the dreamer's inner life, but as a way of conveying information about the impact of the dynamics of the group and the broader social environment as they may be impacting upon the dreamer. The reader will traverse an array of chapters examining this broader communicative nature of dreams, while not neglecting the individual.

It is no surprise that the therapist and the other members appear directly or only thinly disguised in the manifest dream content. The dreamer is no longer the sole owner of the dream, but in presenting dreams in the group context, shares with others, who in turn become participants in a new drama. Communication processes reverberate among the individuals and their image of the group. Dreams can be seen as co-constructed, as part of intersubjective processes present within the group, as part of a matrix, or as a vehicle to evacuate unacceptable aspects of the self into others (projective identification).

These formulations expanding the focus from the individual to consider-ations of the context are reminiscent of the evolution of group therapy in the United States. The major historical trends of group therapy, consistent with the broader American culture of individualism, began with the transporting of individual psychoanalytic concepts into the group setting, with a relative omission of group dynamics (Slavson 1957). Group-as-a-whole approaches were more slowly accepted into clinicians' practice (Whitaker and Lieberman 1964). Integrative efforts followed, modifying the austerity of the Bionian approach (Malan *et al.*1976) with interpersonal and relational considerations (Yalom 1970; Horwitz 1977).

The social aspects of dreams presented in a group setting are highlighted in a shift in focus from the individual to the cultural and social context. 'Social dreaming', in specifically designated groups, in large group settings, or in acting of dreams in psychodrama, serves to highlight the intersubjective, interactive and socio-cultural underpinnings of group reported dreams.

Technical aspects of working with dreams in the broader context are explicated. Interpretations, particularly those made very quickly by others, are seen as resistances to understanding the communicative processes. Instead, members are encouraged to provide their own associations. This is particularly striking in techniques that include acting, and the spontaneous modifications of the dream portrayed by an actor. Thus, the expansion from the efforts in dyadic therapy to gain insight into the intrapsychic functioning of one individual to processes that may have both interpersonal and group focused meaning for the entire membership.

The basic science of dreaming is not neglected. The discovery of dreams primarily occurring during rapid eye movement sleep stages, and subsequent ability to wake individuals during or immediately following their dream, began investigations of the biology of dreaming. We are perhaps on the cusp of understanding connections between biology and psychology, which at this time remain poorly integrated. Psychological theories explicating the meaning of dreams did not stop with Freud. Particularly intriguing, in this respect, is Grotstein's annotation of Bion's contributions to the theory of dreaming. Bion, within his particular lexicon, theorises that dreams convert 'unmentalized emotional experiences' (beta elements) into images that in their recounting contain conscious and unconscious elements, a formulation distinctly different from that of Freud.

This book is not monothematic. We are certainly aware that one size does not fit all. We need multiple perspectives to work with our patients and our groups. The richness of the contributions does not lead to 'easy' reading. The effort involved, I expect, would require repeated excursions into many of these essays. The effort will be well rewarded by the reader's increasing grasp of the manifold ideas related to the understanding and use of dreams in group settings.

Walter N. Stone

Past President, International Association of Group Psychotherapists

References

Horwitz, L. (1977) 'The group centered approach to group psychotherapy.' *International Journal of Group Psychotherapy 27*, 423–440.

Malan, D.H., Balfour, F.H.G., Hood, V.G. and Shooter, A. (1976) 'Group psychotherapy:

A long term follow-up study.' *Archives of General Psychiatry 33*, 1303–1315.

Slavson, S.R. (1957) 'Are there group dynamics in therapy groups?' *International Journal of Group Psychotherapy 7*, 115–130.

Whitaker, D.S. and Lieberman, M.A. (1964) *Psychotherapy through The Group Process.* New York: Atherton Press.

Yalom, I.D. (1970) *The Theory and Practice of Group Psychotherapy. First Edition.* New York: Basic Books.

Introduction

Robi Friedman, Claudio Neri and Malcolm Pines

The idea for this book was born during a meeting on a Roman terrace one sunny afternoon after a congress about 'Dreams and the Group'. The three future editors of this book – relaxing with drinks in hand, chatting about this, that and the recent scientific meetings – concluded that the congress had been very interesting. But their strongest impression was that they were starting rather than ending a journey of exploration.

It was clear to them that although the dream theme strongly links group psychotherapy to Freud's psychoanalytical tradition, dealing with the dream in the group context goes far beyond psychoanalytical paradigms. The most ancient traditions had addressed dreams in order to decipher the future as representing a different level of 'reality', essential to living contemporary social life in a richer, more creative way.

Soon afterwards, Friedman, Neri and Pines found themselves with paper and pen in hand, planning the outline for a book. The plan was to systematically cover different aspects of the complex relationship between the group, dreams, psychotherapy and contemporary reality. The result – the actual book – is very different. It seems less organised, but richer. While this dream book did not become a handbook, as with daily residues, it ended up collecting selected contributions from psychotherapists and researchers from three continents and seven nations.

We – Friedman, the Israeli; Neri, the Italian; and Pines, the Englishman – were in constant communication with each other and discussed the book from a distance. It is hard to imagine achieving the task without the help of email. This new way of communicating, which facilitates sending and receiving messages, shows a strong resemblance to magical processes. For us, the almost instant interaction and feedback from such distances was a dream come true.

The final meeting took place a year later in Haifa, on another terrace, overlooking Mount Carmel National Park. Following Jerusalem's IGPA (International Group Psychotherapy Association) congress, we gathered in order to talk and tour the Jordan Valley and the northern part of Israel during what was still a peaceful situation.

This book draws attention to long-neglected ways of understanding and using dreams. For many centuries, the dream's individual functions have overshadowed its communicative functions in the group or community. From our contemporary perspective, some of these very ancient approaches are worth recovering. Already in the second century B.C., Artemidorus (of Daldia), who, like Freud, wrote a book called *The Interpretation of Dreams*, described the interpretation of dreams for the individual. Both Artemidorus and Freud applied assumptions leading to an individual, rather than a communal, approach to dreams.

Within the urbanised world of the classical Mediterranean – Mesopotamia, Egypt, Israel, and Greece – dreams became items for individual attention rather than group concern. They were regarded as messages to individual dreamers. Being previously transparent and influential within the shared life of the group, the language of the dream now became obscure: the dream bore a significant message, but for that message to be understood, an interpretation was needed. Thus the dream specialist emerged. The need for expertise to interpret the personal unconscious and decode condensation and displacement resulting from intrapsychic 'day's residues' was one of the main contributions of this development. As Artemidorus puts it: 'A man will not dream about things to which he has never given a thought.' Both Artemidorus and Freud assume the existence of a split between the individual's conscious and unconscious. Both privilege allegorical dreams containing multilevel images. And both use the concept of the 'day's residues', already a common topic in Epicurean literature. Dreams were no longer a vehicle of unconscious attunement within the group, possibly requiring a collective response, but rather revealed the fate of the individuated dreamer.

Before the change in Mesopotamia and Egypt (and to this day in many tribal cultures), dreams, like myths, were not only told on a regular basis, but were seriously discussed to ascertain what they 'meant', what event or development they augured, or what state of the spiritual surroundings they reflected. Because the group shared so much through symbols, language, and culture, its members were able to 'read' the significance of a dream without a specialist's assistance. Their ritual specialists were aware of the multiplicity of voices of the communal symbols, but their interpretative discourse was to accentuate, illuminate, integrate and elaborate dreams by poetic resonance rather than to disenchant them. Dream interchange facilitated the adjustment of group members to each other and became especially beneficial in those areas where cooperation and interdependence had to proceed easily, unreflectively and harmoniously. It contributed to tribal life, which demanded collective confrontation of harsh living, hunting and, on occasion, fighting as a unit, entrusting their lives to one another.

The majority of the contributors in this book think that a recounted dream not only increases the group's empathy and harmony but also permits a shared encounter. Joint work may facilitate any previously blocked personal autonomous growth, as well as enrich the group atmosphere. The social approach to dreams is represented in this volume by two contributions: Traveni and Manfredi (Italy) believe the Large Group itself contains some dream characteristics. In both there is not only a frightening momentary loss of identity, but a concurrent access to a complex, multidimensional representation of the 'external' collective, the social unconscious and the individual experience. The therapist may facilitate the establishment of common thought through continuous recalling of memory material, primary and transgenerational links.

The second contribution is the discussion by Lawrence (United Kingdom) and Biran (Israel) about complementary aspects of social dreaming and therapeutic dreaming. Social dreaming is 'the currency of the matrix', not the participants' relationship nor transference to the conductors of the matrix. Only the authority figures in-the-mind that are given flesh in the dreams are important. In social dreaming one 'has to enter a non-therapeutic state of mind'.

The theory of dreams 'occupies a special place in the history of psychoanalysis and marks a turning point. With it analysis took the step from being a psychotherapeutic procedure to being a depth psychology' (Freud 1932, p.7). In 1900, *The Interpretation of Dreams* disclosed the nature of unconscious mental processes. Freud considered dreams to be symptoms of a conflict with a hidden meaning, the disguised fulfilment of a wish, and the means through which the dreamer copes with drives and reality. The 'royal road to a knowledge of the unconscious activities of the mind' consisted of primary and secondary elaboration of latent emotions into manifest content, and disguising mechanisms like condensation, repression, displacement and symbolic representation.

In this volume, Avron (France), in keeping with Freud's explanatory model of basic infantile drives, describes group participants as trying to re-establish situations of primary satisfaction through hallucinatory representations. Through the stimulation of a shared creation – the scenic exposition of the dream – and its receptivity, a non-conscious capacity for basic energy reciprocity can further dialogue and cooperation in therapy. Avron approaches scenic structure and function as an active whole, the dream's sexual energy pushing towards the object of their desire, giving the group an impetus to new organisations of transference dynamics and inter-linking processes.

From a different perspective, Puget (Argentina) considers dreams to have the power of generating unconscious material through their disorganising influence. The group's encounters with the dream's incoherence and consequent anxieties of the unpredictable and fragmentation gradually builds its unconscious. Regarding the dream space as an event, a beginning of the group's attempts to complete the dream thoughts which may further the emergence of a new organisation.

Resnik (Argentina/France) considers telling a dream a transference event, referring always to the analytic session. The therapist should behave like an archaeologist, discovering fragments of either a disintegrated or not yet integrated language. Dream thinking is developed through under-standing the dream stage grammar and the dream's theatre significance. The group members mutually help one another through Foulkes's 'mirroring', by functioning as lead-backed mirrors, proposing different perspectives on the 'unavoidable problem' from which the dreamer and the other patients try hard to escape. Understanding and repairing meaningful dissonance are considered to be the ingredients in the dreamer's and the group's therapy.

Another very important point in Freud's hypothesis regards the dream as the sleep keeper through stimuli-reducing mechanisms. He also maintained, however, that dreams endeavour to cope with stimuli retrospectively, in line with Ferenczi's approach to dreams as 'attempts at better mastery and settling of traumatic experiences' (Ferenczi 1931, p.238). These were the forerunners of most subsequent considerations of dreaming as mental unconscious coping, and as part of 'thinking' (Meltzer 1980). The dream can be compared to children's play and drama, considering dream-work as self-revealing projections of the self. Dreams are relatively protected transitional spaces (Winnicott 1970) in which a child grows through the creative staging of inner plays. They have a 'psychic envelope' giving a safe boundary. It is imperative to create and protect these playful spaces, differentiating between sleep and waking life, between internal and external objects. Moreover, the dream can be considered a coping process by which the dreamer tries to get rid of unacceptable or unbearable feelings (Flanders 1993).

Neurophysiological evidence gathered by REM research corroborated much of these findings, and is described in this book in Lavie's chapter (Israel) and in Schlachet's paper (USA).

Further order may be made by ascribing various aspects of dream and dreaming to a one- or a relational two-person psychology, i.e. studying communication as descriptions of intrapsychic processes or interactions between people. Of course, these perspectives are more complementary than mutually exclusive.

Sandor Ferenczi has probably been a pioneer in understanding dreams in a relational context: he locates their genesis in intersubjective space and sees dream-telling as often being a communication to an audience. In his clinical diary he writes: 'The patient feels that this dream fragment is a combination of the unconscious contents of the psyches of the analysand and the analyst' (Ferenczi 1932, p.13). Earlier in a short article with the poignant title of 'To whom does one relate one's dreams' he states: 'One feels impelled to relate one's dreams to the very person to whom the content relates' (Ferenczi 1913, p.349).

An expansion on dream-telling as a second chance to further elaborate unsuccessfully processed dream material through the help of an audience is central in Friedman's paper (Israel). Dreaming and dream-telling represent two distinct developmental phases: a first autonomous step is attempted through projective identification[1] mechanisms during dreaming itself, and may be followed in a second elaborative effort by dream-telling, considered an interpersonal request for containment. Friedman also discusses the dream material and the diagnostic value of dream-telling. Together with many authors in this volume, Friedman maintains that dreams further the conscious and unconscious communication of messages, informing about the sender's state while having a transforming influence on both the receiver and the sender.

Kaës (France) deals mainly with 'polyphony' and intersubjectivity in dreams which are either born out of the associative process in a group, or told by an individual analysand representing a group in his manifest content. Traumatic events which had remained unthought (meaningless) are elaborated by one or more dreamers at the intersection of their own dreaming apparatuses, through resonance with phantoms, depersonalization anxiety and confusion of identity. Kaës's new proposition is that the dream is a representation of desires and conflicts, which intersect the subject's identification composition or 'code'. Conversations heard from different sources are woven into the texture of the dream. The dream is not a closed statement: it becomes a transformation process as it is acted and addressed.

According to the late Peter Schlachet, patients narrate their dreams for the therapist. In the group everyone is the intended audience, and telling a dream becomes a relational-social event. Through 'going to the movies', the metaphorical pictorial nature of our dreams' inner states, needs, feelings and subjective experiences are communicated in an interpersonal event.

Bion's many important contributions to the understanding of dream-work have been synthesised for this book by Grotstein (USA). Central is the concept of 'dream-work alpha' which marks the transition from a one-person to a two-person psychoanalytical model, i.e. the 'container/contained' unit. The analyst must dream the analysand. Bion believed that reciprocal dream-work between analyst and analysand results in the 'alpha-bet(a)-ization' of raw emotion, which is responsible for thinking. Grotstein considers this concept the main launching pad for the postmodern concept of intersubjectivity.

Rutan and Rice's (USA) use of the concept of 'projective identification' re-emphasises the influencing and transforming aspects of the dynamics of container/contained perspectives in group therapy. If the therapist leaves the dreams' adaptive task as container of both individual and collective anxieties unattended, they can lead to acting in or acting out.

Solomon (USA) describes Tavistock's characteristic 'group-as-a-whole' approach, which places the individual's dynamic in the background. Conductors should always try to objectively describe the group's ongoing process in the here and now, often focusing on Bion's basic assumptions and challenging participants' roles. For Solomon, dreams represent these 'common group tensions' and should be stated rather than interpreted.

Livingston (USA) considers the dream a part of the playful and metaphorical communication between analyst and patient. In line with Kohut's selfpsychology, the therapist (and the group) should attempt to remain close to the patient's subjective experience of the dream, the curative process considered to be empathic attunement. The therapist, balancing between responsiveness and reaction, helps cope with 'self-state' dreams.

In her comments on this paper, Harwood (USA) emphasises that therapists should help distinguish between 'self-state' dreams, requesting organisation and working through, and dreams with a more informational character (transference, problem-solving, memory-evoking, etc.).

Marinelli's (Italy) 'dual-faced' dreams – defined as those with less symbolic quality – are in need of a protective skin around them in order to better endure unprocessed pains and losses. The manifest dream represents the dreamer's individual features, the group's transference concerns and sociopolitical issues. Therapy achieves transformation by facilitating 'protomental' states of confusion, and fantasy representations of somatic and psychic events.

A patient once remarked that when a dream is told it is as if a new member is introduced into the group. This volume is about addressing this 'new member', understanding the complexity of its presence and its contents, and using it for the well-being and growth of the individual, the group and society. Group analysis needs technical revisions in order to make sure that dreams are properly encountered, coped with and used for integration and further individual and group development.

Telling dreams in a group may not be an easy task for a number of reasons. From the outset, the sheer size of the group renders dream-telling and working with dreams different than in a dyadic setting. Dreams, usually messages about intimate matters, may initially encounter neither a receptive nor a discreet audience. The fate of the dreams may be rejection, although intended as requests for containment, resulting in potential narcissistic injuries inflicted on the dream-tellers. Individual therapists may readily accept and even encourage the inclusion of the inner world's most dreadful representations in dreams, whereas in a group there is no guarantee of secure reception of such representations. As an audience, participants may not feel bound to automatically contain every kind of material. Even dream material with strong relevance and relation to the group may engender strong resistance because of the unacceptability of possible group-as-a-whole self-images and other configurations.

While eventual difficulties in group work with dreams are described, many articles in this book emphasise the advantages of the group's coping with loaded dreams. From a technical point of view, all contributors seem to agree unanimously that the therapist should build some sort of secure space by helping the group develop norms of associating to dreams rather than 'interpreting' them.

Pines (United Kingdom), in this volume, gives a *tour d'horizon*, ranging between the individual's approach to dreams in groups, and their social aspects. The dialogue between representational/informational and transformational functions of the dream is synthesised in the notion of the 'widening of vision'. Pines believes that dreaming 'in concert' is the next step to the ecology of mind in our next millennium.

Neri (Italy) describes Fabiana's long group-analytic process, with special focus on two dreams and one dreamlike event. The group transforms the patients' states of mind through gathering up, naming and giving sense, while the analyst helps cope with the unknown and with 'lack of sense'. Together, they help Fabiana find a more secure, alive and balanced identity.

A very interesting contribution comes from Greece. Tsegos and Tseberlidou's supervision approach to dreams in groups consists of recorded formats of presentation, analysis and synthesis, in which mirroring crystallises into fantasies, feelings and main topics.

Common to every one of the papers collected in this volume is the close connection between clinical and theoretical thinking. We believe that this link strengthens a reliable approach to group psychotherapy. The editors – Friedman, Neri and Pines – hope that *Dream and Group Psychotherapy* will contribute to the reader's individual integrative and creative work with dreams in the group setting.

The book ends with a comprehensive index and a glossary composed of entries regarding dreams and psychoanalytic theory, group psychotherapy and group psychology. These apparatuses make it a useful tool for consultation purposes.

References

Aron, L. (1989) 'Dreams, narrative, and the psychoanalytic method.' *Contemporary Psychoanalysis 25*, 108–126.

Casement, P. (1991) *Learning from the Patient.* New York: Guilford Press.

Ferenczi, S. (1913) 'To whom does one relate one's dreams.' In *Further Contributions to the Theory and Techniques of Psychoanalysis.* New York: Bruner/Mazel.

Ferenczi, S. (1932/1988) *The Clinical Diary of Sandor Ferenczi.* (ed. J. Dupont) Cambridge, MA: Harvard University Press.

Flanders, S. (1993) *The Dream Discourse Today.* London and New York: Routledge.

Freud, S. (1900) *The Interpretation of Dreams. Standard Edition 4/5.* London: Hogarth Press.

Freud, S. (1932) 'Revision of The Interpretation of Dreams.' Lecture XXXV, New Introductory Lecture, Standard Edition 22.

Joseph, B. (1985) 'Transference: the total situation.' *International Journal of Psychoanalysis 66,* 447–54.

Langs, R.J. (1978) *The Listening Process.* New York: Aronson.

Meltzer, D. (1983) *Dream-Life.* Worcester: Clunie Press.

Murray, L.W. (1999) 'The angel of dreams: Toward an ethnology of dream interpreting.' *Journal of the American Academy of Psychoanalysis 27,* 3, 417–30.

Ogden, T.H. (1996) 'Reconsidering three aspects of psychoanalytic technique.' *International Journal of Psychoanalysis 77,* 883–99.

Palombo, S.R. (1992) 'The Eros of dreaming.' *International Journal of Psychoanalysis 73,* 637–46.

Wilson de Armas, D. (1993) quoted in Murray, L.W. (1999) 'The angel of dreams: Toward an ethnology of dream interpreting.' *Journal of the American Academy of Psychoanalysis 27,* 3, 417–30.

Winnicott, D.W. (1971) *Playing and Reality.* London: Tavistock Publications.

Endnote

1. The dynamics of projective identification (or any other concepts of a similar interpersonal – intersubjective process) help clarify how information turns into transformation. Freud's view of the dream and its interpretation as the 'royal road to the unconscious' of the patient seems to belong to the representation/information pole of an imagined communication continuum. Levenson (1991), who describes patients' dreams portraying dramatic situations paralleled by the interaction with the therapist, takes a middle position on the communication continuum. The information helps analysts deduce how to extract themselves from neurotic interactions with the patient, leading patients to discover new coping strategies. Joseph (1985) goes even further on the continuum, suggesting that dreams have a tendency to be unconsciously staged and enacted in reality. She describes how 'a dream can reveal its meaning in a fairly precise way by being lived out in the session' (p.451). Ogden (1996) seems to go all the way to the continuum's end by implying that an analyst's understanding of a patient's dream is born in the 'analytic third' (the intra-analytic shared space) through his intersubjective experience.

CHAPTER 1

The Illumination of Dreams

Malcolm Pines

We are such stuff as dreams are made on.

Shakespeare

In solitude we have our dreams to ourselves and in company we agree to
dream in concert.

Samuel Johnson

The history and lineage of dreams is ancient, mysterious and revelatory.
Dreams have been used for prophecy, fortune-telling, for access to the spirit
world and for extending our vision beyond our diurnal limits. Ancient Greece
sought healing through sleep and dreams; Bion asserts the psychotic halluci-
nates because he cannot dream, cannot use normal dream work; Kohut and
self psychologists see dreams as revealing the unconscious state of the self,
giving the therapist an opportunity to aid in self-healing.

Freud's view of dreams has dominated during this century. 'Dreams are
not in themselves social utterances, not a means of giving information', the
dream is an intrapsychic phenomenon which has sleep-preserving functions,
censoring unacceptable psychic contents. Dreams can be decoded by the
expert in the psychology of the unconscious. *Dreams are democratic* because
Oedipal creatures all, we constantly recycle our childhood adventures and
tragedies. In his 'revolutionary' dreams, Freud, the rebellious poor subject in
the Austrian empire together with its arrogant prime minister Count Thun,
are both translated into an Oedipal father–son dyad: social context is
banished, the intrapsychic empire of the family is superimposed onto the
imperial hierarchy. Freud's *dream-work is democratic*: 'Parricide replaces

25

regicide' (Schorske). However, society re-enters the dreamworld in 1913 when Ferenczi asks 'To whom does one relate one's dreams?'.

Dream-telling, the search for the other to whom one can tell the dream, transcends Freud's autonomous intrapsychic dream model. Indeed anthropologists have shown us cultures where dreams are given great importance, are told each morning in the family circle of scenes of communications with the spirit world (Schlachet, this volume).

In a striking phrase Jung writes: 'The dream is a little hidden door in the innermost and most secret recesses of the soul opening into that cosmic night which was psyche long before there was any ego-consciousness.' For Jung the dream comes from the more universal, truer, more whole self, bearer of egohood. Later we shall see how this concept of the dream possessing an unifying capacity has been taken on in social dream-matrix workshops, initiated by W. Gordon Lawrence (this volume).

Group analysts are aware of the universal, pervasive, powerful impact of context and setting. Whatever is experienced, said, whether attended to or ignored, has meaningful connections to the situation, both in the here and now and in its resonance to the there and then. Thus the dream remembered – brought to the group, whether explained, ignored, associated to, amplified, interpreted – belongs to the group context. Does the dreamer dream for herself or for the group? In respect of dreams in the group, Foulkes was still a follower of Freud, who wrote that dreams are not in themselves social utterances, not a means of giving information. Note that Freud here speaks from his one-body intrapsychic model, in contradiction to his later acknowledgement that all psychology is both individual and social. Foulkes (1984, pp.165–6) writes: 'The dream is particularly an individual creation, not meant for publication, for communication to others. The self, as Freud has shown us, refused to accept it even as an internal intra-individual communication.' Foulkes, however, contradicted himself by saying that we should treat the dream like any other communication; according it a dynamic significance. Every dream told in the group is the property of the group, which has a fine intuition to distinguish between 'group dreams' and other dreams which can be presented as resistances. The dream can shed light on the group situation, on the group as a whole, can be an unconscious reflection on group occurrences.

Foulkes considered that the manifest content of dreams relates to the ongoing transference situation; this is the way in which the positive use of dreaming comes into the group situation: dream as told to the group is left to the group to analyse. Often the dreamer reports events in his dream which shed light on his own situation, in particular in relation to the group, on the group as a whole, on events going on in the group and his unconscious reflections on occurrences in the group. This is a valuable aspect of dreaming in group analysis and has to be differentiated from the telling of dreams as a resistance, representing withdrawal from human contact.

So far we have looked at and been confined within the intrapsychic and autonomous model of the dream. Yet within this model, from the object of relations perspective, there is always an internalised group so that the dynamic processes are often recognisable in the theme of the group where the presence of intrapsychic others may threaten or may offer safety to the dreamer. The internal object is used for projection or evacuation of intolerable psychic conflicts so that the dream is an effort to make use of a 'not-me personification'; this is not my murderous aggression, but that of the other who attacks me.

The dream is also an attempt to find a container for the conflicted self, to give recognition and expression to our cultures of psychic forces. How often in a dream do we seek a home for ourselves, just as in childhood we seek security in the arms of parents. Here I recall Freud writing about the child in the dark bedroom calling for the parents, who says that when he hears the parents' voice he feels safe because the light goes on.

Claudio Neri (this volume) has written of the common space of the group, as an imaginary stage by which the participants' fantasies are formed (Resnik, *The Theatre of the Dream*). Neri wisely reminds us that the fact that a patient brings a dream to the group does not imply that the dream becomes a group dream. Sometimes, the group is there to receive a dream with the dreamer making a gift, a fragment of childhood or a precious photo from the family album. But in other dreams it is the group that is in the foreground with the story of the individual in the background.

The imaginative space of the group can represent a fantasy of the interior of the maternal body, a rich space of creativity and a stimulus to imaginative curiosity. In group fantasies and dreams exploration of these obscure spaces becomes part of the group process. Dreams, fantasies and imaginative speculation are ways in which self can be represented in the group.

Any member of the group, or of a social dreaming matrix, may tell a dream with the aim of revealing an inner experience to an audience. This is dream-telling, a narrative. The group's response may be disinterest, evasion; a dreamer in one of my groups was told that before the group could give attention and understanding to his dream, he had himself to become a more responsive and understanding member of the group, moving from his position of self-isolation and self-destruction. Thus the response to his inter-personal relationships is the response to his dream. Other dreams may be welcomed, resonated and responded to as illuminating not only the dreamer's psyche, but those of other group members, amplifying the group's recognition of their shared processes.

Examples

A habitual latecomer had overslept and been awakened by a dream in which she was attacking her father, trying to strangle him and damage his throat. That same night in another dream, she was looking at the group through a TV screen, but wishing that she could actually be at the group. Through the dream she could speak about her fear to damage her therapist by the aggressive things she needed to say to him, a theme resonated to in the group, bringing into consciousness damage that can be done to fathers by their daughters in retaliation to having been physically and emotionally abused by them.

Another dream which could be understood as the group containing and amplifying hidden aspects was from a woman who suffered severe migraines. Her dream occurred during a migrainous attack: she was being attacked by members of the group with others standing by and not protecting her. This dream came at a time when she was becoming more able to assert herself in the group, to put limits onto what another woman, representing her mother, was doing to her. Some two years later, as she was preparing to leave the group, the same person had some headaches and brought a terrifying dream: an aeroplane was taking off vertically, though its back was broken away, leaving everyone vulnerable to falling out. This dream represented both her fear of leaving the group catastrophically and being vulnerable, and the group's potential to disintegrate through a member leaving, again perhaps a fear of her underlying destructive capacities. The capacity to have a horrifying dream and to have it responded to before leaving was important for her and for the group.

Udo Rauchfleisch (1995) has shown that dreams in groups emerge at times when there is a disturbance to the group structure, as when a member leaves, as in the dream I have reported, or when a new member is expected. The dream reveals both the underlying disturbance and the defences of the individual and of the group. Example: a group anticipates welcoming a new member and does not seem to experience conflicts over rivalry, disappointment or difficulty in sharing. However, in a dream the group is sitting together at a garden party and is annoyed because the therapist has chosen to sit at another table, talking to people they do not know. Another dream Rauchfleisch reports is the response of a woman to the departure of another woman from the group. In this dream she is with other people in a lift; she becomes terrified when she discovers that a mirror in which she used to see herself has disappeared and she is faced with a blank wall. Through this dream the group could recognise the loss of mirroring that the former member had provided and appreciate that they themselves now had to develop their own capacity for self-reflection and self-discovery.

It is relevant here to refer to the work of Didier Anzieu who described the dream as a pellicule, a membrane which protects part of an organism and which also functions as a photographic film on which impressions register. The dream acts as a protective shield, putting both external stimuli and internal pressures onto the same plane. This presupposes the existence of the skin ego, the earliest body boundary which is always vulnerable to rupture in the cumulative traumas of everyday life. This skin envelope, this pellicule, can clearly be seen in the dream of a group patient described by Luisa Brunori (unpublished) where in the dream the patient comes out of a tent which is a sort of theatre, a kind of rubber tent, like a membrane. Emerging from this tent it brings the patient into a zone where he experiences the anxiety of being alone. The rupture of the group membrane through the arrival of newcomers gives us evidence of its existence.

Bion and dreams

In his late *Cogitations*, Bion writes that dreaming proper is a continuous process in waking life, akin to a mental digestive process that makes conscious material accessible for storing unconsciously, suitable for transformation from the paranoid-schizoid to the depressive position. If the capacity for dream-work, as in the psychotic, is destroyed, the psychotic is unable to make use of the experience of both external and internal reality and therefore hallucination takes the place of dreaming. The dream also has an integrating and synthesising capacity for achieving 'common sense', linking body senses to one another. Similarly, dreams in the group can make 'common sense' between the members and unify the group matrix.

I have a former individual patient of Bion's in one of my groups. A single woman who is now in her sixties, highly intelligent and a good linguist, she had not risen above a secretarial position, and lived a relatively restricted social and emotional life. After several years in a twice-a-week group, she had achieved a much improved social and emotional level of functioning, in contrast to her previous destructive, explosive, unsocial behaviour. In the group she had often fallen asleep for lengthy periods and had long periods of insomnia. I believe she illustrates Bion's thesis of the pathological effect of the lack of dream-work in waking life, and that she sleeps in the group because she lacks the capacity for normal working-time dreaming, for reverie; mostly she could only hear what directly connected with her preoccupations; without it she becomes unconscious. She had great hatred for persons who had the ability to speak openly about themselves. She rarely brought dreams to the group, but here is one.

In the dream there was a ship and she knew there were many untrustworthy and dangerous persons aboard. The steamer's funnel was belching and billowing intense black smoke which was descending on everyone and she knew that the ship would sink under it. She spoke vividly and was listened to attentively. She had thought hard about her dream and knew that it represented her terrible inner contents, her jealousy, which is so painful, so out of control that sometimes she wants to die of it, yet she also knows that it is healthy and therefore does not want to lose it. Her anger is terrible, uncontrollable, seeps out of her: but in the dream because the smoke came from the funnel of the ship it therefore had some direction and did not seep out. Her dream enabled the group to work on jealousy, exclusion, spoiling, splitting of love and hate, gave direction to the shared voyage, the group as the ship. The dream journey took her from the autistic to the sharable.

Dreaming the self

Dream-work takes place in what Winnicott called the intermediate third area of experience, the in-between, a space for curiosity, exploration, discovery, the playground of experience. Winnicott's ideas have been taken up by the Kohutian self-psychologists (Livingston, Harwood, this volume). They respect the dream as phenomenon, as a 'thing in itself' that communicates meaning, a meaning that does not need decoding, that instead requires empathic attunement by the listener: staying with the dreamer's subjective experience, understanding the particular images and experiences as presented, which are expressions of the state of the self and also attempts of self-healing, through regulation and restoration of psychic structure. 'The dream is the best expression of itself and not a disguise for something else.'

Instead of being an authority of meanings, the primary task of the therapist, or of the other group members, is to amplify and elucidate the patterns of meanings conveyed by the dream imagery. Such a dream was that of a man with a poetic ability who dreamt joyfully of being part of his computer game, a dream which though mad, was a marvellous experience. The dream occurred at a time when he was more able to speak his mind openly to his wife who would say to him that these are mad thoughts, but which he did not mind. In this dream, as in the same session, he had a joyful sense of play, of being released from having to be the healer to his disturbed mother and to other group members.

This is a transformational dream, presenting a change in self-structure, a dream that conveys a powerful and undeniable message. Transformational dreams are recognised as such by other group members and are often compared to earlier dreams of the same person. Important dreams will be remembered, sometimes for years, particularly the first early dreams that patients bring to the group. In dreams we create and survive catastrophes, both for ourselves and for others. A patient about to leave a group after several years dreamt of standing next to a window and seeing a ship wrecked upon rocks, the survivors standing ashore. She could see that they had wires attached to them which enabled them to be rescued and thought what good technology it was! This dream represents the invisible network of connections of the group members to the group matrix. Following the dream the theme of this session was that in the group there is release from self-judgement and the consequences of the judgements of others. Loves and hates within the group do not have consequences that have to be paid for. In the group people stay together and work through issues that would elsewhere have led to a breakdown of relationships: the group is both the container of and a container for emotional experience.

Transformative dreams

These two dreams were spoken by an elderly austere priest, a lifelong bachelor without sexual experience who was soon going to leave the group. He said that both these dreams followed my having used the word transformation in a previous session. The first dream 'was rather wonderful. I was looking at the sea and the sea was full of dirt and mess. Then as I looked at it, there was transformation, then the sea became clear and clean.'

In the second dream: 'I saw a whole lot of food that was old and stale and covered with cobwebs and thought that I had to get rid of it all. Then as I started to look through it, I found that there were statuettes and other valuable objects in it. I broke open a vase and in it was a small bird hanging upside down and to my amazement the bird was still alive. Its beak was open and it was making big movements as if needing something. I knew that what it needed was water and so I ran out across a big grassy space to bring back a small beaker of water with which to feed it.'

The dream was greeted with pleasure, as having a powerful transformational force. One woman excitedly said: 'What a marvellous dream, because here in this group you are always asking to be fed and you've never been able to use it, so there's always discarded food and now you discover that what it wants is not food but water.' The dreamer said that he'd been very inspired by a book entitled *We Drink from Our Own Worlds*, which is about transformational theology. This dry, austere man was leaving the group after several years where he had always thirsted for recognition, in conflict between his thirst for authentic recognition and his compensatory need for grandiosity. The theme of grandiosity resonated. A woman was overwhelmed by her grandiose fantasies of being the only woman singer in her choir: either climbing to the top and singing; or, shitting and farting over everyone below her. The theme of the group seemed to be how to use the power of grandiosity to transform it into something acceptable to others as well as to oneself.

Narcissistic defences of grandiosity lead to interpersonal distancing and failure of intimacy. This priest had often chilled the group by his glacial withdrawals which tested the group's capacity to find warming, containing responses. He saw himself as a baby who, after having been fed and cleaned by his mother, would be left in his pram in the garden and that there would be no response to his cries until it was the correct feeding time again. He repeated this pattern in the group, resenting the intervals between the sessions. Similarly, Rauchfleisch (1995) writes of an isolated man who makes his group members feel angry, helpless and uncaring. He had a dream about a puma with an injured paw sitting in the middle, surrounded by killed animals; he came to see that it represented his compensatory wishes to be big, powerful, to conceal his vulnerability. This dream enabled others to express how they had felt killed off by his aloofness and how this had left him alone in a dead world. The work on this dream brought about significant change in the group configuration: he was less isolated, more open to his vulnerability and others no longer felt killed off.

Another form of transformation is what I call 'widening of vision'. This is when the person's previous narrow view of themselves and of the world becomes widened through internalisation of the group's capacity to have multiple perspectives, multi-visions. Gordon Lawrence (1998) calls this the ability to recognise a 'multiverse' rather than a 'universe'. The ability to use this 'multiverse' entails a movement into confusion and threatened disintegration from which our new visions can emerge and exist together within a coherent frame.

In Rome two Jungian group analysts, Pier Giacomo Miglioratti (1996) and Marco Zanasi (1996), have shown how we can understand the language of dreams on the neurobiological level, work stimulated by their late colleague Romano Fiumara, and also on the archaic archetypal transformational level. Zanasi describes dreams as going on on two levels: the interpersonal transferential, and the activation of the collective unconscious. Dreams that express the collective unconscious represent the activation of what he calls 'the right hemisphere' of the group, giving meaning to shared experiences of chaos, of fusion and confusion, which are intrinsic to the group process.

Miglioratti describes a succession of dreams from the phobic obsessional woman in his group and shows how the patient finds herself inside her symptom, being in the dreaded situation, but at the same time contained by the group situation. Thus through interpretations the patient is able to widen her sphere of consciousness, to recognise the dreads of birth and death that underlie her symptomatology and to remain within the dreaded situation, receiving help and understanding, instead of taking flight.

Social dreaming matrix

I will conclude this paper on dreams by discussing a significant innovation in dream-work, the social dreaming matrix. This is the brainchild of W. Gordon Lawrence (this volume), former member of the Tavistock Institute of Human Relations, a man of originality. He greatly values Bion's thoughts and also Jung's. Bion and Jung are both prophets, mystics who have made dark journeys of discovery into the realm of madness. Jung in 1913 had a series of dreams in which he saw Europe covered by a monstrous flood, though Switzerland was protected by its mountains. He saw the rubble of civilisation, the sea turned into blood. Jung believed that he was threatened by psychosis and did not see a possible political dimension to his dreams. Later, in 1914, he dreamt that the earth was covered with ice as a result of arctic cold, and then he understood the link between the personal and the political as the First World War broke out.

It was by chance that Gordon Lawrence found the book *The Third Reich of Dreams* by Charlotte Beradt, a German psychotherapist who had collected 300 dreams in Germany between 1933 and 1939, dreams that directly expressed the dreamer's reactions to the threatening political atmosphere. This encouraged Lawrence to take the bold step of instituting dream workshops in different countries in which he observed the matrix of dreams related to the different cultures of Israel, Germany, Australia and India.

In a social dreaming matrix where persons gather to explore the social dimension of dreaming, the seating is in a spiral or in a snowflake configuration which enables the participants to differentiate the setting from that of a therapeutic group. Dreams are presented for responses by the dreams and associations of others. It is the dream, not the person, which is the medium for discourse.

Lawrence's language is rich and metaphorical. He differentiates between 'the politics of salvation' and 'the politics of revelation'. The meaning of these terms is that in the conventional meeting between expert and client, therapist and patient, consultant and organisation, there is an expectation from the client that the expert will find a way to solve the client's problems. By contrast, what can be transformative for persons, patients or clients, is when they are able to find their own internal sources for creative change through revelation, which can come through their dreams. In group analysis we know that this is the way people are enabled to develop.

An illustration of this transformation is that of a workshop where a dream-sharing session led to an atmosphere analogous to the improvisations of musicians.

There was 'an inspiring sense of rhythm and wholeness' as a collage of dreams was assembled. From my own experience in the dream workshop, I know that over one or two nights a dream-matrix evolves with the aid of a consultant or consultant team who have the necessary vision to capture the unconscious links between the dreamers. Lawrence has written 'that one can feel disconnected, at times, in the matrix, but a connection can always be found because of the richness of this associative culture that it engenders.' This applies also to our group analytic Large Group experiences where from the disparate utterances a sense of connection emerges that can be registered through imagery and metaphor (Traveni, this volume). At a recent Large Group meeting of the American Group Psychotherpay Association (AGPA) a veteran group therapist, silent through the previous two sessions, said 'I don't know why I keep coming to these sessions, it must be because I like to feel what it is like to be disconnected.' Those words express the sense of discovery of disconnection from the familiar self in a safe setting. The Large Group takes us into the waking dream that Bion tells us is necessary for maintenance of mental and emotional health. I believe that Large Group and dreaming matrix together, are the next steps to the ecology of mind at the beginning of our next millennium.

Jung does not refer to the very similar dream of Raskolnikov in Dostoevsky's *Crime and Punishment*. He dreamt that the world was condemned to a terrible, new, strange plague that has come to Europe from the depths of Asia. All were to be destroyed except a chosen few. Some new sorts of microbes were attacking the bodies of men, but these microbes were endowed with intelligence and will. Men attacked by them at once became mad and furious. And never had men considered themselves so intellectual and so completely in possession of the truth as these sufferers, never had they considered their decisions, their scientific conclusions, their moral convictions so infallible. Men killed each other in a sort of senseless spite. They gathered together in armies against one another, but even on the march the armies would be attacking one another, ranks would be broken and the soldiers would fall on each other, stabbing and cutting, biting and devouring each other.

Raskolnikov's dream is used by Trigant Burrow, the American founder of group analysis, to exemplify the divide between human beings, divided because each claims his own individuality and fails to recognise the organismic indivisible nature of man. For Burrow (1949, pp.57–8) this dream of Raskolnikov is not a prophetic dream of the outbreak of warfare, but instead illustrates the constant warfare that humankind is engaged in through the failure to recognise the depth of our commonality.

Dreaming 'in concert', as Samuel Johnson describes, can restore the sense of primary unity which is our common birthright, unity with the maternal other, and through her with the caring community which she represents. If dreams are always attempts to adapt to traumas, both internal and external, to repair the tears in our psychic envelopes as Anzieu describes, the therapy group offers to its participants the opportunity of weaving a collective skin-container. Within this container dreams reveal the threats represented by newcomers, by the re-emergence of repressed and split-off affects and fantasies, that can now become part of a common narrative journey. This journey can reach mythological and archetypal depths.

In my experience, group members are soon able to feel themselves into the expressed dream of one of their number and to relate both to the dreams, to the group situation and to their own participation. Dreams are therefore both individual and social and dream time is a valuable time in which we can reconnect to ourselves and to the group matrix and through this to society of which each one of us is but a fragment.

References

Anzieu, D. (1993) 'The film of the dream.' In S. Flanders (ed) *The Dream Disclosure Today*. London: Routledge.

Battegay, R. (1977) 'The group dream.' In. L.R. Wolberg and N.L. Aronson (eds) *Group Therapy, an Overview*, 37–41. New York: Stratton Intercontinental.

Bion (1992) *Cogitations*. London: Kornac Books.

Burrow, T (1949) *The Neurosis of Man*. London: Routledge & Kegan Paul.

Ferenczi, S. (1913) 'To whom does one relate one's dreams.' In *Further Contributions to the Theory and Techniques of Psychoanalysis*. New York: Bruner/Mazel.

Foulkes, S.H. (1984) *Therapeutic Group Analysis*. London: Karnac Books.

Kaplan, S.R. (1973) 'The group dream.' *International Journal of Group Psychotherapy 23*, 421–31.

Lawrence, W.G. (1998) *Social Dreaming @ Work*. London: Karnac Books.

Miglioratti, P. (1996) 'Group therapy and the phobic obsessional neurosis.' *Group Analysis 29*, 4, 449–62.

Neri, C. (1998) *Group*. London: Jessica Kingsley Publishers.

Rauchfleisch, U. (1995) 'Dreams as Defence and Coping Strategies in Group Analysis.' *Group Analysis 28*, 4, 465.

Resnik, S. (1987) *The Theatre of the Dream*. London: Routledge.

Schlachet, P. (1992) 'The dream in group therapy: a re-appraisal of unconscious processes in groups.' *Group Analysis 16*, 4, 196–209.

Schorske, C. (1980) *Fin-de-Siècle Vienna*. New York: Knopf.

Zanasi, M. (1996) 'Dreams and the primordial level.' *Group Analysis 29*, 4, 463–74.

CHAPTER 2

Dreams in Psychodynamic Group Psychotherapy

J. Scott Rutan and Cecil A. Rice

A dream not explored is like a letter that has not been opened.

The Talmud

It has now been over 100 years since Freud published *The Interpretation of Dreams*, though the nature and meaning of dreams have fascinated mankind for all of recorded history.

The function of dreaming is mysterious. How dreams are understood in psychodynamic theory is a direct consequence of the hypotheses inherent in that theory. Freud conceptualised that individuals relegate unacceptable affects, memories or experiences to the unconscious. Sleep weakens the monitoring function of the brain so that the unacceptable elements of the unconscious become somewhat more available (Craig 1992). However, the monitoring function is still sufficiently effective so that the awareness is highly coded. There may well be an adaptive purpose to dreaming (Cartwright 1991). Thus, according to psychodynamic theory, dreams represent a potentially important source of information about an individual's unconscious.

In psychodynamic groups, dreams are often communications about unconscious elements of group process: communication to the group about and by a member (Whitman 1973); communication about the group through a member (Kieffer 1996); or dreams becoming linked with other dreams to deepen understanding of particular elements of group process (Rutan and Stone 1993).

A Group Dream

Just before the group therapist's four-week vacation, Ann reported a dream in which she had severely criticised a fellow group member for his repeated tardiness. In the dream, after her criticism, Ann herself returned from a vacation and found the group members voting on whether they should allow her to continue in the group.

Ann's dream hints at previously unstated group concerns about keeping the group agreements (late arrival) and anger about those who take vacations (should they allow Ann to continue after having taken a vacation?). Given that the therapist was about to leave for a vacation, it seemed that the dream might be revealing some unspoken group reaction about the therapist-induced breach in the group meeting schedule. When the group therapist suggested this interpretation, the members quickly and powerfully spoke of their anger and worry about the potential effects the therapist's vacation might have on them. As though to reduce the effect of her dream and the therapist's comment, Ann responded to the initial scattered and agitated conversation by saying, 'Don't worry he'll be back soon.'

Ann, who was in the group in part to understand the effect her comments had on others, sought to deny or reduce those effects quickly, just as she had done during her parents' ongoing fighting. This time, however, Bob (in a departure from his usual purely rational stance) said, 'There are no guarantees, five years ago a crazy bastard walked into my previous therapist's office with a gun and blew a hole in the side of her face.'

Ann and Bob's reactions and associations to the dream begin to elaborate their mixed feelings stimulated by the therapist's vacation – from Ann's glossing it over to Bob's expectation of violence and loss. Bob's expectation of violence is clearly a recollection of a tragic event close to its anniversary. It may also hint at unspeakable wishes toward the therapist for abandoning him as his previous therapist had done. (Though she did not die, Bob's previous therapist never returned to her work. His last contact with her was through a letter she sent in which she told him she would not be back.) Little wonder that Bob could not tolerate Ann's attempt to smooth things over. Later, Bob also acknowledged the sadness he felt about the group therapist's vacation and the loss of his previous therapist.

In groups, all dreams are potentially group dreams and all members are encouraged to associate to the dream material. As other group members associated to Ann's dream, new material emerged. Barbara spoke of a crush she had developed on a television singer whom she described as 'Tall and thin, just like our group therapist!' After a great deal of embarrassment, she acknowledged that the television singer was probably a substitute for the group therapist. Then she briefly investigated her yearning to be close to men – her father, her husband and the group therapist in particular. Yet she kept all at a distance. She said she feared men. Ann suggested that she might fear something else – 'maybe your own sexual wishes?'

The Use of Dreams in Psychodynamic Groups

So far we have used our brief example to illustrate how the content of dreams may well provide important clues to individual and group unconscious material. The fundamental premise in psychodynamic theory is that dreams represent a highly coded 'message' directly from the unconscious. The job of the therapist is to assist the patient (and in this instance the group) in decoding the dream. We have also implied some techniques that may be useful in harvesting the rich fields that dreams in groups provide. The guidelines include the following:

Value dreams

Group therapists subtly reward or do not reward content that appears in groups. Therapists who do not appreciate the power of dreams will find patients do not present dreams in their groups. If a therapist desires to use dreams to explore unconscious data, then all dreams that are presented should be considered important.

Allow group members to associate interactively

When a member shares a dream the other members and the leader may feel an urge to interpret it. This is rarely helpful, especially at first, and it usually results in a cognitive discussion. Rather, the leader should help the group develop the norm of associating to dreams rather than 'interpreting' or 'understanding' them. (This would be the group version of Freud's free association.)

Although the example above is brief, the process amongst the members leading up to it was long and circuitous. Tolerating the uncertainty of this circuitous process, and avoiding premature closure through too early interpretation, allows the group members to more fully understand what is happening. It allows them to elaborate the intricate meanings and relationships among them, and between them and the therapist. Members learn to tolerate the discomfort of not knowing until richer meanings and understandings can emerge.

Allowing the process to evolve slowly also gives the therapist a chance to reflect on what the dreams and related behaviour might mean. The following assumptions can help inform that reflection.

The dream relates to the adaptive task of the dreamer

The adaptive task (Langs 1978) for Ann's dream included coping with the loss of the therapist and the group. This task had special meanings and difficulties for Ann, who aspired to be a writer. It turned out that Ann's present project was a biography of her mother, who was a very well known figure. However, the book had still a long way to go, and Ann had yet to publish anything. Her mother, now in her nineties, was even more difficult to relate to than when she was younger. Interviewing her about the book was the most comfortable connection Ann could make with her. Ann's connection with her mother was ambivalent and made all the more complicated by the fact that she was supported by a trust fund her mother had established for her. Ann raged about how her mother controlled her via money, and yet she could not make her way in the world without it. For Ann, connecting with her mother and separating from her was torturous. Her connection with the therapist and the group had the same ambivalence. As Ann explored her dream, and all the feelings stirred by the therapist's vacation, she gained new and richer understanding of her complex relationship with her ageing mother.

The dream relates to the adaptive task of the group

In this instance, the adaptive task of the group was coping with the loss of the therapist and the group. As with the individual dreamer, the members' and the group's earlier experiences of loss will profoundly influence that adaptive task. To cope with the current loss, the members will use behaviours and skills that, though once successful, may now be a frequent source of discomfort. It may be a pattern that led to the dilemmas that brought them into therapy in the first place.

The dream may enable members to rework earlier losses

As the members seek to cope with the current loss in the group, they will, as suggested above, reach back to earlier losses and associated behaviour. However, the dream will also give the members an opportunity to address those earlier losses again and seek a fuller resolution of them. In the current example, Ann, Barbara and Bob all indicate how dream material makes available earlier loss experiences.

The material of the dream may be represented in the group and vice versa

Through projective identification the dreamer and the members may recreate the dream or its genetic roots in the group dynamics. That is, the group members may play out the dream giving it more immediate vitality.

Projective identification is a defensive and coping process by which individuals deal with unwanted aspects of themselves, usually unwanted feelings and fantasies. (People may also use it to protect aspects of themselves that they feel are under threat.) Essentially, the individuals deny the undesirable in themselves, but see it in others, even if it is not there. That is, they project that which is undesirable onto others. However, unlike simple projection, these individuals – through body language and looks; through the tones, rhythms and cadences of speech; through humour, feelings, mood, behaviour, clothes, perfumes and aftershave lotions, and much else besides – bring pressure to bear on others to play out their undesired parts. Ogden (1982) put it this way:

> Projective identification…addresses the way in which feeling-states corresponding to the unconscious fantasies of one person (the projector) are engendered in and processed by another person (the recipient), that is, the way in which one person makes use of another person to experience and contain aspects of himself. The projector has the primarily unconscious fantasy of getting rid of an unwanted or endangered part of himself – and of depositing that part in another person in a powerfully controlling way. In association with this projected unconscious fantasy there is an interpersonal interaction by means of which the recipient is pressured to think, feel and behave in a manner congruent with the ejected feelings and the self- and object-representations embodied in the projective fantasy. (p.1)

Bion crisply described the subjective experience of the recipient by saying it was like living in someone else's nightmare. Dreams often contain and give voice to parts of us we wish to disown. Thus, a dreamer through the process of projective identification may invite the group members to contain and enact the undesirable within the dream, rather than own it. As the last phrase suggests, this is especially true if the dreamer or group does not examine the dream.

The group was low-key, but unusually tense. Barbara had been to her recently deceased uncle's place in Maine. 'I felt so uncomfortable,' she said, in a disgusted tone, 'being there with my parents. And my father – ugh! – he seemed just too physically close to me for comfort.' Then she told the following cryptic dream. Her father was in bed with her and she tried desperately to get away from him. She was reluctant to explore the dream and was angry with the therapist for inviting her to wonder about it and its relationship to the group. She felt that, like her father, the (male) therapist was robbing her of what was hers. Eileen, another group member, associated to her own experiences of incest. First, she spoke about the incest experience of her friend, whom we later discovered was her lover. From there she jumped to her father describing the rage he generated in her, and then spoke about her fantasies of dismembering him and her friend's father. Throughout this slow-burning tirade she acted as though the therapist was not in the room. Again the daughter had desperately distanced the father in the proverbial bed.

In this example, Barbara did not want to think about or own her fears, wishes and desires hinted at in the dream. Very quickly others picked up her unwanted feelings, especially Eileen, who, with the other members, played them out. The therapist, as the father, had dared to wonder about the meaning of the dream and was pushed farther and farther away. Although some of the group members had distanced him, the men in the group became the containers of the dreamer's anxiety, conveyed to them through threats of dismemberment and other more subtle communications. The anxiety silenced them. The group would have remained a mere enactment of the unexamined dream, had not one man finally spoken. Andy, after describing his fears, said he felt the therapist had been right in raising the dream as a group issue because it was affecting everyone in the group. This allowed for a tentative exploration. The group had contained the projection and stopped the enactment.

Just as a group may enact an unexplored dream, so a dream may contain unexamined behaviour of the group. In short, a group member may be the recipient of the other members' projections and feel compelled to struggle with it. That struggle may be manifest in a dream.

The group was dealing with loss. The therapist's summer vacation was approaching, and the successful termination of two members, Carol and Darlene, was occurring around that same time. Evelyn (another member) reported a dream in which she had come to the therapist's home. She assumed she had come for a group session, though she did not recognise any group members in the dream. Instead she found a very young boy alone in the home. Then she learned that the therapist would be back in an hour and a half (the length of a group session). She felt very anxious and angry that the therapist could abandon a child like that. It also meant that the boy had to take care of things in the therapist's absence. The group played with the dream for some time. They saw the infant as Evelyn abandoned by the therapist, Carol and Darlene. Later, Evelyn noted that she never knows how she feels about the therapist going on vacation until during the vacation itself, when she experiences all kinds of physical problems.

This dream is worthy of exploration in its own right. However, for our purposes it has the following significance. The session before this one the members of the group had talked at length about adoption and loss in their families.

Jane mentioned in passing that she had cut out articles from the papers about adopted children and shared them with her adopted daughter. Chuck reacted quite strongly, suggesting that her daughter might experience that as intrusive. Don added that it might suggest to her daughter that she wanted to abandon her, which was her fear and her daughter's. The session continued with many similar discussions of abandonment in the members' families.

The session was powerful and dealt with many personal concerns of the members. However, the members were reluctant to explore beyond those concerns, which focused largely on events outside the group. In Foulkes's terms, the group-related concerns remained somewhere within the group matrix, unexplored. Or in more classic psychoanalytic terms they remained within the unconscious of the members, unwanted and unexplored. Thus, it seems Evelyn became the primary recipient of those unaddressed concerns, which found their initial encoded expression in the dream she reported in the following session. That is, parents leaving their children unprotected, or 'giving them away', comes up as a topic in response to the therapist's upcoming vacation. This indicates how groups rarely 'change the subject', and this week's dream may reflect unconscious feelings from a prior group session.

Multiple Dreams

If two or more members present dreams in the same meeting, it is useful to consider them as one 'group dream'. Often, perhaps through a mechanism akin to Jung's collective unconscious, members tend to reflect different aspects of important group issues in dreams reported at the same time.

The group had been exploring some angry feelings between Bill and Carl. Both men came from families where physical violence and substance abuse were common occurrences. They always sat next to one another and chatted amicably prior to group, but in recent weeks they had got into ferocious arguments during group sessions. In the prior session Bill had stood up in a threatening manner and then fled the group 30 minutes before it ended.

Elizabeth reported a dream she had the night before the present group – 'I was on a beautiful, peaceful beach enjoying the sun. Then I felt the ground shake, and I saw two giant dinosaurs coming toward me, one from my left and one from my right. They were huge and they looked very angry. Gradually I realised they were not coming for me, but they were going to have a huge fight to the death right in front of my beach chair. I was paralysed with fear. Then I woke.'

John said he, too, had dreamed a vivid dream last night. 'I was a boxer and I was sitting in my corner looking across the ring at my opponent. He was enormous, and his face never changed. It was as if it were made of concrete. I went from feeling very confident I would win to knowing I would be killed. But the fight was about to begin and there was nowhere for me to run.'

The group quickly associated to the frightening exchange between Bill and Carl the prior week and the members, including Bill and Carl, spoke of how frightened they had been. Bill said he fled so that he would not strike Carl, just as he had often left the house rather than fighting back when his dad would beat him.

Summary

Since time immemorial, dreams have played an important role in understanding human desires, and many have explored how best to use dreams in a group therapy setting (Schlachet 1992). In this chapter we have outlined some ways in which dreams may be particularly helpful for individuals in therapy groups. We illustrated how dreams can enrich the members' understanding of themselves and help them change. Additionally, we have shown how the dreams of individuals may also reveal shared concerns among the members, and throw light on group dynamics and tasks the members may fear addressing, which often lie outside their awareness. Thus, dreams may be the containers of both individual and collective anxieties, which if left unattended can lead to acting in or acting out. Yet, when members understand those dreams and give voice to their meaning, separately and collectively, they gain a better understanding of themselves and their interactions with each other. They also gain understanding of their collective struggles. In brief, effective exploration of dreams can lead to intrapsychic, interpersonal and group-wide change. In addition, working with dreams reinforces the psychodynamic assumption that there is an 'out-of-awareness' world that influences our perceptions.

References

Cartwright, R. (1991) 'Dreams that work: the relation of dream incorporation to adaptation to stressful events.' *Dreaming 1*, 3–10.

Craig, E. (1992) Paper presented to the Association for the Study of Dreams. Charlottesville, VA.

Freud, S. (1900) *The Interpretation of Dreams. Standard Edition, 4/5*. London: Hogarth Press.

Kieffer, C.C. (1996) 'Using dream interpretation to resolve group developmental impasses.' *Group 20*, 273–85.

Langs, R. (1978) *The Listening Process*. New York: Aronson.

Ogden, T.H. (1982) *Projective Identification and Therapeutic Technique*. New York: Aronson.

Rutan, J.S. and Stone, W.N. (1993) *Psychodynamic Group Psychotherapy*. 2nd edition. New York: Guilford Press.

Schlachet, P. (1992) 'The dream in group therapy: a reappraisal of unconscious processes in groups.' *Group 16*, 4, 195–209.

Whitman, R. (1973) 'Dreams about the group: an approach to the problem of group psychology.' *International Journal of Group Psychotherapy 23*, 408–20.

CHAPTER 3

Dream-telling as a Request for Containment in Group Therapy

The Royal Road through the Other

Robi Friedman

The traditional, intrapersonal way of working with dreams can be enriched by an interpersonal approach (Ferenczi 1913; Kanzer 1955). Dreaming may no longer be viewed as an exclusively internal and autonomous working-through process, as classic one-person psychology approaches suggest (Freud 1900, 1933; Meltzer 1983). From a two or more person psychology frame of reference, a dream is shared not only in order to represent the self, but also to 'use' significant others to further previously incomplete processing by the dream-work. A dream met with unsatisfying intrapsychic containment may initiate a search for a less damaged, better external containment, thus unconsciously replicating what the dreamer may have done in childhood. Dream-telling will often have a compelling unconscious emotional aspect, which will manipulate the audience into feeling, and even acting out, a certain relation to the dreamer. The therapist and the group have to be ready to work the dream through instead of allowing its enactment. Both intra and interpersonal theoretical and technical approaches to the work with dreams will be described.

Introduction: What is a dream?

Classic intrapsychic aspects

Dreaming was considered a way of coping with the 'exciting and dreadful', and mainly an *intrapsychic* process executed by autonomous mechanisms. Freud described the personal and idiosyncratic ways an individual protects him- or herself from difficult and conflictual emotions in order to preserve sleep. These tension-reducing 'solutions' can be evaluated by their degree of psychic development, e.g. projections, evacuation or symbolisation. Dreaming provided Freud (1900, 1933), and all of us since, with evidence of the patient's ego strengths and defences, id and superego manifestations, etc. Thus a dream – the result of this fascinating process – was thought to be the self's picture and the royal road to the unconscious of the dreamer. Many aspects of classical psychoanalysis are rooted in dream theory: the presupposition of a 'primary' thought process during dreaming; a differentiation between the dream's manifest and latent components; and perception distortions such as condensation, inversion and displacement. These aspects should be considered in understanding the dream-work, and bear witness to the endless creativity and richness of the human mind (Sharpe 1937).

Dreams have been understood as symptoms, as compromise formations between instincts and inhibitions, at once born out of unconscious conflicts and reflecting them. Starting with Freud (1900), who for many years analysed his own dreams, the aim has been to understand unconscious conflictual processes – as if dreams were a microscope, helpful in detecting and magnifying hidden elements in the psyche. 'The dream is like a newspaper in a dictatorial regime which absolutely must come out every day, but must never tell the truth, and the work of the editors is to cover up the truth as much as possible or tell it between the lines' (Freud 1900, p.69). This conceptualisation belongs to a '*one-person*' *psychology*, addressing mainly 'diagnostic' and intrapsychic aspects of dreaming rather than those of relational and 'two-or-more-person' psychology. Ego- and self-psychology have added further diagnostic aspects – helping us to deduce the patterns used by the ego in problem-solving, mastery, and adaptation, as well as the self's unconscious efforts towards self-representation and cohesion (Stolorow and Atwood 1982; Neri 1998). Elements like movement, colour (Erikson 1954), the nature and relations of objects in a dream, and the dreamer's distance from the dream's events (Steward 1973) contribute to an assessment of the personality's strengths and weaknesses (Morgenthaler 1986). Jung's contribution, that of viewing the dream as compensation of the ego in the individuation process, may be included in this same category (Adams 2000). Approaching the dream as if it were 'a text' has many clinical uses in both group analysis and supervision. It may further an understanding of the patient's psyche and state of mind, and provide the group participants with initial tools with which to reflect on their dreams.

Intrapsychic aspects in object-relations contributions

Dreams are a way of thinking (Meltzer 1984), of trying to give meaning (Bion 1962) to an encounter with a difficult emotion. These intrapsychic working-through container-contained processes (Bion 1962b) have soothing and organising functions. Their origins can be traced back to interpsychic processes between mother and child. In order to transform primitive and unbearable feelings (called beta elements) into thinkable and tolerable (alpha) elements, the threatened, immature child needs his mother's transformation capacity, called alpha function. This is fulfilled by 'reverie', a natural but complex unconscious thought process – through which the mother 'digests' (contains and elaborates) for the child's still inedible sensorial input. His own developmental task consists of going through a process of introjecting his mother's alpha function, which gradually enables him to autonomously metabolise the exciting and threatening. Maturity makes dreaming (i.e. coping with difficult emotions) possible, without usually having nightmares.

Dream projective identification

Unlike for psychotics, who may be lacking alpha function, excessive fears and excitement may be worked through in the self without the need for an 'expulsive component' (Bion 1963, p.27) which exports ('evacuates') the intolerable emotions into an external object. Coping with conflictual emotions during dreaming makes use of a projective and evacuative function that may be called 'dream projective identification', which functions as an integrator of split-off emotions. Fairbairn (1963), introducing an additional intra/interpersonal viewpoint, saw the dream stage as a space divided between self and 'others'. On this stage intolerable excitement and dread can be split-off and projected onto a 'not me' dream object. For example, dreaming of being attacked by a stranger may serve the purpose of putting some distance between one's self and one's aggressive emotions.

The dream 'stage director' (Grotstein 1987), an unconscious inner-self agency, chooses the 'right' character able to contain hitherto intolerable elements during the dream play. The 'other' in the dream is never an arbitrary choice: I think he is retrieved out of an unconsciously stored collection of 'containers' perceived as being able to work through the 'unbearable'. The containers on the dream stage range from familiar symbols – like a parent figure – to a classmate 'forgotten' for a quarter of a century. This conceptualisation is in line with investigations of the use of the emotional timeless memory for unconscious coping with conflicts in dreams (Palombo 1992).

Working with a dream 'as text' – the 'diagnostic' approach

Clinicians diverged significantly when considering the dream material, and often took completely opposing positions. Decades-long disputes about the merits of decoding manifest versus latent dream material, or deciphering 'contents' versus preferring 'function', took centre stage (Segal 1980). In practice, intermediate positions may be taken between these polar approaches. There are benefits to considering manifest together with latent specific contents, to approaching the dream material as ever-deeper representations of different levels of consciousness, as well as to understanding the dream processes. Rather than the meanings of specific contents, the dream's organisation often represents a patient's level of maturity and the structure of his neurotic patterns even more accurately. A poorly structured, chaotic dream weighs against a seductive 'interesting' content. All these approaches may provide important clues to therapeutic directions.

Understanding unconscious dynamics and patterns in the dream's hidden and covert manifestations helps the therapist assess the level of ego-functioning, and attempt to improve it. Ego-maturation, the ego's ability to contain and organise emotional experience, determines the level of the dream's processing function. The distance from the dreadful in the dream may measure ego-functioning (Steward 1973). The higher the symbolisation ability, reflecting the level of alpha function, the less evacuation of feelings and subsequent acting out in the waking state (Khan1972). 'The structure of the dream reflects the structure of personality' (Segal 1980, p.100). Working with the dream's structure helps to deepen the knowledge of the individual participant's rejected, intolerable sides. In group analysis[1] it may promote therapy and growth of the entire audience, including the analyst and the group-as-a-whole, by reowning the split-off (Scharff 1992).

Analysing a dream 'as if it were a text' will be described step by step as follows: retelling the dream, analysing its content, deciphering 'latent' material and interpreting the dreamer's relations with the group's patterns. These techniques will be exemplified by the same dream that will be used later on to explore interpersonal approaches to the work with dreams.

'Retelling the dream' or the dream-structure as a play / narrative

A male participant (36), well into his second year of therapy, tells the following dream:

> In the kibbutz the word spread that the Nazis were coming. I fled with my girlfriend to a place that was crowded with people who were hiding. A male Kapo[2] carrying a club came to hit us, and we could barely persuade him to remember he was Jewish and join us. A similar encounter happened with a female Kapo who wanted to attack us with a club. Then we both continued trying to escape, and hid inside two separate large drawers. A Nazi soldier came by with a barking dog that even scratched under the cupboard doors with his paws – but somehow the soldier went away and we were saved. Then I found myself in an orphanage, incessantly asking the question: Where is E? Where is E? [the dreamer's own name]. I decided to return to the hiding place, wishing only not to find that E. had already rotted. I open the cupboard and see him small and shrunk like a fetus. I take him back to the orphanage.

'Retelling the dream' is (like most of the consequent techniques) what this way of working with the dream has been called by group participants over the years. The dreamer helps the group retell the dream, but from that moment on usually profits most from the process by remaining passive and watching the group work. Only at the end of the work does his feedback help provide evidence of the work's relevance (which often seems incredible).

The group starts by narrating the dream together and elaborating on different aspects of its manifest structure, deliberately postponing the debate on latent contents. The group looks together for the dream's narrative organisational structure, and tries to divide it into acts, as if it were a theatre play. Following Morgenthaler's (1986) dream-diagnostics and similar contributions, the organisation of a story is used as developmental evidence similar to the TAT test.[3] We look for the following parts:

- Introduction
- Acts (I, II, etc.)
- End

In the introduction we examine the dreamer's capacity for a preliminary basic (defensive) preparation for an encounter with the exciting and threatening, and investigate their quality. Existent protection offered by the dreamer's affiliation with human or other objects in a defensive space,[4] and the introduction's connection with the succeeding parts of the dream, determine the narrative's nature.

In the acts we mainly watch for recurring patterns and their course. We explore the characteristic pattern of relations between people, as well as the course and end of the narrative.

In the end we evaluate ego-strength by its ability to find a solution and integrate all parts.

The dream shows a clearly weak introduction by a very exposed, 'skinless', dreamer: the kibbutz setting and even the accompanying girlfriend do not offer any protection. They are invaded without providing him so much as a hiding place. The introduction reveals the familiar, almost post-traumatic unprotected psychic existence common among 'second-generation' Holocaust survivors. (The dreamer's parents were freed from concentration camps at the end of the Second World War.) In addition to arranging a protective stage, the usual function of a good introduction is to prepare for an encounter with the exciting and threatening by surrounding the dreamer with protective actors: 'I went shopping with my sister…', 'my mother and I were travelling in Pisa…', 'I was sitting with friends in our usual pub…'.

Act I starts with the escape, and centres on the two meetings with the Kapos. In this act, the dreamer repeats a similar pattern twice: encountering 'external' aggressors, with 'almost' catastrophic endings, but managing a magical last-minute escape. In Act II this same pattern of encounter with aggression is repeated once again (the Nazi and his dog 'almost' detect his hiding place). In the final act, the 'solution' to another repetition of the same pattern (the orphan finds that he is a shrunk fetus in the war space) is even more impotent, magical and lacking control. According to the dream sequence, it seems that with every repetition the dreamer regresses and feels less potent. This pattern may be adumbrated as a man encountering threatening parental figures on his mental stage, and, as an increasingly impotent victim, barely surviving the (disowned and projected) aggression.

Morgenthaler called these emotional–behavioural configurations the 'central emotional movement in the dream'. They may also correspond to core conflictual relational themes (Luborsky and Mark 1991).

However, in spite of the repetitions, this dreamer undoubtedly has a complex yet very creative and strong ego-organisation, which enables him to work on coherent intra- and interpersonal themes.

Analysing the dream contents

In this part, the group deliberately takes a deciphering view (like decoding the hieroglyphs on the Rosetta Stone) of the dream's manifest contents as another reflection of the dreamer's personality structure. For trained therapists/testologists, the similarity with the Rorschach test is evident. Manifest contents signify special features with possible meanings, which can even be explored together with the dreamer. Below are some examples:

Content	Feature	Possible meaning
Girlfriend, Kapo	Kind of objects	Object representations
Fleeing together, being attacked, being chased	Relation between objects	Maturity of attachments (ability to separate; bear aggression, envy and complex relationships)
Fleeing, raising clubs, patrolling, asking, holding	Movement	Psychic energy, libido, mental status
Crowding, being 'hiders', Kapos, hiding places	Audience's place	Group, therapist and member representations and internalisations
'We' versus him, the fetus	Distance to dream drama	Ability to encounter the exciting and threatening

The dream exposes the relations with familiar objects along with parts that symbolise some kind of primal aggressive parent, who may be better understood in the context of intergenerational transference in 'second-generation' (Vardi 1990). The dreamer's relations alternate between being a parent (or parental child) and being an almost helpless victim. The only exception is the convincing dialogue with the Kapos, marking a great therapeutic development. The group's reflections raised the possibility that the dreamer may be investing most of his psychic energy in trying to distance himself from the threatening, which stems from every external source including the group, and seems to endanger his psychic existence.

Deciphering 'latent' material

Group participants relating to dream contents help clarify hidden meanings. This kind of work is usually very creative and furthers the dreamer's and the group's mutual involvement in an insightful process in which everyone becomes a 'detective'. Understanding the hidden meaning of a scene or symbol transforms 'known' but hitherto 'unthought' features into thinkable insights (Bollas 1987).

In our example, there were many associations and allusions to the dream content. These included the following: the Kapos were considered to represent the aggressive parents on the one hand, and the dreamer's own violence on the other; the difficulty in accepting his own aggression, its projection, followed by his unconscious preference to be a victim, were pointed out as well; and the Kapos (representing the most vicious, cruel and treacherous Holocaust survivors) were linked by the group to 'being an orphan', and understood as a devaluation of the parents. Many associations with Benigni's film *Life is Beautiful* also disclosed the great creativity of this 'dream-director'.

Interpreting the dreamer's patterns and his relation to the group

The relational patterns disclosed in dreams may potentially be re-enacted in the therapeutic setting through the dreamer's transference and by the group's unconscious relations. In a group, the objects of this pattern may be the analyst, a member, a subgroup or the whole group. Interpretations should try to show unconscious links between the dreamer's inner world and his relations with the object world in order to contain the re-enactment (Steiner 1995).

In our dreamer's unconscious relation to the therapist, hidden fears of (projected) aggression seem to have echoed similar fears in the group. While exploring his hatred and feelings of victimisation, the group's ambivalence

towards the analyst, who was sometimes perceived as aggressive in his interpretation (and penetration), surfaced.

Before sharing an understanding of these links, the therapist may have to
consider transference and countertransference processes, the dreamer's
maturity, his or her relations to the group, and the group's developmental
stage. The group analyst also has to match the depth of interpretation to the
participants' level of consciousness. This technical approach may be best
suitable for first dreams or in preparing therapy groups for them.

By creating the dream narrative together and training in working with
dreams,[5] participants are coached in understanding and conceptualising
emotional and behavioural patterns. A technique for analysing dreams may
enable the group to better cope with difficult surfacing emotions.[6] In time,
the participants become less dependent on their therapist, and the narration
becomes a first effort to 'make the dream material one's own'. Working with
dreams through identification with the 'other' and the dreamer's relation
with the exciting and threatening may generally be considered to represent
the essence of the group process.

'Dream as text' in supervision

This approach has ample use for supervision purposes. Like the dream-teller
in a therapy group, the therapist reporting a patient's dream in a supervision
group should passively listen to the group's work. The dream-teller's turn to
share his insights and reaction to the group's reflections should come only
after the work on the dream is finished.[7] Working on a dream in supervision
may be a good opportunity for inexperienced therapists to learn from the
model of their supervisor's approach to a dream. Rereading a dream in a
supervision group, as text already read in the space between patient and
therapist, may also facilitate the 'parallel process' (Ekstein and Wallerstein
1958).

Dream-telling as a request for containment

The following material integrates new understanding from a *two- (or more)
person psychology* into the technique of dream interpretation. The main contribution is that a dream, often a message loaded with excessive exciting and
threatening contents unsatisfactorily processed in a first autonomous
attempt, may in a second attempt fulfil further working-through functions if
told to a receptive audience. Projecting these difficult emotions onto an

identifying audience may enable elaboration. Thus projective identification seems to be the main unconscious interpersonal relational process active in groups (Rafaelsen 1996), as well as central to the dream's unconscious function. Projecting disowned feelings onto an identifying group may fulfil at least three tasks: building some kind of object relation with the recipient of these messages; changing this significant 'other' through communication; and changing the self through the transformation this 'other' will accomplish for him.

What is containing ?

In an early description of containment, Bion compared it to a mental skin (in Echegoyen), a sense of envelopment like a skin around oneself, which protects and enfolds (Bick 1968). A container gives a sense of being in a safe place and 'being inside something good'. Britton (1998) described a patient requesting containment as searching for two things: a sanctuary, and meaning. Containment may be achieved by a variety of defined holding objects, even by words providing semantic boundaries around the emotional experience, as in therapy.

The relation with a container is also a process which transforms experience (Bion 1962b). Intolerable feelings may be evacuated or projected onto related containers (e.g. the good breast), and if they are processed and modified there, may become tolerable enough to be re-introjected. Bion thought that the model of transformation already described (projection, identification, processing beta into alpha through reverie), which he called the container/contained relationship, is a basic relationship, a predetermined form, a pre-conception. If the processing capacities generated in the link between infant and mother are lacking, they have to be improved in therapy. Similarly, I think that a 'dreamer's request for containment' constitutes an early basic and latent relationship, which may be re-established in therapy through initial external containment and subsequent re-internalisation. Ongoing failures in the container/contained relation/link damage unconscious processing of conflicts (Palombo 1992) and determine the development of thought and K (knowledge).

Internal and external containment are not the same. Internal containment is the capability of the self to process the contained, which is the difficult material. By external containment I mean the possibility to communicate, evacuate and project intolerable contents onto a better able containing object for further elaboration. Since container and contained mutually influence each other, both undergo transformation and learning processes, causing all involved parties in the group to develop.

'Container-on-call', 'dreaming with precautions' and the need of the dream-teller for an audience

Children's nightmares have compelling interpersonal functions: over-whelming emotions that cannot be contained and elaborated by the child's as yet immature ego (alpha function) wake the child up in panic. His shriek is a communication almost impossible for his parents to ignore. If they function as 'container-on-call', they will make themselves available and calm the little dreamer, mainly by their presence and receptiveness to the child's evacuation. I believe this kind of basic responsive interaction is internalised and continues to be more or less potentially active throughout life. In adult life, this containing 'presence' may also be described as 'dreaming with the analyst' (Bion 1992, p.38), or better still, 'dreaming with precautions' (p.40), allowing the dream to develop when the dreamer knows someone is there. It is natural to use significant others in order to cope with anxieties or other difficulties, such as a murderous superego (p.38), aroused by a dream and its contents. Sometimes even traditional dream-interpreters are enlisted in this containment effort which may be defined as part of 'the interpersonal functions of dream-telling' (Michael 1995; Ferenczi 1913, p.349). The dreamer needs a relation to an available and responsive object ('on-call') who is willing to envelop him in order to contain the exciting and threatening.

The difference between dreaming and dream-telling

Any disclosed content indicates both a surplus of tension and a request to further its containment by the group. As M. Khan maintains, a dream may be considered unsuccessful if the working through of an emotion is unsatis-fying, and surplus tensions raise the probability of the dreamer's acting out. Dream-telling as a request for external containment may be an alternative to its enactment, given the right interpersonal situation (psychotherapy, love, friendship). This development of external dialogue about his dream may be the 'unsuccessful' dreamer's last coping opportunity. The related to and iden-tifying audience, perceived as more able to process the unconscious intoler-able dream contents, becomes a target of projection. In this sense, dream-telling in a group (or elsewhere) always has communicative purposes. According to the level of its successful elaboration, any dream story may be evaluated as ranging from 'sharing elaborated information' (a 'known thought') to 'sending unprocessed messages' (an 'unthought known'). The elaboration levels are similarly reflected in what the dreamer and the therapist feel as ranging from low urgency 'dreams (thoughts) which found a thinker' to those 'still in search of a thinker.'

The unconscious connection between an audience and a dream may be further complicated by the possibility that dreams may be unconsciously created in the individual by others or the group (Pines 2000). Citing Ferenczi (1932, p.13): 'The patient feels that his dream fragment is a combination of the unconscious contents of the psyches of the analysand and the analyst.'

'The group' may be considered the relational space between the dreamer and his audience (the *'psychoanalytic third'* (Ogden 1996)). If a 'dream...is being generated in the intersubjective analytic dream space'(p.896), then the group certainly influences the dreamer not only to process his own problems, but also to identify with an evacuated group content and dream it up.[8] Dreams about participants and barely disguised analysts bear direct evidence of the group's matrix influencing the arousal of unprocessed intrapersonal conflicts. The dreamer's function in group therapy is often to tell the appropriate dream that may help a group's hitherto disowned content (e.g. some kind of latent sexual or aggressive feeling) be contained, elaborated and subsequently better integrated.

The group's ability to contain

Why are dreams more easily told in individual therapy than in a group? Early experiences (e.g. 'container-on-call' relationships) cause dyads to be a priori perceived as the preferred audiences to share intimate and conflictual emotions. Individuals seem also to be tempted into dyads where their dream-telling is (unconsciously) expected to have projective influence.

However, despite wishful thinking, in post-dyadic connections the possibility to be as tuned-in and understanding as in a mother–child relationship gradually diminishes. This may sometimes even be true of individual therapy, which, although representing the highest level of understanding and acceptance, may still have strong distorting biases when reacting to threatening and ambiguous contents.[9] Thus although a dream-teller may initially be naturally more distrustful of the group's containment ability, he should often be more suspicious of a dyad's possible misunderstanding of his dreams and their unconscious messages.

Because relevant reactions are of an emotional rather than cognitive nature, 'echoing' the multifaceted fragmented split-off carried by a dream is a very complex endeavour. Expecting it from an individual therapist, sensible as he might be, often seems to be a fantastic demand – and it can be handled more successfully by a number of receptive individuals. In order to cope with this complexity, analysts tend to unconsciously select central themes, which seem to represent their own idiosyncratic tendencies.[10] A responsive group's greater diversity and complex unconscious sensibility may enrich possible reflections of the intolerable material.

Psychic change can be conceptualised as taking place in two basic stages: an initial autonomous effort to work through stress, and, if unsuccessful, the subsequent possibility of completing it by external elaboration, especially through projective identification. Dreaming and dream-telling are thus different prototypes of change, representing two complementary models of the human mind's development. Therefore, dream-telling as a powerful vehicle of projective identification may be *the royal road to the self through the other's unconscious*.

The 'emotional echo' technique: a relational response to a request for containment

The group therapist, listening to the dreamstory together with the group and inviting everyone to share his or her own personal emotional resonance, helps contain the intolerable exciting and threatening feelings in the message. Instead of rejecting it under the cover of 'interpretations',[11] the participants are asked to associate personal material to the dream told, 'as if it were mine'. Although these '*echoes*' may seem at first idiosyncratic/individual/detached and even chaotic, the responses represent unconscious encounters with the message. They may be considered unconscious identifications which adumbrate and usually amplify various split-off emotions attached to the dream material. Together with the therapist's own emotional resonance (which includes his spontaneous tendencies to interpret), they should be regarded as part of the 'reverie' process, which not only decodes messages but also processes them by projective identification.

After sharing the 'echoes', an attempt is made to integrate all associations into an effective relational narrative. The therapist helps 'think the dream' by including opposing echoes in an effort to use them as split-off parts of a narrative in which the dreamer and the group-as-a-whole are put in relation.

The group's contribution to the individual dreamer starts by considering the different splits echoed by the participants as fragments of their inner worlds. As in Fairbairn, a first dialogue between the dreamer and his split parts is facilitated in the group.[12] On the group level, a similar integration should be accomplished between the split voices. Witnessing other participants linking with 'the disowned' also furthers working-through. As Betty Joseph (1987) states, containment is not only the (external) digestion and returning of the better elaborated, but already the *watching of containment* by another person is a corrective experience, may be therapeutic. 'There was a shift in mood and behaviour as my patient started to accept understanding and face the nature of his forcing into me, and he could then experience me as an object that could stand up to his acting in, not get caught into it, but contain it' (p.156).

Men's aggressive dreams requesting a feminine container – a clinical vignette from a 'dream-group'

The description of a difficult containment process and the use of dreams in group therapy will exemplify this relational approach in the following paragraphs. In the group, female participants processed their own defensiveness against the request for containment of emerging male primitive aggression. At the beginning they reacted with identificatory tendencies towards the aggressive men, and subsequently integrated overt assertive and aggressive behaviour.

In a 'dream-group', therapy is carried out through the telling of one, sometimes two dreams in a session and working through associations with the described relational technical approach. This particular ongoing group of eight members, most of them therapists, had been meeting twice a month for three hours for over a year and a half. Although 'dream-group' sessions without dream-telling are frequent and important, dreams are the main overt vehicle for representation and processing, and are approached as in analytical group therapy.

After the summer break, the group of seven women and one man became a group of five women and three men, as three women quit and were replaced. A difficult integration process started: the newcomers felt left out, did not understand many of the group codes and had bad feelings about their place in the group. Although the 'veterans' tried to elaborate on their ambivalence, it was obvious that subgroups of new versus old members made integration into the group difficult.

Dream-telling as an integrating experience

The newcomers' first attempts to become part of the group were not made through dream-telling: one female newcomer's sharing of an intimate sexual abuse experience she had had as a child induced identification, and one man's passive behaviour invited external active engagement. The most direct encounter between the subgroups was enacted by a very angry and frustrating rejection of another, more active male newcomer by one of the veteran women after he had touched her chair.

Work on these direct interactions could possibly, gradually and unconsciously, build a bridge towards integration, but in the present group this process was experienced consciously only after dream-telling. For some months, there was a good deal of tension and mostly unspoken hostility in the air while, at the same time, an aggression-container for the dreams of all participants was gradually developing. We tried to build a stable and open relationship between participants and subgroups, which sometimes bore the appearance of the dreaded split-off aggression. This aggression was 'known' but 'unthought' (Bollas 1987) and we had only vague and mostly unconscious warnings about it.

Aggression had taken a very mild and gentle 'feminine' form until the newcomers' arrival. During its first year, the group had normally been very open and honest, and mostly kind to one another. Despite interventions, the central affective theme could be described as 'hurts, pains and sorrows', which had always been met by identification and acceptance. Judging by the dream material, there were many losses, ambivalent relations with partners, and victimisation by external aggression. The 'echoes' in the group were mostly of neglect and hurt. Examples of the strongest aggression up to that point were dreams of a conflict with a fatherly boss, a baby who slipped from parental 'caring' hands and hurt his head, and some far-away intifada (Israeli–Palestinian violent armed conflict) in the 1980s. Aggression could also be detected in a dream in which a frustrated participant leaned on a huge window, causing it to fall from the 16th floor.

Male aggression in dreams

Four months after the newcomers had joined, the quality of dreams in the group began to change. The only male participant until then lifted the aggression threshold, as if (unconsciously) joining the male subgroup now permitted it. Dreams about terror attacks and 'army' dreams (which, contrary to expectations, are not often aired in Israel) came like an avalanche. The passive male dreamt about snakes, and in the third male's dream his little son, though babysat by his sister, fell out of a window. A man he had warned and threatened became the victim of his displaced violence. Later on we understood that our group had also been warned about surplus aggression. This set culminated in a dream told a year after it had been dreamt, actually by a man who had participated in the group from the start. Though the dream had shocked him, he could not tell it to the group in real time – presumably because he considered the 'feminine' container not yet ready to help him contain fears of his own aggression. The dream about 'Nazis invading the kibbutz' can now be used to demonstrate the relational approach to the work with dreams.

The group's immediate emotional response included identification and memories typical to 'second-generation' Holocaust survivors – mostly full of aggression and self-pity. Some were connected to the film *Life is Beautiful* by Roberto Benigni (1998), linked by emotionally detached associations, partly praising the hero's fatherly protective role, others diametrically opposing it as a 'fatherhood' and 'manhood' in need of containing. The strongest voice representing the repression of fears and aggression came from one female participant who thought the dream was 'optimistic'. After a participant objected to this 'optimism', I started to consider the possibility that these opposing feelings toward aggression were put on stage in order to better work through fears of destruction. Voicing my thoughts, I raised the possibility that the optimism was a reaction formation of both the group and the dreamer, in order to continue to repress hate and destructive aggression. The group now 'echoed' a process of decreasing distance between subgroups by talking rather freely about emotional differences and difficulties.

One member asked the dreamer if the Kapos were really his parents. I thought that although right, this 'interpretation' was now being used as a defence. It was an attempt to displace the encounter with aggression to a psychologically 'correct' but distant stage. I went on to raise the hypothesis that the encounter between the aggressor with the club and the victim provided a possibility to meet, identify and incorporate aggression for both the individual and the group here and now. The group responded by remembering the rejection of the newcomers.

Integrating aggression and sexuality

The next sessions' dreams, atmosphere and behaviour gave dramatic evidence of an effort to integrate the aggression. This was achieved mainly by first accepting angrier behaviour in the group, which subsequently transformed itself into assertiveness and a joining of genders, with sexual connotations. An ambivalent welcome to a newcomer combined one very rejective comment by a woman with an intimate sexual dream told by another. A party dream followed, including tender scenes 'without sexual feeling' between the female dreamer and a man.

This process seems to represent the struggle of the women in the group to form a transitional space together with the men that would be receptive to the fantasmatic, threatening and unacceptable aggressions. It seems that men, while unconsciously struggling with their masculine violent feelings, may be afraid of exposing these intolerable contents if suspicious of rejection.

We may speculate that this inter-gender process replicates the difficulties boys as young as four or five years old encounter in dream-telling because of lack of motherly containment. Mothers often seem to reject their boys' pre-dominantly violent dreams, preferring their daughters' more accepted contents. As a result, masculine dream-telling may be generally inhibited. Furthermore, those male aggressive contents (raw beta elements) which are not worked through by the mother's reverie, tend to be acted out instead of transformed into thoughts. Unfortunately, fathers may lack the ability to contain and elaborate dreams due to the rejection they experienced in their own childhood. This may well be nature's way of perpetuating male aggression.

The process that enabled participants to accept hitherto dreadful material was achieved by the group's work with dreams.

Preparing the container

Preparing the group

Preparing the group to contain dreams is a prototype of all engagements with difficult emotions and contents. The therapist has to help his group emotion-ally and technically. Helping the participants not to be too defensive, such as by facilitating the reowning of the 'other' in the dream, and encouraging them to trust and voice their emotional 'echoes' of the dream voices, often makes receptiveness possible.

The main emotional help is to let insight about the participant's tendency to project difficult emotions gain access to consciousness. In group therapy there is always a delicate balance between understanding interpersonal reactions as projections, which bear 'only' on the projector, versus accepting those reactions as feedback, which may enhance self-understanding for the 'container'. For example, a man with an aggressive dream may detect strong distancing and even (projected) hate in the audience. If the splits are too difficult to contain, potential rejection makes it imperative to help the participants bear distress in order to make themselves available to external threatening material. Better integration can be achieved if the rejection of projections is not too pervasive, which results in disabling free communication between members, and may have defensive roots. The working-through of projective identification, which is one of the most important sources of change, is made possible through closeness, openness and spontaneity. A sanctuary is often first built by a maternal holding function, including some kind of support (Winnicott 1960a), followed by a more active containment and elaboration through the group-as-a-whole and its therapist.

This feeling of security has a different meaning in every stage of the group's development. In the first stage of the therapist-centred group, the group analyst's personal support is important, leaving this function later in a group's life to the participants themselves. When strong cohesion threatens individuality, it is imperative to emphasise containment of differences and personal development. The feeling of secure containment despite variance is most important when conflict with other members or the therapist threatens autonomy and independent thinking. This development is achieved mainly by experiencing the ability of the therapist (representing the group's containment) to contain and process a great range of emotions. Another segment of the work is done cognitively through interpretations that help make splits conscious and integrate them in the reowned self of the group.

Preparing the therapist

Usually the therapist is in danger from a number of sources. Often the therapist unconsciously tries to use 'knowledge' as a means of establishing his superiority in the group. Blindness in the counter-transference may easily involve him in the enactment of hidden dream dramas. For example, he may be enlisted by the group to play the omnipotent analyst who, like Freud, deciphers every dream. By engaging in this role, he could contribute to the infantilisation of the group. Facing difficult dreams, the analyst may also forget that in order to make change possible cognitive approaches alone are not enough. Most of the transformations in therapy result from processing difficult emotions through the therapist's psyche, often by initially partici-pating unconsciously in difficult interpersonal patterns. Counter-projective identification has far-reaching implications in the group process, influencing the therapist's actions and hindering his maintaining a therapeutic stance. Ferenczi (1932) thought that because of the counter-transference 'in clinical psychoanalysis the dreams of the patient may provide a road to the uncon-scious of the analyst too' (p.2). Understanding his or her own reactions and projections are the prototypes of containment and elaboration. Most important, the therapist should have good contact with his own dreams, accepting them as being a meeting space with the exciting and threatening.

Summary

Psychoanalysis began by considering the interpretation of dreams to be the main road to the unconscious of the dreamer. Now it seems the royal road to the dreamer's unconscious is through audience identification, and a main road to change for all involved. Dreaming and dream-telling represent two complementary models of the human mind's development and transforma-tion. If preliminary autonomous attempts to process conflicts through dreaming remain unsuccessful, dream-telling may be used in a second inter-personal attempt as a powerful vehicle of projective identification onto a willing audience. Tentative theories about men's difficulty in sharing dreams, especially those of an aggressive nature, and the subsequent lack of elabora-tion were hypothesised.

References

Adams, M.V. (2000) 'Compensation in the service of individuation – Phenomenological essentialism and Jungian dream interpretation. Commentary on paper by Hasel Ipp.' *Psychoanalytical Dialogues 2000 1*, 127–42.

Bick, E. (1968) 'The experience of the skin in early object-relations.' *Internationl Journal of Psychoanalysis 49*, 484–6.

Bion, W. (1962b) *Learning from Experience*. London: Karnac Books.

Bion, W. (1963) *Elements of Psycho-Analysis*. London: Aronson.

Bion, W. (1967) *Second Thoughts*. London: Karnac Books.

Bion, W. (1992) *Cogitations*. London: Karnac Books.

Bollas, C. (1987) *The shadow of the Object*. London: Free Association.

Britton, R. (1998) *Belief and Imagination*. London and New York: Routledge.

Ekstein, R. and Wallerstein, R. (1958) *The Teaching and Learning of Psychotherapy.* New York: International Universities Press.

Erikson, E. (1954) 'The dream specimen of psychoanalysis.' *Journal of the American Psychological Association 2,* 5–56.

Fairbairn, W.R.D. (1963) 'Synopsis of an object-relations theory of the personality.' *International Journal of Psychoanalysis 44,* 224–5.

Ferenczi, S. (1913) 'To whom does one relate one's dreams.' In *Further Contributions to the Theory and Techniques of Psychoanalysis.* New York: Bruner/Mazel.

Ferenczi, S. (1932/1988) *The Clinical Diary of Sandor Ferenczi.* (ed J. Dupont) Cambridge, MA: Harvard University Press.

Freud, S. (1900) *The Interpretation of Dreams. Standard Edition 4/5.* London: Hogarth Press.

Freud, S. (1933) *New Introductory Lectures on Psycho-Analysis. Standard Edition 22,* 5. London: Hogarth Press

Freud, S. (1937c) *Analysis Terminable and Interminable. Standard Edition 23.* London: Hogarth Press.

Grinberg, L. (1979) 'Countertransference and projective counter-identification.' *Contemporary Psychoanalysis 15,* 226.

Grinberg, L. (1987) 'Dreams and acting out.' *Psychoanalytic Quarterly.* LVI. *Group-Analysis 30* (2), 187–202.

Grotstein, J.S. (1979) 'Who is the dreamer who dreams the dream and who is the dreamer who understands it.' *Contemporary Psychoanalysis 15,* 1.

Joseph, B. (1987) 'Projective identification – some clinical aspects.' In E. Spillius (ed) *Melanie Klein Today, Vol. 1.* London: Routledge.

Kanzer, M. (1955) 'The communicative function of the dream.' *International Journal of Psychoanalysis 36,* 260–66.

Khan, M. (1972) 'The use and abuse of dream in psychic experience.' *International Journal of Psychoanalytic Psychotherapy 1.*

Luborsky, L. and Mark, D. (1991) 'Short-term supportive-expressive psychoanalytic psychotherapy.' In P.C. Christoph and J.P. Barbar (ed) *Handbook of Short-Term Dynamic Psychotherapy.* Basic Books.

Meltzer, D. (1983) *Dream-Life.* Worcester: Clunie Press.

Michael, S. (1995) *Victoria.* Israel: Btb.

Morgenthaler, F. (1986) *Der Traum.* Frankfurt: Qumran.

Neri, C. (1998) *Groups.* London: Jessica Kingsley Publishers.

Ogden, T.H. (1996) 'Reconsidering three aspects of psychoanalytic technique.' *International Journal of Psychoanalysis 77,* 5, 883–900.

Palombo, S.R. (1992) 'The eros of dreaming.' *International Journal of Psychoanalysis 73,* 637–46.

Pines, M. (2000) *Funzionegamma.* Vol. 1.

Rafaelsen, L. (1996) 'Projections, where do they go?' *Group Analysis 29,* 2.

Scharff, D.E. (1992) *Refinding the Object and Reclaiming the Self.* Northvale, NJ and London: Aronson.

Segal, H. (1980) 'The function of dreams.' In S. Flanders (1993) (ed) *The Dream Discourse Today.* London: Routledge.

Segal, H. (1988) 'Sweating it out.' *Psychoanalitical Study of the Child 43,* 167–75.

Sharpe, E.F. (1932) *Dream Analysis.* London: Karnac Books.

Steiner de, C.M. (1995) 'Analysing children's dreams.' *International Journal of Psychoanalysis* 76, 45–9.

Steward, H. (1973) 'The experience of the dream and the transference.' In S. Flanders (1993) (ed) *The Dream Discourse Today.* London: Routledge.

Stolorow, R. and Atwood, G. (1982) 'Psychoanalytic phenomenology of the dream' in S. Flanders (1993) (ed) *The Dream Discourse Today.* London: Routledge.

Ullman, M. (1996) *Appreciating Dreams – a group approach.* London: Sage.

Vardi, D. (1990) *Memorial Candles.* Jerusalem: Keter.

Winnicott, D.W. (1960a) 'The theory of the parent-infant relationship.' In (1965) *The Maturational Processes and the Facilitating Environment.* London: Hogarth Press.

Endnotes

1. Most of the described approaches may also be used in individual therapy.

2. KZ-Polizei or Jewish police in concentration camps.

3. It is also possible to say that universal structures of primary processes are reflected in the structure of a play.

4. For example, post-traumatic patients often lack a protective introduction and seem to be 'attacked by surprise' by the threatening dream.

5. It especially improves the patients' ability to continue working on their dreams after the end of therapy in their never-ending eternal analyses (Freud 1937c).

6. The lack of appropriate group technique in working with dreams may explain Foulkes's difficulties with dreams.

7. Another technical (unanswered) question arises about the necessity of knowing the dream's context or the possibility of dealing with it as an independent 'text' representing a stable organisation relatively autonomous of situative influences.

8. A dream may also be a result of projective identification, much as action is in waking life.

9. Grinberg's counter-projective identification (1979) is an example of this kind of process.

10. Morgenthaler shows, for example, how Freud's interest in dreams centred on eliciting evidence for his unconscious theory and the Oedipal aspects (1986).

11. Ullman (1996) prohibits interpretations because of the so-called 'security factor' – not to enter the dreamer's inner space too strongly and endanger the dream-teller. Although the dreamer's fragility of personality is an important issue, it seems doubtful that his defences should break down as a reaction to even the deepest of 'wild' interpretations.

12. Gestalt and psychodrama also do this part of the work.

CHAPTER 4

The Polyphonic Texture of Intersubjectivity in the Dream

*René Kaës**

Interest in dreams amongst groups that follow the Freudian psychoanalytic pattern has produced three main research courses. The first is based on the analogy of the group with the dream. Anzieu (1966) proposed this approach, claiming that the group is like the dream. The second course studies the statute and function of the dream, the report of which becomes part of the association process of the group; this approach pays particular attention to the group oneirism, meaning the common dream or the shared one. I suggested a third research axis: it is based on the hypothesis that the dream is developed in the polyphonic texture of the interdiscourse. The dream is one of the most peculiar and private of our symptoms. The emphasis I put on the interdiscourse in the dream and in the group owes a lot to the work of Bakhtine and his followers. In his analysis of literary structure, Bakhtin introduced the idea that it emerges at the crossing of other structures, just as the word is a polyphony of several writings: those of the writer and his characters, of the addressee and of the historical, ethical and cultural context. The overdetermination of the word is revealed by its ambivalence or, better, by its polyvalence (Bakhtin 1929, 1963)

Polyphonic organisation is typical of the area of language. Bakhtin extends this principle to semiotic production in general: the logic organising

---

* English translation by Marie-Christine Reguis.

it, is not the logic of the linear determination and of identity, but instead the transgressive logic of the dream or of the revolution – another law is ruling.

The conception of polyphony is interesting here for another reason: it questions the belief of the author's uniqueness. In conclusion, Bakhtin believes in the idea of an inner social audience, which is specific for every individual, in the 'atmosphere of which his deduction, reasons, appreciations are produced' (Bakhtin 1929, p.123).

Finally, Bakhtin says, the word is oriented by two determining factors: 'it is at the same time determined by the fact it proceeds from someone, and by the fact it proceeds towards someone... Every word is used as a form of expression to the one related to the other one...the word is the common territory of the locutor and the interlocutor' (Bakhtin 1929, p.124). I tried to work on these ideas with regard to dreams. My research hypothesis about the polyphonic texture of the intersubjectivity in the dream rests on two bases. The first deals with the analysis of the dreams that are born from the group associative process (Kaës 1994). The second is concerned with the dreams whose manifest content stages a group and that are recounted on the couch. Could the analysis of such dreams clarify the general processes of the dream?

Dreaming in a group situation

In *The Interpretation of Dreams* (1900), Freud made the dream a private matter, pointing out its operating principles and suggesting a conception strongly based on its intrapsychic function: the dream is the halluncinatory realisation of an unconscious desire, a waking-state desire and an infantile repressed sexual desire.

In the group, the dream is expressed in accordance with other factors, as are the associative process and the patterns and contents of transference. In the group situation, what I call interdiscourse is the effect of the multiplicity of the speakers: the result is a double associative chain, one strand formed of the single subjects and the other formed from the succession and simultaneity of their statements. My hypothesis is that the dream 'in the group' is elaborated by one or more dreamers, at the crossing of their own oneiric apparatuses with the group psychic apparatus, that the group members build in common out of identificatory and fantasmatic resonance with other subjects. The dream is a polyphony of several conversations and figures; its origin is found in a series of utterances and statements which have been heard in the group during the previous day. The dream-carrier's 'factory of the dream' transforms the polyphonic productions to give them back to the group associations, equipped with a new representation, a preconscious one, and thus has an interpretative effect.

A woman dreaming in the group

I will briefly describe the context in which a dream appeared in a time limited group (16 sessions), conducted by a colleague (here her name is Sophie) and by me.

During the very first sessions, different members, particularly Marc, complained they lost their 'reference frames' because of the fact they came into that group. Considerable confusion occurred and subsided only when some of the group members explained the reason why they chose to join it. Marc declared that he joined the group 'because of my name' (which was the same as the conducting therapist's). The following session, he 'confessed' what was the 'marking' episode: in a similar group he had been strongly struck by an interpretation offered by the therapist who conducted it. This episode happened 15 minutes before the end of the last session. We did not know anything about the interpretation content; Marc communicated the emotion in all its violence, only through the tone of his voice. The lack of information about the interpretation content increased our confusion and difficulty in thinking.

Fifteen minutes before the end of the following session, Solange made herself the spokesperson of a 'secret' Anne-Marie had told her during a break: her daughter was to be hospitalised because of cancer, and she felt guilty about coming into the group. Though Solange said the words on behalf of another, she remembered the threat of cancer her mother had uttered against her when she was the same age as Anne-Marie's daughter.

There developed a common point of reference for traumatic events which had remained unthought (meaningless) on the basis of the first phantoms of loss of reference frames, of depersonalisation anxiety and confusion of identity. The memories of violence in relationships between parents and children, with their stake of life and death, were taken into the mechanism of transference on the therapists and on the group. How does the group organise itself during the very first sessions? I would say that the unconscious organiser of the group psychic apparatus is a phantom whose formula is: 'a parent threatens–repairs a child.' The fact that it is impossible to state this formula in only one way is an argument in favour of its polyphony: the scene includes a reversibility of the positions of the subject, the object and the action (acting the threat, suffering it). The internal group structure is recognised. In it, each subject benefits by a scene and by a related place which make him unique, according to the version of his secondary phantom.

The first session of the second day began with Michële telling us about her dream of the night before. She was making love with Marc's father or, maybe, with hers, in a room with everything in a mess. Both of them had grey hair. Surprised by her own words, Michële added that she did not really know what she was saying about fathers. Each element of the dream is the origin of different associative series. The first series are organised starting from the uncertainty of the father's identity (Marc's father or Michële's?), from their common features (grey hair) and the insistence and displacement of the incestuous desire. The chain will come up against the resistance of the transference on me ('the same grey hair') and on the silence of Marc, whose place in Michële's dream will often be recalled. The second associative series – 'the room in a mess', the love disorder – has a different origin. On the previous day there was a 'battlefield', a violent and chaotic primal scene. The third series takes its origin just from recalling this catastrophe: the sudden and violent death of one of the participants' fathers, the disappearance of a friend on the mountains, the death of an elder brother, the paralysis of a mother because of a road accident.

The evocation of these traumatic events and of death will provoke a further libidinal cathexis which supports a fourth associative link. The main reason of the dream is taken into consideration again: there, in the group, is it possible to make love without breaking the prohibition of incest between siblings? Or is it that the requirements of the abstinence rule are valid only for the relationships between therapists and participants?

Let us go back to Michële's dream and let us stop on the representation of 'Marc's father' as an object of the displacement of her incestuous desire, which is here expressed directly. Michële's dream is also Michële's interpretation of what she unconsciously picks up about what has been put at stake in a traumatic event in Marc's life. In fact this involves her too, because it deals with her own phantom of seduction by the father. The associative work of the group makes the variations of the phantom of seduction larger, expressing its connections to other phantoms. Michële's dream is co-determined by the associative process of the group; Michële dreams of an unknown side of herself.

The dream marks that interdiscourse. Starting from Michële's dream, in the core of the organising phantom of the group, a transformation is formed:

the reprisals phantom is linked to the seduction phantoms, particularly the phantom of sexual seduction of the son by the father.

The dream tale in the group

The clinical example allows us to analyse the structure of the dream and that of its narration in the group more precisely. The first question concerns the dreamer: as far as the cited situation is concerned, who dreamt the dream? Obviously, Michële did: above all and to the highest degree, the dream is 'selfish', as Freud reminded us. It consists of its function of hallucinatory satisfaction. Is this also the case with the making and the addressing of it?

If we take into consideration the group associative work during the previous sessions, we have to suppose that, in the group, day psychic residues have been produced. These psychic residues have been picked up by Michële to formulate the dream thoughts, and have been used and transformed according to her own fabricating processes. We could say that, as an oneiric representation, Michële realised her own desire and at the same time what she perceived about the phantoms and psychosexual and unconscious conflicts mobilised in the group.

The dream is Michële's interpretation of what is still repressed in the group and close to becoming preconscious in herself. We can apply to the dream of the group what Freud wrote in the analysis of the dream of the botanic monograph, by recalling Goethe's metaphor about the weaver: 'here we are in the core of a thoughts factory' (Freud 1900, p.289). Michële's dream is the original fabric that she weaves on the loom of the weaver–group. It also gives us a representation of the psychosexual conflicts and phantoms moving in the group. As a dream-carrier, she loads herself with everything that the group can't dream about.

The second issue is about the addressee of the dream. Of course, Michële dreams for herself, for a part of herself whose representation she delegates to the characters of the dream. However, she also dreams for the group participants who take on the characteristics of her transferred objects: Marc, me, Sophie, the group as a whole, the addressees of her dream. In the group, the interpretative function of the dreamer has been recognised by the group and the dreamer dreams to keep on this function by which, 'selfishly', she receives some benefit. The dream-carrier is formed through the same process Levi-Strauss described to produce the sorcerer. In the very same way, the group attributes to one of its members the function of interpreter–dreamer: it invests him with a function the dreamer couldn't grant to himself by himself.

Thus he becomes and recognises himself as a group dreamer, just as the sorcerer holds his power and function since he knows he is the sorcerer and he is recognised as the sorcerer by the others: 'He is proclaimed sorcerer; since there are some, he could be one' (Levi-Strauss 1958, p.189).

What is the nature of the associative work which is realised in the group? Pontalis (1972, pp.251–68) pointed out the contrast between the poverty of the dreamer's associations on his dream in the group, and the interest the group members' associations show about the dream. I suppose that this phenomenon depends on the fact that the group recognises itself as the beneficiary, the maker and the addressee of the dream. Therefore, the group interprets it as material built for an interpretation. We shall say therefore that the dream narration made by a dreamer in the group is a tale offered to the associations of the group members.

I identify five functions of the dream in the group:

1. A function of return of the repressed in a representation that is acceptable for the preconscious. A female member will have access to her own incestuous phantom after the narration of Michële's dream and the group members' associations having issued some signifiers that she can use.

2. A function of intersubjective treatment of the day residues which are carriers of meaning still unconscious and charged with instinctual investments repressed the day before.

3. A function of container and contained of the representations (Bion's alpha elements).

4. A function of representation dramatised and staged, coupled with the subjective positions in the group.

5. A function of granting the dreamer a privileged position in the group topic, dynamic and economy and thus in the transference dimensions. This function is the one of the dream-carrier.

We can verify that the five functions are those performed by Michële's dream tale in the group. Before Michële's dream, Marc's symptom is based on the assertion of the reality event which 'marks' him, the reason that he had the 'mark'.

The dream tale, the associative work and the transference analysis open the access to the meaning of the symptom: the incestuous and confusing relationship with the father will put into action a process of transformation of his traumatic representation.

The figure of the dream-carrier

Some subjects such as Marc, Solange and Michèle guarantee the intermediate functions which are necessary to the process of the intersubjective connections: in the family, in a couple, in a group or in an institution. These subjects provide those functions for personal reasons, but also after an intersubjective determination to which they were subdued: they are the spokespeople, symptom-carriers, dream-carriers, death-carriers, ideal-carriers... I suggest the concept of 'phoric' function to specify these positions and functions. The dream-carrier teaches us about the 'phoric' function of those 'group dreamers', such as we find in some families or in some psychiatric centres amongst the medical staff as well as amongst the patients. I tried to show how these dreamers dream their own dream, but also that some events from the day before produce the dream's content and destination.

The content includes events shared by the group members and common traumatic experiences. The destination is determined by the transferences, which are often very strong and by the identifications régime, often of a protective type. The dreamer dreams in this situation, giving and telling his dream to the group, posing the question of dream making. Starting from here, we pose the question of its further use in the group intersubjective relationships. We could formulate the following hypothesis. The dream-carriers make dreams from the interdiscourse polyphony which contributes to dream making. Like all analysands, they dream of someone or for someone. These dreamers dream in somebody else's shoes. They become dream-carriers because of the inner need to establish a psychic room larger than their own, through projective identifications. They need to deposit it in an external container: an other, or more than an other, or a whole group. The dream-carriers play the interpreting role of their preconscious function. This is the basis of group oneirism: dreams travel amongst the members of a group, there is an exchange of characters and letters and the exchange implies a porosity of psychic wrappings, as contained in the narcissistic wrapper of the shared dream by the mutual identifications.

In the psychoanalytic clinic of the group, the position held by the dream-carrier is placed at the crossing point of three spaces: that of the shared phantom, that of the associative discourse and that of the intersubjective structure witnessed by the transferences.

The dream as interdiscourse and intersubjective texture

If we say that the dream is an interdiscourse organisation in which the work is done and the elements are anchored to the intersubjectivity in the 'factory' where each element is distinguished, is the polyphony conception productive when it is applied to the dream analysis outside of the group situation? Which are the dream production processes which are responsible for its polyphonic character? I will use a particular kind of dream to try to give an answer: the group dream.

This is a dream in which the dreamer takes on the roles of different characters linked together by different kinds of relationships: often, many people meet in a familiar setting (an apartment, a house), in a guest room (the living-room, the dining-room or even the therapist's studio), or in a 'passing-by' space (the entrance, the corridor, the hall), but sometimes also in public spaces (an amphitheatre, a meeting room, a church).

These people are parents, friends, other analysands, work colleagues, school friends or social acquaintances. The people who are met can constitute a restricted group: a family, staff, guests, a crowd, an assembly with characters more or less identified.

The associations which are stimulated by these dreams are based on the pleasure of being together in the space where the family members meet together, of meeting important people, of giving a party; or, on the opposite side, on the basis of the sorrow of being alone in the midst of strangers, of being lost in a crowd and being invaded, observed and threatened; or, being rejected and forgotten. However, it can also happen that the dreams do not produce any association.

Freud had applied to the analysis of these dreams the basic principles he had elaborated in *The Interpretation of Dreams*. Some dream processes can explain the relationships between the dreamer and the characters grouped in the dream. In group dreams, the plurality, the multiple and the composite figures are effects of identification, condensation, diffraction and multiplication.

Identifications and the dream: conglomerate-people, diffraction and multiplication

The reference to a plurality of objects or of psychic characters is present in Freud's theories defining identification, dating from 1897: 'the plurality of psychic people: the fact of the identification maybe authorises the literary use of the expression' (Freud 1900, p.133). This first observation is contemporary to the studies on hysteria and it goes together with Fliess's debate, particularly at the moment of the operation on Emma Eckstein's nasal trumpets. This will be a useful guiding thread for the analysis of the dream called 'Irma's injection', and will provide the explanatory principle of the dream called 'of the butcher's wife'.

The analysis of the dream of the butcher's wife shows how the identification binds two (or more) people in a community:

> Identification is a highly important factor in the mechanism of hysterical symptoms. It enables people to express in their symptoms not only their own experiences, but those of a large number of other people, it enables them, as it were, to suffer on behalf of a whole crowd and to act all the parts in the play singlehand-ed. (Freud 1900)

All of a sudden, we have a group version of the identification, of the phantom, of the dream and of hysteria.

This grouped representation of the dream objects will be evidenced by the formation of the conglomerate-persons: the work of grouping is realised through the mechanism of condensation of the dreamer's objects. Thus, in the analysis of the dream of Irma's injection, Freud shows that in the back of the Irma of his dream are dissimulated many people he knows: his patient (Emma), his elder daughter (Anna), his niece, a girl in the hospital, another patient, his wife and other people. The dream analysis explains what the condensation work has collected: '"Irma" of the dream...so she has become a general image, made up of a series of contradictory features. Irma represents all the people sacrificed during the condensation work because it happens to him what happened to them' (Freud 1900, p.254).

My opinion is that each Irma who was dreamt, survived the sacrifice which the censorship had imposed.

Their identical and different features produced the polyphony of the dream crossed by all the different 'people' forming the Irma-group. The principle which binds the self of the dreamer to his dream characters is still identification. On this basis, Freud observed that the dream of the butcher's wife fulfilled the desire that there was something common to two people: and it was expressed by the exchange of one person with the other (Freud 1900, p.155).

Diffraction is one of the primary processes which contributes to the creation of group dreams. The representation process combines with the decondensation, displacement and multiplication so as to produce a specific mechanism which is responsible for the multiple representation of the self-aspects which are represented by the dreamer's characters or objects, making up a group. The different elements of the dream's content represent only one idea, in fact: an object, an image, the very person of the dreamer is decomposed into multiple representatives, identical or otherwise. Just as, for a subject, different members of a group can represent different aspects of his inner universe.

> There are also dreams in which my ego appears along with other people who, when the identification is resolved, are revealed once again as my ego. These identifications should then make it possible for me to bring into contact with my ego certain ideas whose acceptance has been forbidden by the censorship. Thus my ego may be represented in a dream several times over, now directly and now through identification with extraneous persons. By means of a number of such identifications, it becomes possible to condense an extraordinary amount of thought material.

The dream of the group: effect of the dream work or typical dream?

I have attempted to show that in the dream, the group is a particular effect of the representational processes used by the dream. I would like to carry on the analysis from another point of view, putting the dreams of the group next to the typical dreams. In effect, the group, a number of people are often present in this category of dreams. In the analysis of dreams of nakedness, Freud observed that the dreamer dreams himself naked or partially dressed in front of strangers. He suggested the following interpretation: '"A lot of strangers" who take no notice of the spectacle that is offered – is nothing more or less than the wishful contrary of the single familiar individual before whom the dreamer exposed himself.' (Freud 1900). Freud made his suggestion general: 'A lot of strangers frequently appear in dreams in many other connections, and they always stand as the wishful contrary of "secrecy"' (Freud 1900).

In the dreams about the death of loved ones, Freud suggested another example of the presence of a great number of characters. He reported the dream of one of his patients: 'Lots of kids, her sons, her cousins, everybody was playing on the field. All of a sudden, everyone had wings and they flew away and disappeared.' Freud proposed to imagine that, having asked what happened to dead babies, she had heard people say they grew wings and became little angels. In the dream she gave the wings to her younger sons and she made them disappear as butterflies which flew away.

What do the multitude or the group represent in the typical dreams? The group is not only a representation of the inner group of the analysand. It does not represent only the multiples making up the self which are represented in the difference of characters and their common link. The group is the representation of the inner audience, owned by each person. Finally, and this is the new proposition, it gives a representation of desires and of 'conflicts' which cross the identificatory 'composition' or the 'code' of the subject: the conversations heard from different sources are woven in the texture of the dream.

The polyphonic and intersubjective texture of the dream

The dream is polyphonic, it is elaborated at the crossing point of many structures of many processes and the materials it organises, transforms and interprets are heterogeneous. As the word is a polyphony of many writings, the dream is built on the basis of the productions and inner process of the dreamer, but some daily remainders and traces or marks of others are inscribed in the identifications of the dreamer. The dream which is dreamt is a composite construction. The dream is not a closed statement, it is acted and addressed: it is a transformation process, it is crossed by utterances or by other people's perceptions, sometimes by their dreams. The trace of this overdetermination of the dream shows in its ambivalence, better in its polyvalence. The dream is heterogeneous, heteromorphous, heterologous (Bakhtin); this last characteristic is a consequence of the diversity existing amongst the psychic apparatus structures, the dream sources, the making process and the addressees or the people to whom the dream is devoted. The dream tale is *a fortiori*: its explanation tends to reduce the diversity, but its interpretation must give it back. Who is dreaming in the dreamer? For whom does he dream? So to support the polyphony perspective in the dream, we have to imagine another dream navel to be found in the intersubjective chain. I have tried to show that in the group the dreamer is also the dream-carrier of another or of a collective of others. Now, we have to think about the limits of the intrapsychic space and its overflowing in a different way. As Breton, Artaud, Borges and Tabucchi suggested, maybe every dream is crossed by the signs and the dreams of desire of another.

References

Anzieu, D. (1966) 'Étude psychanalytique des groupes réels.' In D. Anzieu *et al.* (1998) *Le groupe et l'inconscient. L'imaginaire groupal.* Third edition. Paris: Dunod.

Bakhtin, M. (1929) *Le marxisme et la philosophie du langage.* Paris: Les Editions de Minuit, 1977.

Bakhtin, M. (1929) *La poétique de Dostoïevski.* Paris: Les Editions du Seuil.

Freud, S. (1887–1904) *Briefe an Wilhelm Fliess.* Frankfurt and Main: S. Fischer Verlag.

Freud, S. (1900) *The Interpretation of Dreams. Standard Edition 4.* London: Hogarth Press.

Kaës, R. (1994) *La parole et le lien. Le processus associatifs dans les groupes.* Paris: Dunod.

Levi-Strauss, C. (1958) *Antropologie structurale.* Paris: Plon.

Pontalis, J.B. (1972) 'Rêves dans un groupe.' In D. Anzieu *et al.* (1982) *Le travail psychanalytique dans les groupes, 1. Cadre et Processus.* Paris: Dunod.

CHAPTER 5

Sharing Dreams in Group Therapy

Peter J. Schlachet

Introduction

Some time back, I had a patient who reported turning around in bed to her sleeping husband in the middle of the night, slamming him over the head, and screaming 'How dare you, you scum!' It seems she had had a dream in which she had caught him in bed with another woman. Now, aside from being tempted to interpret the dream, you might perhaps think, 'Well, this Schlachet fellow obviously had a borderline character on his hands, one who had some difficulty distinguishing her dream from reality.'

But consider. Was she really that far afield? When I decided to entitle this 'Sharing Dreams in Group Therapy', the double meaning of the title was quite intentional. When we tell a dream in the context of a therapy group, we are indeed sharing our dream with the other members. But is there another kind of sharing going on? Is the dream we are relating really solely and completely our own, the product of our singular, unique and circumscribed psyche, independently fashioned solely from the elemental material of our own inner world? Or, is there perhaps some additional dimension, some participation by the other members in the construction the metamorphism, the symbolisation, the feeling tone, or perhaps other aspects of the dream?

A hypothesis

What I am leading up to here is a hypothesis about what happens in groups – and perhaps even in societies – of which dreams, already recognised since Freud as 'the royal road to the unconscious', may well be the gauge and mirror. The unconscious to which he was of course referring was that of the individual patient with whom he was consulting. The context in which his patients reported their dreams encompassed only himself and the patient He was the one for whom the narration was intended. And, of course, his own dreams, which he reports in his *The Interpretation of Dreams*, existed only for himself – and, naturally, his readers. Can we say the same about our patients – one of five, six, seven or eight – all of whom we are dealing with simultaneously in our groups?

In that group context, matters are considerably more complex. Not only is the therapist addressed in the recitation of a dream, but the other members are as well. In addition, they have participated in the antecedent events of the dream, they both comprise and construct the context in which it is reported, and they, along with the therapist, are the intended audience. So, in addition to being a relational event, as in the dyadic situation, the dream narrative becomes a social event in which all the members of the group participate.

This is not unique to our small groups. Various societies recognise that the dream is not necessarily a solitary event, but rather a socially contextualised experience, to be shared both in its production and its use. Among the Senoi of Malaysia, dreams are an integral part of the social fabric and of daily life, shared, discussed and acted on by all, from children to ancients (Greenleaf 1973). The Australian aborigines consider dreaming an entré into the underlying unity of things, including the social system itself; the Mapuche Indians of Chile share their dreams with other family members, especially during times of stress; and the Cuña Indians of Panama view dreaming as an important part of shared experience. In still other societies as well, dreams have social functions. 'Dreaming has been regarded as an important source of transpersonal information by many sociocultural systems', writes Arden (1996, p.104), noting that 'the Naskapi Algonquin in Labrador, the Cushininahua in Eastern Peru, the Siberian Chuckahee and the Australian Unambal constitute a small sample of the sociocultural systems for which dreams play an important shamanic role... In fact, dreams are regarded as so important by the Parintinin tribe, Kagwhahiv, of the Amazon, that they have constructed a single linguistic form for the description of them' (Arden 1996, p.104).

Background studies

But I am getting ahead of myself. Before getting into the specifics of what a dream might express or embody in a group, let me backtrack a bit and talk for a moment in more general terms about dreams. Before Freud, the dream was seen largely as an other-worldly manifestation, an emanation from either divine or demonic sources. Freud's (1900) monumental and groundbreaking work demystified the dream and brought it within the realm of scientific scrutiny. Recognising dreams as a form of mentation, albeit a primitive one, taking place during sleep, and, he felt, rendering it undisturbed – or relatively so – he saw it as an important form of psychic activity, one that had far-reaching implications for the entirety of psychological functioning. It is interesting to note, and a cogent salute to Freud's inferential genius, that Solms (1995), many years later, found physiological evidence in his neuropsychological studies to support not only the notion that dreams protect sleep, but that they have symbolic value. He observed that patients in whom brain lesions had totally eliminated dreaming, contrary to the expectation that their sleep would be less disturbed and hence more sound, had more difficulty staying asleep than the comparison group of control patients. And, he noted that in patients in whom the seat of symbolic thought was destroyed, that is, the frontal lobes, dreaming was completely eliminated.

Kleitman's description of REM sleep back in the 1950s, and his and Dement's subsequent research on dreaming during REM sleep, provided a resurgence for the study of dreams and cast the entire enterprise in a new light. In addition to interest in the psychological and psychodynamic character of dreams, numerous studies emerged exploring both the possible functions and the physiological underpinnings of this phenomenon. Questions not only of how we dream, but 'what's the point', have been sparking debate now for years. Some, like Hobson and McCarley (1977) and Crick and Mitchison (1986), see dreaming as mere random activity of the nervous system in the process of 'refreshing network links' (Van den Daele 1996) and of retuning itself. Others, such as Winson (1990) and Vanderwolf (1969) see it as an essential part of the nervous system's information-processing efforts. It is this view that sparked my interest and that I found particularly intriguing and potentially relevant to understanding some of what I had observed when dreams were reported in my therapy groups.

Vanderwolf (1969) was able to demonstrate that most mammals 'display a prominent electroencephalographic signature' in situations where species-specific survival behaviours are especially significant. These

5-cycle-per-second 'theta' waves occurred in cats during predation, in rabbits when apprehensive and in rats during exploration. Whishaw and Vanderwolf (1973) showed that these *same* waves occurred in animals during periods of REM sleep, which presumably coincides with dreaming. Winson (1990) used this evidence to develop the hypothesis that species-specific primary adaptive behaviour and dreams are linked, and that this dream activity functions to 'rehearse, consolidate, and enact species-specific adaptive strategies' (Van den Daele 1996) during the brain's 'down time', that is, sleeping. In primate species, 'theta activity occurs in children and adults when emotionally aroused in wakeful states, and when falling asleep...and in REM states' (Van den Daele 1996, p.256).

Extrapolating from this line of thinking, in my 1995 paper (Schlachet 1995) I propose that in humans, the most salient species-specific survival behaviour is social interaction and interpersonal responsiveness, and that the process of consolidating 'species-specific adaptive strategies' revolves around these interpersonal events. Van den Daele (1992) made a similar observation. In categorising dreams by content, among other things, he notes that what he calls 'relational orientation' is one of the motifs which tend to organise dream themes.

So, what can we glean from all this so far? First, that there are particular neurophysiological events underlying dreams, that dreams are functional and even necessary (and there is a good deal of other evidence which I haven't mentioned here to corroborate these points), they are contextual, that is, related to ongoing events and circumstances in the life of the dreamer, and they are adaptive for the dreamer. I might also add that in being contextually adaptive, they also represent efforts at solving problems – of whatever kind. These can be circumstantial or internal to the dreamer, embody some reality difficulty or some imagined challenge, but they always include some effort, even if ultimately unsuccessful, to overcome a problem. The fulfillment of a wish represents one such problem-solving effort, which a dream, in hallucinatory fashion, can resolve quite readily. Extrapolating somewhat loosely from the various thoughts I have been offering, we might say that in humans, the adaptive and problem-solving function of dreams has to do largely with an internal effort to resolve what goes on between people, particularly if what goes on between them has some emotional intensity, and that their dreams serve to integrate and metabolise these experiences.

So, this is a process that goes on within individuals. Now let's look at how what happens between them might affect this process.

More about dreams

In groups, members often display an uncanny knack for understanding the communications inherent in one another's dreams. How is this possible? We mentioned earlier that dreams are a form of mentation. I would like to suggest that in many ways they are very similar to ordinary conscious thinking and communication. Bonime (1962) has even quite explicitly described dreams as a form of thinking.

Freud (1900) discerned a number of presumably special mechanisms which appeared to be specific to dreams, the nature of which enabled him, in his famous Chapter 7, to infer much of the workings of the psyche. These included displacement, substitution, using part for whole, inversion, and condensation, among others. On what basis can we assert the similarity to conscious thought and language? Let's consider ordinary speech. Carefully scrutinised, it can be seen to contain a wealth of metaphor and other 'poetic' devices. It reveals itself to contain almost all the mechanisms which are also present in dreams, and it utilises these to create impact, to express feeling or to communicate affect. That the two are intimately interrelated – perhaps even reciprocal – is also mirrored, it seems to me, in the converse: dream images often represent a spoken expression pictorially. I recall a dream of my own of many years ago, about my father, in which a horse appeared, but its teeth were all on the outside of its head. It turned out, as we worked on the dream, that I was 'looking a gift horse in the mouth'.

But to return, consider expressive forms such as synecdoche, metonymy, metaphor, and displacement. In poetry, we take these forms completely for granted as natural expressive tools, but we often do not realise that they also exist in our most ordinary daily speech. When we spend a lot of money on a 'big-ticket item', say, a car, we hardly expect to take home a huge piece of paper, but rather we are expressing a certain awe at how much money we've just been induced to spend, describing the experience using metonymy, the substitution of one thing for another; or when you ask someone to 'give me a hand', you don't really expect to receive a bloody stump. Rather you are quickly and economically conveying your momentary and imperative need, using synecdoche to get the message across, that is, using a part to represent the whole. I am sure the 'roaring twenties' were no noisier than today's world, in which traffic jams and the sound of jet engines abound, but the descriptive metaphor certainly expresses the ambience very effectively. We use hyperbole for emphasis – 'The greatest show on earth!' – or ironic inversion to express opposites, like speaking of 'his saccharine smile'. When we talk about 'the hand that rocks the cradle', aren't we using displacement? And so it goes. And isn't that expression also a metaphor? Nothing is 'going' anywhere, but the device indicates a sense of progression, doesn't it?

These and various other forms of speech are how we communicate verbally with one another to convey our inner states, our needs, our feelings, our subjective experiences. Virtually our every utterance conveys images or creates images in the listener. The most salient difference between speech and dreams is perhaps that normal dreams, rather than conveying such states verbally, do so pictorially. Granted, there are other types of dreams, but these with visual images seem to predominate. One patient described her nocturnal experiences as 'going to the movies', which I thought was a rather cogent way of getting across not only the pictorial nature of her dreams, but also what her dream experiences felt like to her.

Just as various forms of consciously articulated communication depict affect, so do dreams convey the subjective, affective, emotive, experiential world of the dreamer. Their language, however, is entirely metaphorical. Whereas spoken and written language uses denotation as well as connotation, dreams are limited to the latter: the language of dreams is completely affective. An attempt to understand dreams in objective, denotational terms, will invariably go astray. Put somewhat differently, to understand dreams we must suspend secondary process and immerse ourselves in primary process thinking. We must tune into their poetry. That is the medium of dream exchange.

Yet, unless there is some psychic difficulty, we all naturally understand communication in these poetic forms, because that is after all how we spontaneously communicate with one another. Denotation is an astoundingly small part of what transpires between people. It is no particular surprise, then, that patients can often communicate in dream symbols, that telling one another their dreams can become a cogent, powerful means to intimate mutual understanding, a mode of exchange which can quickly create a sense of commonality and bonding.

Events between members in the group situation itself

By now you must be wondering, 'This is all very well, but what does it have to do with what happens in my groups around the dreams they bring in?' A good question. Well, let's talk for a moment about the experiences people in groups have with one another. Let's look at the group context within which dreams are spawned. Presumably, the situation is one which is highly emotionally charged, one in which members affect and influence one another, often in powerful ways. We have already talked about how language can convey charged emotional interchanges, but we have not yet considered what else there is that is simultaneously going on. The words being exchanged are only a small fraction of what is actually taking place. The levels and types of interaction are varied and multifaceted. They include, to mention a few, gestures, attitudes, body posture, limb position, facial expression, vocal pitch, timbre and inflection, eye orientation and movement, synchrony and asynchrony of various kinds, among many others. Even without hearing the words being spoken, like in a video without the sound, we could discern most of what is transpiring among the members of a group. I would like, then, to dwell for a moment on these other facets of group interaction; I would like to consider questions of emotional contagion, facial expression and the nonverbal interpersonal communication of affect. I believe this is the medium, the matrix, if you will, out of which dreams in groups arise.

Hatfield, Cacioppo and Rapson (1993, 1994) have described some interesting findings about how people affect each other emotionally. They define emotional contagion as 'the tendency to automatically mimic and synchronise expressions, vocalisations, postures, and movements with those of another person's and, consequently, to converge emotionally' (p.96).

They cite the fact that infants are capable of mimiking facial expressions of emotion very shortly after birth (Emde 1983), and refer to the Condon (1982) study which showed that college students could synchronise their movements with one another within one twentieth of a second, about the time it takes to show one movie picture frame. They point out, and cite considerable experimental evidence for the fact, that 'people tend from moment to moment to catch other people's emotions' (p.99). This happens spontaneously and instantaneously. Hatfield *et al.* (1994) quote Condon's fascinating assertion that 'For people to match their behaviours within 50 milliseconds requires some mechanism unknown to man.' Perhaps most importantly, all this transpires without the participants having any awareness of what they are doing.

Ekman (1993) found not only that people tended unconsciously to imitate one another's emotional facial expressions, but that individuals imitating a particular facial expression began to feel the emotion. You have all undoubtedly made these observations yourselves in your groups. But Ekman also discovered that not only were facial expressions universal and could be recognised similarly across cultures – at least those for fear, anger, disgust, sadness and enjoyment – but that they had underlying neurophysiological implications, they had both autonomic and central nervous system correlates. (Now isn't that interesting: so do dreams.) Going beyond postural and facial coordination, mutual synchrony can in fact be so profound that women have been observed unconsciously to coordinate their menstrual cycles with one another (McClintok 1971).

Similar things happen in groups, where members pick up one another's affects in a whole variety of ways: by contagion, by imitating one another's facial expressions, by synchronising their gestures with one another and with the leader (have you ever noticed how your own gestures are mirrored by your patients' gestures?) and, of course, by responding to what they are saying to one another. But the point here is that the channels of affective interchange are multiple, many-tiered, instantaneous, largely unconscious, and quite powerful. These are some of the constituents of what Foulkes calls 'the matrix', aren't they? Moreover, members share contextual and situational circumstances. They are all 'in it together', all sharing the same challenges to the group, the same struggles within the group, the same traumatic experiences and memories, the horrific fantasies, the lurid dreams which are placed there for all to shoulder jointly. And all of this can be, and often is, highly emotionally charged. So their autonomic nervous systems (viz. Ekman's research) are working overtime during the group and, if Winson's hypothesis holds any water (another metaphor) they are all processing these shared feelings, experiences and interactions in their limbic systems after and between group sessions. Each person in the group is striving to integrate and metabolise emotionally charged experiences, material that the work of the group has elicited, which in turn has stimulated in each one current affective reactions as well as affective residua. And each person in the group, in the adaptive work ongoing during their sleeping and dreaming, is struggling to metabolise and integrate these new exposures. The dreams which they then produce in their efforts to cope with the emotional impact of their shared experiences, and which they bring into the group for support in that coping effort, will quite naturally and understandably have overlapping elements, attenuated and filtered, of course, through each individual's unique psychic apparatus. The presented dreams can then as a matter of course be expected to reflect, in one fashion or another, feelings, concerns, responses, preoccupations, problems, themes, challenges, etc., which the group as a whole is confronting, and these will thread through all of the dreams presented in any given session. The Senoi know this about their dreams and use it as a lubricant to their social machinery. In our ongoing groups as well, we can observe that – given individual variations – members' dreams express their shared common circumstances.

Shared dreams in new groups

In groups in which members have known one another for a period of time, this phenomenon may not be unexpected. One can at times, however, discern that something similar seems to happen even in new groups, where dreams which members bring into the group seem to have common thematic material. How can this be, given what I've been saying up to now? If in this instance we view the dreams not as some very special form of communication amongst intimates, but rather as another in a chain of shared group associations, this phenomenon becomes easily comprehensible. The dream is then understood as another way of bringing feelings and issues into the group for scrutiny, or as an oblique commentary on the events transpiring either in the group itself or in the context in which the group in embedded. I led a workshop on dreams at one conference in which – even though the people did not know one another and the group had never before been constituted with these members – a number of dreams were presented, all of which seemed to have the same underlying thread. It turned out, as the group associated to the various recounted dreams, that all the group members were responding to their shared experiences in the conference as a whole, and the dreams were in essence the affective associational material reflecting this. Once this was identified, the group was able to work on their shared unresolved traumas and dissatisfactions with the conference at large and experience a good deal of relief from the pent-up tension they had brought into the workshop.

Dreams as associations and associations to dreams

What happened in that workshop is what so often happens in groups: when one dream is brought in it seems to stimulate the recitation of other dreams by other members. It is akin to an associational chain, except that the associations, instead of being thoughts, words, fantasies, etc., are dreams. That in itself might be a clue to connecting threads existing between them, but the implications are more far-reaching than that. The dream recitations seem to have both a horizontal and a vertical vector: horizontal in their ongoing associational context, but vertical in appearing to tap something much deeper and to serve a more profound function for the group as a whole. In light of the shared context, the shared affects, the shared group experiences, and the shared group-wide problems and circumstances (for instance, losses, new members, vacations, illnesses, important anniversaries, etc.), the dreams which members report, both as associations to contextual ongoing events in the group and as expressive utterances, can be understood as serving a 'container' function, that is, expressing some deeper group-wide issue or concern, in which, to a greater or lesser extent, all the members of the group participate. Similarly, and for the same reasons, reported dreams can be eloquent expressions of the group's culture, its state of development or its prevalent feeling tone. And it is for this same reason as well that the reactions, of whatever kind, of other group members to the dream (obviously, in addition to associations by the dreamer) can serve as extremely enlightening elucidations of the dream itself, analogous to the associations provided by the dreamer in individual therapy.

From this vantage point, however, every response must then be understood as an association, even apparently 'analytic' ones where one member of the group 'interprets' the dream of another. These represent, after all, merely one kind of response to the dream presentation, albeit a highly intellectualised and defended one. By the same token, dream symbols can readily become expressive metaphors for the entire group. For example, in one group of mine, a member dreamed of a house floating in mid-air with a room barely attached, almost falling off. Subsequently – for years – this image of a room falling off a house became a shorthand expression for all the members of this group whenever tenuous connection or detachment was brought up. In another group, a member dreamed of being a spy and of protecting his brothers in that context. The theme of that group, eloquently expressed in that image as well as in the group's subsequent associations, was discovering and protecting secrets as well as protecting each other from intruders, most notably, of course, the therapist.

There is, however, another interesting facet to all this. As often as not, when a dream is recounted in a group, and other members also recall dreams, and often more than one member will have such a recall, especially if the group is used to dealing with dreams, it is fascinating to note that almost invariably the recounted dreams will have a *common thematic thread*, one which points to or identifies these shared underlying issues with which the group is dealing or which is preoccupying it.

A research idea

One can readily extrapolate an interesting potential research based on this hypothesis, for those of you looking for doctoral dissertations. It follows, of course, that as a group's culture develops and it becomes increasingly cohesive, the convergence of member dreams will also increase; but also, as the group matures into an effectively working therapy group, its members' dreams will continue to show common themes, with the addition, over time, as members individuate, of divergences dealing increasingly with individual members' idiosyncratic emotional issues: an empirical question which warrants exploration and may shed some light on the extent to which the membrane around the psychic life of each of us stretches to encompass others.

So, returning, for a moment, to my original hypothesis, and putting together the various pieces of information I have been describing, I think there is sufficient evidence to lend credence to the notion that dreams are far more of an interpersonal event than we have heretofore believed. Not only is the manner in which they are generated and metabolised a common denominator among individuals, but the events which stimulate them and to which they are responses are also both shared and mutually elicited. In addition, they often constitute a shared, private and very intimate 'in-group' language. Hence, there is as much in them that is social as is uniquely singular.

Some clinical vignettes

Now I would like to illustrate some of what I have been describing with some clinical vignettes.

Vignette 1

The following dreams, all presented in a single session, were presented in a previous paper of mine, but I think they are quite germane here.

The last new member had entered a particular group of six individuals a year earlier, rendering the therapist, who had taken over the group only two months previously, its most recent arrival. Members had been typically reticent during recent sessions, preferring to leave the more intensely emotional material for both informal 'after sessions', unofficial gatherings in the anteroom or the building lobby, and meetings of individual members between sessions, most particularly N. and P. Both practices were a legacy from the previous therapist. Pressure had been building from the new therapist for the group to articulate within the group meetings proper, the feelings which these 'sessions' and extra-group contacts served to contain or to decompress, with emphatic suggestions to discontinue the outside meetings. As a result, strong indications of resistance had surfaced in the group sessions themselves, primarily in the form of silences, flights to outside concerns, and absences.

DREAM 1

Around the middle of a session marked by cautious ventures toward confessions of sexual feelings, longings and experiences, N., a highly intellectualised, primarily silent member, suddenly came alive, announcing that he had had a dream. Earlier he had confided to the group that he had been unable to consummate a sexual intimacy with a woman he had recently begun to date.

In the dream, he is watching from the wings as people perform on a stage. Outside after the performance, he recognises one of the performers, whom he spies entering a car containing another, waiting, man. This man, who has apparently not liked the first man's performance, proceeds to take out a gun and shoot him. Completing his recitation, N. giggled and adopted an expression as if to say, 'Imagine that!' Whereupon the group fell silent.

The most obvious and superficial interpretation of this dream, as well as one limited only to N.'s individual dynamics, would focus on the castration anxiety stimulated by his recent, problematic sexual encounters. A broader view, however, reveals additional dynamic roots out of which this dream emanates. It reflects experiences that the other members, too, were having. The fear of retribution for both exposure and 'inadequate' performance that it expresses for him individually is equally true of this entire, very reluctant group, while the shooter – the one who punishes for that exposure and the poor performance – is easily seen as the therapist, someone to be avoided by all. Consider their 'hiding' their most intense feelings in their 'after sessions', just as the observer in the dream hides in the wings (and just as the observing N. hides in his silences in group), their reticence to speak openly of intimate feelings, and their collective avoidance of sexual material, at least up to this catalytic session, not to mention the actual 'performance' – in which N. is a prime player – of their extra-group contacts, relative to which the therapist is the waiting outsider. The terror of retribution, the fear of punishment for 'forbidden games', are concerns shared by the whole group, but reflected through N.'s individual dream.

During subsequent sessions, the entire group responded to the observation that 'N. seems not to be the only one frightened of performing centre stage', with quite a surprising array of graphic sexual confessions, moving quickly to admissions of dread around intimate relationships, including those within the group itself, a response which was seen as validating the interpretation offered them.

DREAM 2

Later during the same session, another member of the same group, O., related the following dream:

> Five or six people are in these buckets for trimming trees and a crazy who is operating them is spinning them around from underneath. I finally get off, but the others are still up there. Then I am with my boyfriend; we go to a movie called The Rose Arbor. Then he is showing me some roses; how beautiful they are! Then I am with my friend, Judy, and I insist on going to her house at the beach with her, even though she says she doesn't want to go there this year. Finally, I am with both my boyfriend and his therapist, who he is socialising with. The therapist is high on something. The stuff is in this long salt shaker. I try it, putting it on my food even though I know it is poison. When I shake some on to my food, I get very dizzy and woozy.

Both she and the other group members associated to the dream. She realised immediately that the therapist is the 'crazy' driving the buckets, that his efforts to deal with unconscious material have been confusing and disorienting, his attempts to control the group disconcerting. She described her boyfriend's therapist as very strange, socialising with his patients, getting drugs for them, being often high himself (an obvious allusion to the present therapist's 'strange', 'incongruous' behaviour). They spent a weekend at his home and she felt very uncomfortable. She identified her desire to go to Judy's house – to which she had escaped every year but this one – as her strong impulse to flee the newly reorganised group, to isolate herself.

Becoming very animated discussing this other therapist, group members warned her of potential dangers and traps, pointing out that she was blinding herself, anaesthetising herself, and buying into problems, letting herself be, as they expressed it, 'led down a garden path' (the rose arbor?) – all depictions of their highly ambivalent feelings about the present therapist.

In the dream, she contains and expresses the group's confusion, its suspicions of the therapist, and the strong temptation the members are experiencing to run away and close their eyes to feelings and issues, feelings that the whole group has been enacting in their 'after sessions'. Other members, in fact, own some of these feelings for themselves, admitting to their own confusion and anxiety, as well as their wish to escape to the more benign atmosphere of the previous group culture (Judy's house last year) in which the insistence on analytic exploration and identification of unconscious processes was less focused and intense. Their sense of danger and threat from the therapist, and the impulse to run away and hide expressed in this dream, echo the expression of the sense of threat in N.'s dream. The depiction of capricious threat, of arbitrary and unpredictable behaviour on the part of the threatening individual, is clearly depicted in both dreams. Both patients are grappling with these shared feelings simultaneously, portrayed by each in a unique way, while the rest of the group, struggling with the same feelings, work on them vicariously via tackling N.'s and O.'s depiction of them in their dreams.

DREAM 3

Shortly after these first two dreams were brought in, a third member, P., in the same group, related the following dream.

> I am on a kind of roller-coaster, on a track, holding my nephew in my lap, my sister holding the other nephew on her lap in the seat behind. The countryside around looks like a burned-out forest. Suddenly the roller-coaster begins going down a grade, going faster and faster. It jumps the track and I see someone – not my sister, maybe my other sister – smash her head against a tree. I am OK, and so is my nephew.

Kadis *et al.* (1974) point out that not only can associations of other group members be helpful in overcoming the dreamer's resistance to material reflected in a dream, but the manner in which the group handles the dream and associates to it also reflects both their resistance and the group's collusion around it.

In this instance, the group's associations were very delicate and flattering, focusing on her 'being on track', 'having warm family feelings', being 'related to her family', merely expressing congratulatory sentiments that she was being more active in the group, and particularly that she was bringing in dreams, which she had never done before. Pointedly, the anxiety aspects of the dream were ignored, as was the fact that there is danger and death present, and that while these are depicted, the affect that belongs with such experiences is conspicuously absent.

Here again there is notable convergence with both the manifest and latent content of the dreams presented by the other members: the sense of danger, the sense of being driven, that is, the feeling of being out of control, with someone else in control (both the buckets and the roller-coaster), that one can be killed by not being passive (in contrast to the dreamer of this dream, the sister is someone who liked to take over; if access to Judy's house in Dream 2 cannot be gained in order to escape, poisoning results; if a 'performance' in Dream 1 is too outspoken and apparent, one can be shot), and that the material, that is, the sexual talk, feelings and actions beginning to emerge in the group, is like a roller-coaster out of control, going faster and faster, impelled by some unseen, lethal force. Finally, it seems worthy of note that this last dream was presented by one of three women in the group (the two sisters?) and that the previous dream had been presented by one of the other women (the sister who gets killed in Dream 3?).

Vignette 2

In a small group containing only three members, the final session before the summer break, an unusually long one, produces the following dreams.

DREAM 1

A young woman who has throughout her life been completely immersed and entwined with the parental family which is currently threatening to dissolve in the face of the imminent demise of the father, dreams that her family has disowned her. Immediately after recounting this dream, she launches into talking at some length about her sense of incompetence at work.

DREAM 2

The second member dreams that she is with a number of people, women, who are all describing how many suitors they have had, how many men have admired them. She herself responds to them by gesturing 'zero' with her hand, and, while doing so, feels shame. Then, she is looking for a particular man, but when she finds him, she discovers it is the wrong man (this is how she tells it). The man has a beard.

The third member is absent, having mistakenly thought that the vacation break was starting this particular week.

The theme of being unwanted, 'disowned', is stimulated by the impending vacation, and resonates with the individual issues of each, one whose relationship to her emotionally detached parents was so tenuous that she could never individuate from the family, the other who, as the only one of four siblings to have been sent away from the home of her European parents as a child to live with a relative – ostensibly because she was so difficult, or so she believes – is extremely sensitive to issues of separation or exclusion. The absence of the third member is itself a form of association and response to the impending break, but expressed in action terms. Furthermore, the feelings of both blame and shame for being victims of exclusion or neglect, are expressed in the associated sense of incompetence, one which the other member echoes in terms of her own experience of being seen as stupid or difficult by her father. The issue of 'acceptability' – or the lack of it – and its consequences, reverberates in both dreams. The bearded man – the 'wrong' man – is clearly the therapist: wrong not only because seeing him as a suitor is taboo, but also because seeking him augurs more feelings of rejection – which the vacation break both stimulates and enacts. And it is this 'inappropriate' suitor who is now rejecting her, and 'disowning' her fellow group member in this 'family'.

The convergence of themes and issues in the dreams of this little group illustrates with abundant clarity, I believe, the various concepts which I have been talking about: that the group themes, resonating among members and intertwined with their individual issues, are shared and processed in reciprocal fashion by the members, and their sharing the dreams within the group setting represents a cooperative effort at grappling with and resolving simultaneously both group and individual problems and dynamics which the dreams depict.

Vignette 3

As a final illustration, I would like to tell you about an experience with a dream in a workshop group in which only one dream was presented, but it turned out to have a most interesting function in the interactions, both conscious and unconscious, of this group and its work.

I had made an error at the beginning of a workshop on dreams in group therapy, by asking participants about their training in dream analysis, something people took amiss in light of the highly variable levels of training in this particular group. While one or two members rather timidly expressed resentment, others were quiet about it. One member, one of the quiet ones, stated she had a dream, but was very reluctant to relate it. Another previously quiet member attempted rather energetically to get her to tell it, and when she was unsuccessful, attempted to enlist a third member, one of those who had expressed some irritation, to help her in the effort. Finally, they succeeded: the dreamer – hesitatingly – told her dream. In it, she discovered an intruder in the bedroom shared by herself and her partner. In a fury, she hurled a boot at the interloper. The gender of the intruder was ambiguous, but by implication in the dream recitation, male.

As the group proceeded, it soon became apparent that the member who had tried to get her to recount her dream was actually enraged at me, but had said nothing about it before. Did she know the dream would express intense rage and indignation at an intruder – like the therapist? Somehow, it seems, she had discerned that the dreamer might express for her what she was feeling but could not assert. When all this was pointed out to her, she, the dreamer, and the other expressive member all confided shock and surprise, but also voiced recognition as well as relief.

It must be remembered that the related dream is selected from among an infinity of possibilities present among the members, and the one which is recalled resonates with the group's ongoing interaction and primary affective state. Thus, the shared feelings – and especially their intensity – had been expressed via her dream by one member who, without realising it, not only felt them, but contained them for the others in the group and, in this way, brought them into the group arena. What is especially interesting in this group is the implicit communication among the members, which was mirrored in the urging by one member of another whose unconscious expression would reflect her own feelings, and of this same member's somehow – without explicit or overt consultation – finding just the right other member who would resonate with the dreamer – one who also shared their joint feelings – to aid her in her urging.

Conclusion

How can the therapist encompass these kaleidoscopic phenomena? How can he or she best listen to the dream presentations, their antecedents and the subsequent group interactions, so as to 'hear' all these different facets and dimensions of the dream utterances, to grasp the multidimensionality of what is being introduced? '[W]e are to remain innocent listeners, sustaining attention that is loose and free', writes Aragno (work in preparation):

> …we are to be fluid and bound at the same time, able to linearize what is simultaneous and freeze what is continuously moving. This makes excellent

sense if we consider that our analysis is never textual but contextual... Balance is the key: in the confluence of content, form, subject and style; the dialectic between what is told and what is hidden, between word and action in interaction – unconscious meanings appear at the hub of these three.

This quotation refers to the therapist's stance in individual analytic therapy, but, I think, it is eminently applicable for the group situation as well, an eloquent and accurate depiction of the essential stance for the group leader. Context, however, is a multifold phenomenon, encompassing diverse tiers in the group therapeutic situation. The group analyst must maintain an open, receptive posture, listening and observing 'between the lines', simultaneously hearing and responding to the 'poetry', the metaphors and other expressive forms, noting the symbols, resonating to the feelings, observing the associational matrix in which the dream is recounted, relating the ongoing recitation to the history, both recent and long-term, of the group, being aware of its current status and how the individual issues of the dreamer play a meaningful part, both at the moment and in the ongoing life of the group, and vice versa, and, of course, maintaining an awareness of the feelings, thoughts and associations which the recounting arouses in the leader him- or herself. All these, and many more – like the interweaving threads of a fine lace or the intricate entwining of harmonious voices in a fugue – the many swirling currents of the group, offer the leader an opportunity for creative immersion, a challenge both for comprehension and for apprehension of the inner recesses of its psychic life, and in so doing, as Aragno illuminates, thereby to discern the emergence of the multifaceted meanings of its dreams.

References

Aragno, A. (in preparation) *Forms of Knowledge: A Psychoanalytic Study of Human Communication.*

Arden, J.B. (1996) *Consciousness, Dreams and Self: A Transdisciplinary Approach.* Madison, CT: Psychosocial Press.

Bonime (1962) *The Clinical Use of Dreams.* New York: Basic Books.

Condon, W.S. (1982) 'Cultural microrhythms.' In M. Davis (ed) *Interaction Rhythms: Periodicity in Communicative Behaviour.* New York: Human Sciences Press.

Crick, F. and Mitchison, G. (1986) 'REM sleep and neural nets.' *Journal of Mind and Behaviour* 7, 229–50.

Ekman, P. (1993) 'Facial expression and emotion.' *American Psychologist 48,* 4, 384–92.

Emde, R.N. (1983) 'The prerepresentational self and affective core.' *Psychoanalytic Study of the Child 38,* 165–92.

Freud, S. (1900) *The Interpretation of Dreams. Standard Edition 5/6*. London: Hogarth Press.

Greenleaf, E. (1973) '"Senoi" dream groups.' *Psychotherapy: Theory, Research and Practice 10*, 3, 218-22.

Hatfield, E., Cacioppo, J.T. and Rapson, R.L. (1993) 'Emotional contagion.' *Current Directions in Psychological Science 2*, 3, 96–9.

Hatfield, E., Cacioppo, J.T. and Rapson, R.L. (eds) (1994) *Emotional Contagion*. Cambridge: Cambridge University Press.

Hobson, J.A. and McCarley, R.W. (1977) 'The brain as a dream state generator: An activation-synthesis hypothesis of the dream process.' *American Journal of Psychiatry 134*, 1335–48.

Kadis, A.L., Krasner, J.D., Weiner, M.F., Winick, C. and Foulkes, S.H. (1974) *Practicum of Group Psychotherapy*. New York: Harper & Row.

Lawrence, W.G. (1998) *Social Dreaming @ Work*. London: Karnac Books.

McClintok, M. (1971) 'Menstrual synchrony and suppression.' *Nature 229*, 244–5.

Schlachet, P.J. (1995) 'The dream in group therapy: A reappraisal of unconscious processes in groups.' *Group 16*, 4, 196–209.

Solms, M. (1995) 'New findings on the neurological organisation of dreaming: Implications for psychoanalysis.' *Psychoanalytic Quarterly LXIV*, 43–67.

Solms, M. (1997) *The Neuropsychology of Dreams: A Clinico-Anatomical Study*. Mahwah, NJ: Lawrence Erlbaum Associates.

Van den Daele, L. (1992) 'Direct interpretation of dreams: Typology.' *The American Journal of Psychoanalysis 52*, 1, 99–118.

Van den Daele, L. (1996) 'Direct interpretation of dreams: Neuropsychology.' *The American Journal of Psychoanalysis 56*, 3, 253–68.

Vanderwolf, C. (1969) 'Hippocampal electrical activity and voluntary movement in the rat.' *Electroencephalography and Clinical Neurophysiology 26*, 407–18.

Winson, J. (1986) *Brain and Psyche*. New York: Vintage Books.

Winson, J. (1990) 'The meaning of dreams.' *Scientific American 263*, 5, 86–96.

Whishaw and Vanderwolf, C. (1973) 'Hippocampal EEG and behaviour: Changes in amplitude and frequency of RSA (theta rhythm) associated with spontaneous and learned movement patterns in rats and cats.' *Behavioural Biology 8*, 4, 461–84.

CHAPTER 6

Singular Dream

Dream of Link Scene and Discourse

*Janine Puget**

'I had a dream' – and the analyst or whoever is listening is immediately put in – or switches to – another state of mind, and prepares for action: something will have to be done, said or thought. The same happens with a group, a family, or a couple, but in this case an additional element arises, in the form of conflicts caused by the effect of an other's presence, and especially the presence of a scene that has unfolded elsewhere and implies something else, 'the dream'. One of the axes operating in the foreground is the axis of inclusion–exclusion, which leads those who are listening to try to find a place for themselves in the scene, or, on the other hand, to easily feel excluded from the scene. This special mode of listening relies not only on the presence of a scene, but also on the curiosity aroused by an *enigma* which is to be unravelled, of which we expect…something, not forgetting the *evocative power* that the dream has, like a poem. We therefore have several variables at play here.

However, I will suggest here the thought that the dream *does not originate from the same register as the discourse* and that the 'dream which is dreamt and narrated' by one of the members of the link introduces a space-time which is different from that of the discourse. It therefore introduces conflicts related to the overlapping of countless space-times which are not articulated; the space-time related to the dream subscribes to the order of a pictogram. This

---

* English translation by Dan Shalit.

is, I think, how Freud (1900) had already referred to it when he pointed out that 'the content of the dream is given to us in the form of hieroglyphics (*or pictography, which is the term used in the translations into Spanish and English*) the signs of which must be consecutively translated into the language of the thoughts of the dream'.

I see the dream as belonging to the register of the *scene* which has unfolded in some 'elsewhere' and which is about to be enacted and seen by others. Once the dream is narrated or spoken, it does not belong to the dreamer only. This scene is awaiting meaning, discovery or a production of thoughts and actions originating from the dream.

The dream has the capacity of *generating a cognitive structure*. There's something new, and therefore what is awaited and expected is a new way of taking a place in a whole, a new way to deal with the overlapping situations. 'New way' does not mean necessarily a way which is in harmony with other ways. Each narration of the dream evokes in the listener as well as in the dreamer infinite interpretations or commentaries. But here lies a paradox: the dream is a summons for action and therefore tends to participate in the action (inclusion) but, at the same time, it imposes an irreducible otherness – one forever estranged (alienated), which causes a feeling of exclusion. As for the dreamer, the narrated dream is always inevitably lacking, incomplete, due to its pictographic quality. There's always a missing piece, a part that's forgotten, the dreamer is trying the impossible because at the moment of waking up, the dream is no longer with us, repression is in action and the dream becomes yet another disorganising dream and, consequently, has the power of generating unconscious material.[1] The dreamer remains a stranger to his own dream, for the dream in itself puts him in contact with that which is forever strange-alienated.

First Question

Is this therefore a new way of saying something that was already here – an unconscious production corresponding to a past which keeps returning under different guises? Or is it a way of saying something that was not here, and will make possible the exploration of a new present? Or is it simply a way of saying something else that cannot be said differently? Furthermore, could it not be one of those contacts with that which cannot be said but which is nevertheless here? So is it a repetition – something that is already here – or is it a new production or, still, is it a way of saying that which cannot be said in any other way? All three options are indeed possible. I tend to believe that the dream must be given space as an event, a start after which something will necessarily be different, and that this event narrates that which, in a way, will forever remain strange, estranged. Other authors have also suggested in various ways similar ideas about the dream's being an event as a new production.[2]

Second problem

When a dream is narrated during a link session, will it have the same status as in an individual session? It is my suggestion that in a link session the dream offers a dramatisation, or staging, which allows the others to participate in it. It thus emphasises not only the dreamer's otherness but also his imposed presence that is soaked with irreducible otherness. But since the question of the link's subjectifying force depends on the work its members are capable of performing, which has to do with the effects of a presence in which otherness and estrangement are fundamental elements, the dream is necessarily a call to a worrying but also necessary strangeness. It is therefore necessary to work on the space in-between, on the shortcomings of language, the overlapping scenes and a certain degree of incoherence. At times, others try to and indeed find their way into the other's dream, searching for a certain coherence between their own ideas and those appearing in the dream. The fact that the dream narrates does not necessarily mean that it includes, it can also exclude! Let us not confuse narration with inclusion.

Comments elicited by the dream, which we refer to as associations, are often attempts to complete the thought of the dream, which are often accepted by the dreamer. And then the dream is enveloped and thus becomes bearable. This practice, which satisfies the members of the link originates from the activation of unconscious pacts that seal the link and that allow them to verbalise that which is not meant to be verbalised at all! But is there any other way of participating in a scene?

Who does the dream belong to?

To the dreamer or to those who, by listening, participate in it? Assuming ownership over the dream consolidates the feeling that one belongs to the proposed framework. We could therefore think that the dream belongs to whoever is capable of dealing with it and become part of it by working on the effect of presence elicited by the dream following the inclusion–exclusion axis. But since the dream imposes a register and an impossible – putting a presence in words – all the members of the group will participate in this or that way.

These ideas lead me to believe that a dream will not have the same function in one framework as in another. And that the dream effect matters. The dream in a link session becomes bearable when members manage to cancel that which they cannot share, that which cannot be expressed in words. Should this be thought of as resistance or does the psyche have the ability to manage that which it cannot think?

Very often, theories about the functioning within the framework of links suggest that the dreamer is the relation's representative – in French the word is *porte-parole*, literally meaning the 'carrier of the word'. Kaës refers to the dreamer as the *porte-rêve*, the 'carrier of the dream', or, if you will, a scapegoat who will have to bear the other's projections. Probably, this way of seeing the problem cancels the impossible of a dream. Working through the dream during the analysis of a link offers each member an opportunity to change their positions and rediscover themselves in the proposed space-time, since there is generally an overlapping of space-times.

All that I have said here about the dream in a link session is related somewhat to that which happens to the dream in an analysis said to be 'individual', due to its origins in the scene. But for that we need to believe that one of the qualities of transference/ counter-transference is that the analyst's presence intervenes in a dual register: the analyst as an internal–external object which is in relation with the patient's world of objects, which is the more traditional view, and the analyst in a relation of externality, as an other, with whom the analysand creates a new relation – a link – in which questions of belonging, which are inherent to the link, are enacted and explored. Here there is no question of repetition but, rather, of novelty. But the dream narrated in the course of an individual session does not always lead the analyst to actively take part in the scene proposed by the patient's dream, even if very often he wants to be included on the basis of transference. What I mean here is that the result will not necessarily be a new organisation of the analytic link.

The dream as imposition

The dream imposes itself, which returns us to the basic conflict of belonging to a link that originates from precisely those dynamics of imposition. Here I rely on the notion that a link may be defined as a rapport between various othernesses, which mutually impose themselves and cause disorganisation.

One cannot not belong to a link and that belonging originates from the effect of 'imposing otherness'. This is how the narrated dream causes the emergence of anxieties related to subjectivation's inherent *inevitable dependence*: to feel suffocated, compelled, or, on the other hand, to feel unrepresented, that is to say, not recognised as existing.

Returning to the issue of the overlapping of space-times and scenes, it will be crucial to work through the psychic effects caused by the lack of coherence between the different scenes and between this register and that of the discourse. In a dream's manifest content, it is rare not to find some mention of a part of the dream that does not coincide with the superficial productions of the conflict, which are of the order of the misunderstanding and due to the lack of coherence, and of that which the misunderstanding might lead to. The dream does not respond to the questions posed by the discourse, rather, it interrogates, interrupts the course of association and forces the recognition of the existence of another imperceptible psychic organisation. This is how the understanding of the dream shifts, from seeing it as fragments that need to be deciphered, endowed with a meaning, emphasising its evocative and disorganising power, and the new momentum it gives the material.

Another problem – the dream and the unconscious

The classical approach maintains that the dream provides access to the unconscious, to the insatiable desire, to the trauma, to dissatisfaction, to memory. Since I suggest here that the dream is of the order of the pictogram, in continuation of the concept of Piera Aulanguer who endows the pictogram with a status *sui generis* that does not necessarily depend on the unconscious, I tend to think that *the dream creates the unconscious*. It produces a new repression which goes in the opposite direction to what is usually described. The state of waking up, 'that was a dream', introduces a break between the dream-dream and day-life. But making things even more complicated, the unconscious of a single psychic apparatus and the unconscious of a link are not of the same order. Although this is not the right moment to start an in-depth discussion on this question, I will say that the unconscious of a link is being built gradually, as the link is being built, and must have its own unique topology.

The question of coherence

Most reports of session material show – and this is true, naturally, also during sessions – a search for coherence, probably related to a necessary condition of the discourse, as well as to some sort of resistance. This resistance may feed on a rationalist position that underlies certain hypotheses emphasising first and foremost integration, harmony, complete forms, the explaining power of childhood past, genetic continuity, linear causality and so on. Maybe this is how we avoid sinking into anxieties of fragmentation, of overlapping of space, or anxieties related to the unpredictable. It is to postmodernism that we owe the answerless questions of virtuality, non-integration, disharmony, these new realities that change the way we see how we can access a conflicting potential, which is the only kind capable of enriching our patients' – and our own – subjectifying world.

The scene: production of structure

Being pure image, how could the scene be spoken, narrated?

Usually, when presenting material from a link session, we start by trying to describe a scene: where they are sitting, how they are dressed, do they look into each other's eyes and so on. That is to say, the base on which the discourse relies. Then we try to articulate bases and form, or interpret the lack of articulation in terms of split or dissociation. This is what we do in order to speak of the structure in which the account unfolds.

When a dream is told it describes a link (I was, we were, *j'étais, nous étions*…). It defines a position vis-à-vis characters placed in a space which usually only partially coincides with what is known (I was at, we were at, *je me trouvais, nous nous trouvions*…) – it tells or expresses emotions that do not coincide with what the patient imagines that he should feel, and sometimes, while telling the dream, he alters or revises it.

Can an emotion be told outside of a context? Clearly, the answer is no, but I have noticed that often we forget the context in order to deal solely with the emotion (I felt, I could feel that, I was not afraid…).

All that depends on certain events (this or that was happening, it was…): an event that produces something new, or an event that renews a story. This is an event that does not only refer to desire, to impulse life, to the Oedipus, to possible historical traumas, as I have been saying throughout this text, but puts a new scene in place, that gives meaning to a composing element of the link, that element which determines the constitution of the subjectifying function.

Session

This is a group that tends to think that what everyone thinks or says must always be coherent and logically related, and that they must be able to help and be helped by others. This leads them to give advice and orders to one another, and to classify what is being said into good or bad, normal or abnormal, allowed or forbidden. The act of helping provides meaning to their belonging to the group and comes out as resistance. Helping is, clearly, an ambiguous concept. When a member is even slightly late to a session, this is immediate cause for concern, as it represents an ominous sign of *danger*: losing a place, not having enough place to speak, not being able to make oneself heard, or simply the danger of the disappearance of the group, and so on. Some time ago, one of the patients died suddenly. The empty chair was hard to accept, but it was also not easy to admit that although the group could not exist without them, the loss of a single member did not threaten to take the rest of the group out, too.

Only after a while I realised that my tendency to attribute their concern to the death of one of the patients originated from a hypothesis that only took mourning and its elaboration into consideration, whereas what needed to be considered was: what did the fragility of belonging, apparent in certain instances, represent? It was related to work on the unpredictable, and consequently was related to the daily analytic work on the link.

In the beginning of a session, S. tells a dream, happy of being able to tell it, not only because he was worried by the dream but also because he was about to be heard.

In the dream something clings to his back, maybe an animal, but it's difficult to describe. It strangles him with its two paws which hold him like a pincer. He cannot get it off his back. He woke up very anxious and his wife tried to calm him. Then R. says that he too had a dream. He dreamt that he went to the balcony and suddenly realised that the balcony did not have a railing and he was afraid of falling. The 'he too' was thought by me as a means of clinging to the other's dream. He immediately explained that he often feared heights and that this dream must be related to a past experience he had. This is a patient who tends to want to explain, and thus make the worrying effect of the dream disappear. I see this sort of explanation as belonging to the order of resistance. The others are listening as if waiting for something to happen.

There were two different scenes to be resolved: one related to suffocation and the other related to the loss of support.

In S.'s dream there is something that imposes itself, a presence of which he cannot rid himself, and moreover, a mode of relation which is intolerable. S. tends to cling to someone, but is this relationship between him and the animal of the same order? The dream imposed itself upon him and he is now imposing the dream upon the group, assuming that the group, like his wife, must be able to do something or simply take interest in him. He imposes a presence which has to do with otherness.

But R. says 'I too', and what does this mean? Is he trying to cling or just to make place? These are two different dreams which must suddenly coincide. One speaks of an imposing presence, the other speaks of the void, loss, manifested through the lack of a railing. The projection of absence leads to a memory. The presence leads in this particular case to an experienced worrying strangeness – as there is no sign that could allow the presence to be named. To R., who is accustomed to resolving problems, an imposing presence cannot be resolved, except if he manages to force the others to associate which, to him, means finding perfect articulation between one and the other.

So we have two scenes, offering different situations, which one of the members of the group tries to articulate by saying 'I too'. One speaks of an imposing presence, a link that is suffocating, and the other speaks of the loss of equilibrium. How can the void between these two dreams be resolved? What followed was caused by the need to find a way to escape the malaise produced within the group. So S. speaks of a disappointment, which does not originate from the group but from a different scenario. It has to do with the expected marriage of her son, a son who imposes a way of doing things which has nothing to do with the parents' ideals. An intergenerational breach that cannot be resolved. A new scene in which the other imposes and disorganises. Then F. speaks of the fear of losing the group because of his economic difficulties. The others listen.

The work of thinking was directed to the thinking of the pain activated by the overlapping scenes, ideals, codes, etc. And also there was an attempt to realise the extent to which – when trying to give coherence to something that cannot be coherent – the world can shrink and become suffocating.

Scenes of loss and scenes of presence, two dangers of the terrifying dependence and the other's radical otherness. To cling to another who imprisons or to go up-front, defenceless. But at the same time, usual associations, such as those related to the future marriage of one of the patients' sons, could lead to a reflection in which each of them could find himself again.

This interpretation differs from that which could have led us to interpret the projection of drive elements and the dereliction or loss of the protection of the maternal object.

Another example

A couple now struggling with problems of infertility starts the session. After having given it much thought, she has made up her mind and although she would have been extremely pleased if they had another child, she does not want to keep enduring all the difficulties of more treatments, and has decided to allow nature to take its course, and if she conceives naturally, fine, and if not, well, so be it. He adds that there are many things that they can do together, go travelling, etc., that their daughter is now older, and that the issue of another child is not her problem. That is what he had always thought. Apparently he is the one who has the physical problem causing the couple to be sterile.

She is afraid, because of a professional change, to find herself *with nothing to do*. She finds the idea of being only a housewife terrifying. He quickly says that he trusts her completely, that he feels much closer to her, etc.

Then she tells a dream, which, she says, *has nothing to do* with this (note that in French the expression she used is, literally, *has nothing to see*). She was in a room and her husband was leaving with a young woman who had long black hair. She was angry, tried to keep him from leaving and asked herself what she would do without him. He interrupts her and says that it was because last night he had to go out. He includes himself again. She insists and says that she was terribly worried. He remembers that a lady friend had told him, when they got married, that he was about to be married to a wife who liked to oppose and contradict. And he adds that it is like that today, every time they have to make a decision she opposes, as if it were a matter of principle. She gets angry, and says that he just will not listen to her. They need to find a way to make a decision. He wants to keep explaining the dream or, rather, concealing its meaning. He was out last night to attend some sort of political meeting, and he thought that he would have to stay over, but luckily he managed to return on the same evening. To him it's very clear, his wife's dream is due to him.

This is a couple for whom one's body imposes upon the other not only a narcissistic wound but also an irreducible otherness. The dream transforms this conflict into an Oedipal scene of simple jealousy, in which she is being excluded from a couple. Realising that his wife suggests the idea that the couple could disappear, he explains that he is in fact the centre of the dream.

He imposes an explanation which is supposed to put an end to what could be dangerous. Does the scene propose a new couple? She remains alone and jealous. Their relation produces jealousy as well as a new organisation of the couple, that is what the dream means. But the dream also means that something will have to be produced that will allow to accept the otherness, even though otherness is never accepted. Cancelling all that the dream may suggest – all that has to do with the issues of fertility, decisions and how they should be made, how to recognise the other's place, how to accept what one member's body imposes upon the couple and so on – the only thing left for them to do is fight, which is precisely what happened towards the end of the session. For the scene offered by the dream was about being excluded from the dream; about feeling the pain of dependence, which probably has to do with the feeling of being excluded from motherhood; and about wanting to fill what the husband's body is imposing.

Another example

S. has recently lost a person who was very important to him, and he had a dream.

> Last night, unlike other nights before, I slept very well, and when I woke up I remembered a dream. I don't know whether I really remember it but I have the feeling that I did dream it and I felt that I was remembering it. Anyway, I woke up, and I remembered a dream that seemed very strange. Now I don't remember many details but the entire dream was a *good-bye* (in French, *adieu*), I don't know how to say it, it was like preparations for an *adieu*, as if I was preoccupied with, or spoke about or approached some sort of parting, an *adieu*.

I interpret that there are different ways to say *adieu*. I suppose you do not know how to say *adieu*. Now, in order to get in touch with the concept, you remember funerals, but it is only one moment, when you had to feel the weight of the coffin, the weight of the deceased, but there are surely many other moments and other ways to say it, and that is why you feel that your commentaries are not enough to describe the scene of *adieu*. S. says that it is beyond comprehension, I tell him that he wants to reduce into an image or a comment all the scenes which could have to do with an *adieu*.

> When X. died I felt that I had not managed to say *adieu* to him, but I don't even know what I would have wanted to say to him!

I interpret: is it not what death is? Not being able to say something to someone who is not here, an other.

> What you are saying brings up many things. It was difficult for me to say it. I remember many scenes which are unrelated to one another. Many different scenes. I just thought of it, it's something that I cannot resolve. It has to do with being able to say, or being able to be with someone who supports me, embraces me, I don't know how to say it. All the material that followed was full of: not being able to say...the pain of that which cannot be said in words.

I told S. that what he had suggested in his dream could not be said, but had evoked in him many ideas, each putting him in different positions vis-à-vis his different relationships.

He then speaks of a change. For some years now, the bathroom curtain has been in a bad shape, and only now he suddenly saw it and realised that he could replace it. I tell him that his dream made him realise a new way to see where he is, realise that there is something wrong which is old, which is not up to date with him as a husband, a father, a nephew, colleague, etc.

I tell him that *à Dieu* (English *to God*) is a way to find a God who is always here, who allows him to see what he could not see before, but also who allows him to feel that he belongs to a context in which God has a meaning.

Last comments

To be able to listen to dreams as a new cognitive structure could make it possible to avoid repetition or to introduce some new possibilities during an analytic session.

References

Freud S. (1900) T*he Interpretation of Dreams. Standard Edition 5*. London: The Hogarth Press.

Guillaumin, J. (1976) 'Du rêve.' *Revue Française de Psychanalyse*, February 1976.

Meltzer, D. (1976) 'The changing use of dreams in psychoanalytic practice.' *International Journal of Psychoanalysis 29*, 57.

Pontalis, J.B. (1972) 'La pénétration du rêve.' *L'espace du Rêve, Novuvelle Revue de Psychoanalyse 5*, 1972.

Puget, J. (1998) 'Afectos singulares y afectos vinculares. Autencicidad, credibilidad, malentendido.' 20th APDEBA Symposium, Buenos Aires, October 1998.

Puget, J. (2000) 'Rêve singulier–rêve de lien. Scence et discours.' 4th International Congress, Metz, June 2000 and Asociación Uruguaya de Psicoanálisis y Psicoterapia, September 2000.

Endnotes

1. It might be necessary to explain what I mean when I speak of generating unconscious material. I have in mind that as an effect of the presence of two or more subjects and therefore effects impossible to disappear – this will generate an unconscious with different quality than the one which is known as unconscious, created once and forever in accordance with repression mechanism. In the case of presence's effect, it will be due to the suppression of the unbearable alienness of the others and to the suppression of what is impossible to enter in a link.

2. I do not wish to dwell here on the numerous approaches that stemmed from the investigation of the dream. In this article I mainly retain those suggestions that the dream belongs to a different psychic entity, as does Pontalis (1972) when he considers the dream as a dream object, or as does Guillaumin (1976), who proposes that the dream is a pathway between reality and the imaginary. Also, Meltzer (1976) thinks of the dream as an event that introduces something new, and hence a break that has to be handled and coped with. Bion sees the dream as participating in the digestion of the truth. Dream-work for this author must produce thoughts which may be preserved in the memory.

CHAPTER 7

'We Are Such Stuff as Dreams Are Made On'

Annotations on Dreams and Dreaming in Bion's Works

James S. Grotstein

Introduction

When one begins to reflect upon Bion's radical revision of psychoanalytic theory, one usually cites such ideas as container/contained, attacks against links, L, H and K linkages between self and object, alpha function, transformations, emotional turbulence, catastrophic change, and group psychology *inter alia*. His conception of dreams and of dreaming itself has never been a subject of separate study, as far as I have been able to determine. Yet his ideas about dreams and dreaming constitute some of his most original and far-reaching innovations of psychoanalytic thinking. In this contribution I shall synopsise the epigenesis of Bion's venture into dreams and dreaming and try to call attention to the unusual importance Bion assigns to them in regard to 'learning from experience'.

Background

Bion's first period of creativity lay in his work with groups in which he not only established the now famous template for the hidden psychology of groups, i.e. work groups and basic assumption subgroups, but he also laid down the foundation for a later notion, that the individual himself constituted a 'group' of sub-personalities (1961), a finding that achieves its utmost realisation in the manifest content of the dream. In his second period of creativity he studied the psychotic patient, not only from the standpoint of psychoanalytic technique but also from its unique phenomenology. Toward the end of this second period, he began having 'second thoughts' about his observations (1967). These 'second thoughts' ushered in his epistemological period of immersion, one that was to continue for the remainder of his life. He set the task for himself of comparing psychotic with normal and neurotic states of mind to discern the fundamental aspects of thinking, dreaming, and feeling. In brief, his work with psychotics propelled Bion into the highest strata of epistemology and ontology, the later refinements of which were to constitute his greatest legacy. His theories about dreams and dreaming constitute an unusually significant portion of that episteme, one which has hitherto remained unaddressed.

Freud (1900) said that dreams constitute disguised wish fulfilments of hidden wishes and function to preserve the sleep. In other words they are defensive and obscuring by nature. Bion, on the contrary, states that we dream, not just to protect sleep, but to be able to create a contact barrier between the realms of consciousness and the unconscious. Further, we dream – by day and by night – in order to transform (process) the moment-to-moment flow of our experiences of ourselves and others. In short, dreaming is an essential component of epistemology, as well as phenomenology and ontology. Put another way, dreaming is the obligatory beginning of thinking. Furthermore, Bion also discovered and described the phenomenon of pathological dreaming in the psychotic where hallucination in conjunction with evacuative projective identification occurs instead of introjection in the service of learning from experience. Bion (1962, 1965) will later include the former under the category of 'K' phenomena and transformations in hallucinosis.

Caveat

The reader will note that I distinguish between the idea of dreams and the function of dreaming. I do so in order to emphasise Bion's own distinction in this regard. Parenthetically, this distinction seems analogous to another distinction Bion (1962, 1963) made, that between thoughts and thinking. His distinction in both regards reflects the clarity and incisiveness of his thinking. I hope to make clear the relevance of this distinction as I proceed.

[Bion seldom chose dreams and dreaming as such, as topics for a contribution. His ideas about these phenomena are scattered throughout his works, however. I have surveyed all his works and have selected relevant passages for presentation. My procedure in what follows is to cite archivally as much of Bion's significant contributions on the theme of dreams and dreaming as I can, while at the same time annotating these citations as I proceed – these will be bracketed.]

Dreams and dreaming in psychosis

One of the first references to his ideas about dreams and dreaming was in his 'Notes on a Theory of Schizophrenia' (1967 [1956]), in which he states the following to his schizophrenic analysand: 'It must mean that without phantasies and without dreams you have not the means with which to think out your problem.' The reference to the inhibition of phantasy as a severe disability hindering development supports Melanie Klein's observations in her paper 'A Contribution to the Theory of Intellectual Inhibition'. (pp.25–6)

[Bion was the first to posit that the psychotic patient suffered, not from too much primary process, but from a defective or inadequate access to it from his/her mother in infancy, but he acknowledges that the origin of this insight lay in Klein's adumbrations. He was later to discard Freud's (1911) concepts of the primary and secondary processes and replace them with his idea of alpha function (Bion 1962) or dream-work alpha (1991). He formulated the idea that the psychotic's thought disorder is due in part to his/her difficulty in employing phantasies (by day) and dreams (by night) to enable him to think. Bion was later to speak of the continuity of dreaming throughout the day as well as the night. The point for now is that dreaming has something to do with thinking.]

Meanwhile, in his 'Development of Schizophrenic Thought' (1967 [1956]) in which the concept of alpha function first emerged (although there were adumbrations of it in earlier works), he states:

> The patient now moves, not in a world of dreams, but in a world of objects which are ordinarily the furniture of dreams... [H]e cannot synthesise his objects; he can only agglomerate and compress them... [T]he unconscious would seem to be replaced by the world of dream furniture. (p.40)

[I understand this to suggest that the psychotic, lacking the capacity to dream (lacking alpha function), cannot properly transform (synthesise) his emotional experiences with objects to garner the legacy of those experiences for internalisation. Instead, he is left with the concreteness and therefore the meaninglessness of events which fail to become internalised experiences, only useless, persecutory 'furniture'. Later, Bion (1962, 1963) will conceptualise this 'world of dream furniture' as 'beta elements' which the psychotic patient has been unsuccessful in transforming into mentally 'digestible' alpha elements.]

His prefatory ideas about dreaming and thinking and their alteration in psychosis are now revealed in the following passage, in the paper, 'Differentiation of the Psychotic from the Non-Psychotic Personalities' Bion (1967 [1957]) states:

> I must now draw your attention to a matter that demands a paper to itself and therefore cannot be more than mentioned here. It is implicit in my description that the psychotic personality or part of the personality has used splitting and projective identification as a substitute for repression... [T]he psychotic part of the personality has attempted to rid itself of the apparatus on which the psyche depends to carry out the repressions; the unconscious would seem to be replaced by the world of dream furniture. (p.52)

[What Bion seems to be saying is that the psychotic cannot repress (because of the heightened employment of splitting and evacuative projective identification). The consequence of this is the disappearance of the distinction between consciousness and the unconscious. This catastrophic state results ultimately from the psychotic's inability to dream; thus s/he lacks consciousness and unconsciousness, but is left with the shards of his/her erstwhile capacity to dream, the dream furniture, which can be equated with bizarre objects. Later, Bion will ascribe this deficit to the psychotic's failure to create a contact barrier that is capable of separating consciousness and the unconscious.]

In 'On Hallucination' Bion (1967 [1958]) states:

> ...I had already been led to some conclusions about the nature of psychotic dreams. I had noticed that much work was needed before a psychotic patient reported a dream at all, and that when he did so he seemed to feel that he had said all that was necessary in reporting the fact that he had dreamt... I felt that the 'dreams' shared so many characteristics of hallucinations that it was possible that actual experiences of hallucination in the consulting room might serve to throw light on the psychotic dream. It is a short step from what I have already said about hallucinations to suppose that when a psychotic patient speaks of having a dream, he thinks that his

perceptual apparatus is engaged in expelling something and that the dream is an evacuation from his mind strictly analogous to an evacuation from his bowels... In short, to the psychotic a dream is an evacuation of material that has been taken in during waking hours. Much development must take place before the psychotic dream becomes sufficiently coherent to be communicable at all. Before that, I doubt whether its connexion with objects perceived is ever made. After that, I think it always is. (pp.77–8)

[Here was another brilliant clinical insight of Bion's: that the psychotic uses his sense organs to evacuate tension, not to take in the images of objects that are disturbing in order to process them. The evacuation he talks about here will later become integrated with his idea that the psychotic uses projective identification to evacuate, not only bad internal objects, but also his very ego which is inescapably engaged with them. The result of this double evacuation is the production of bizarre objects, one of the pathonomonic characteristics of psychosis. In regard to dreams and dreaming Bion is stating that the psychotic 'dream' is a hallucination in which the psychotic seeks to evacuate (disown, disavow) the sense impressions of his/her emotional feelings.]

In 'Attacks on Linking' Bion (1967 [1959]) sharpens his focus on the psychotic's experience with dreams and dreaming:

> The psychotic patient seems to have no dreams, or at least not to report any, until comparatively late in the analysis. My impression now is that this apparently dreamless period is a phenomenon analogous to the invisible-visual hallucination. That is to say, that the dreams consist of material so minutely fragmented that they are devoid of any visual component. When dreams are experienced which the patient can report because visual objects have been experienced by him in the course of the dream, he seems to regard these objects as bearing much the same relationship to the invisible objects of the previous phase as faeces seem to him to bear to urine. The objects appearing in experiences which we call dreams are regarded by the patient as solid and are, as such, contrasted with the contents of the dreams which were a continuum of minute, invisible fragments. (p.98)

[Bion, true to his Kleinian heritage, was always fond of the alimentary and other somatic part-object metaphors for illustrating many of his ideas. Here he seems to be saying that, as the psychotic analysand improves in analysis, he evolves from what we might call 'diarrhoea' ('urine') – of beta elements – to the ability to form solid faeces; i.e. toward the development of 'retentive' alpha elements. The preceding citations are taken from Bion's papers on psychosis, which were reprinted in *Second Thoughts* in 1967. It seems that

Bion in fact did have second thoughts about some of his formulations about psychotic thinking. In the progress of their original development, these papers were clinical and phenomenological. With the last of the series, however, 'A Theory of Thinking', Bion (1962) seems to have shifted to epistemology, a propensity that has characterised the remainder of his work, beginning with *Learning from Experience* (1962).]

In *Learning from Experience* Bion (1962) stated:

> Emotional experiences must be worked on by alpha function before they can be used for dream thoughts... Beta elements are not amenable to use in dream thoughts but are suited for use in projective identification [for evacuation]. (p.6)

> If the patient cannot transform his emotional experiences into alpha elements, he cannot dream... Failure of alpha function means the patient cannot dream and therefore cannot sleep. As alpha function makes the sense impressions of the emotional experience available for conscious and dream-thought the patient who cannot dream cannot go to sleep and cannot wake up. (p.7)

> The more general statement of the theory is this: To learn from experience alpha function must operate on the awareness of the emotional experience; alpha elements produced from the impressions of the experience; these are thus made storable and available for dream thoughts and for unconscious waking thinking... Alpha function is needed for conscious thinking and reasoning and for the relegation of thinking to the unconscious when it is necessary to disencumber consciousness of the burden of thought by learning a skill. (p.8)

[This passage succinctly announces Bion's metatheory for a psychoanalytic epistemology, i.e. how we realise what we know, or how we learn (and develop) from fully processing and experiencing our emotional experiences.]

> The sleeping man has an emotional experience, converts it into alpha elements and so becomes capable of dream thoughts... A man talking to a friend converts the sense impressions of this emotional experience into alpha elements, thus becoming capable of dream thoughts and therefore of undisturbed consciousness... He is able to remain 'asleep' or unconscious of certain elements that cannot penetrate the barrier presented by his 'dream'. Thanks to the 'dream' he can continue uninterruptedly to be awake, that is awake to the fact that he is talking to his friend, but asleep to elements which, if they were to penetrate the barrier of his 'dreams', would

lead to domination of his mind by what are ordinarily unconscious ideas and emotions.(p.15)

[The capacity to dream, which means the capacity to render experiences into dream (alpha) elements, allows them to be stored, remembered, thought about, or repressed, depending on the use to which we wish to put our attention.]

> The 'dream' has many of the functions of censorship and resistance. These functions are not the product of the unconscious but instruments by which the 'dream' creates and differentiates consciousness from unconscious-ness… Alpha function theory of the 'dream' has the elements of the view represented by classical psycho-analytic dream theory, that is to say, censorship and resistance are essential to differentiation of conscious and unconscious and help to maintain the discrimination between the two. This discrimination derives from the operation of the 'dream', which is a combi-nation in narrative form of dream thoughts, which thoughts in turn derive from combinations of alpha elements. In this theory the ability to 'dream' preserves the personality from what is virtually a psychotic state. (p.16)

[Here Bion consolidates his belief that the psychotic is unable to conduct the normal transformations of the sensory impressions of emotional experiences (beta elements) into alpha elements suitable for emotional digestion and for selective relegation both to conscious awareness and for the formation of dream thoughts for memory storage. But Bion is also propounding something else: the role of alpha function in creating a protective contact barrier which effectively separates sleep from wakefulness and dream thoughts from consciousness. As alluded to earlier, these passages represent a distillation of Bion's epistemological metapsychology for psychoanalysis and a radical revision of Freud's theory of dreaming. Eventually, when he discovers transformations in 'O',[1] he will postulate that one's alpha function (dream-work alpha) constitutes an emotional sense organ that is responsive to one's intersections with evolving 'O', from which transformations from 'O' to 'K' take place in order to facilitate 'learning from experience' (Bion 1965, 1970). This idea alone is unique. What makes it even more unique is that dreaming is in the centre of this transformation – by day and by night!]

In discussing a psychotic analysand's treatment, Bion states:

> In the light of the theories of transference and projective identifications the material poured out could be seen as the link between patient and analyst and I could interpret in the way described in 'Attacks on Linking'… It then occurred to me that he was doing what I earlier described as 'dreaming' the

immediate events in the analysis – that is to say, translating
sense-impressions into alpha elements. This idea seemed to illuminate but
became dynamic only when I related it to be defective alpha function, that
is to say, when it occurred to me that I was witnessing an inability to dream
through lack of alpha elements and therefore an inability to sleep or wake,
to be either conscious or unconscious. (p.21)

[I think this passage can be understood as Bion's assessment of the psychotic's attempt to dream, thus what he terms 'dreaming', which is more in
accordance with hallucination because of the absence of alpha function
(dream-work alpha) which is required to transform beta (β) elements into
alpha (α) elements for dreaming proper. The idea of defective alpha function
is reminiscent of Bion's 1962) concept of 'alpha function in reverse'.]

He then discusses the contact barrier more fully:

The man's alpha function whether in sleeping or waking transforms the
sense-impressions related to an emotional experience, into alpha elements,
which cohere as they proliferate to form the contact-barrier. This contact-barrier, thus continuously in process of formation, marks the point of
contact and separation between conscious and unconscious elements and
originates the distinction between them. [p.17]... The contact-barrier may
be expected to manifest itself clinically – if indeed it is manifest at all – as
something that resembles dreams. (p.26)

[Here again Bion is instituting a paradigm change. He is propounding that
the subject must employ alpha function upon the raw data of emotional
experience (beta elements, Absolute Truth, Ultimate Reality, 'O') not only in
order to create alpha elements but also to create and maintain a necessary
contact barrier to be interposed between System Ucs. and System Cs. so that
each can be protected from the other and can cooperate with one another so
as to facilitate each other in their respective functions. This concept alone
transcends Freud in many dimensions. What is implicit in these ideas is that
alpha function is the function of an intact container that is able to contain the
raw data of emotional experience, beta elements, 'O'. He also seems to be
stating that dreams themselves, by their very nature are the contact barrier! If
this is so, then Bion has elevated dreams and dreaming to a much more
important level of function than Freud ever 'dreamed' of.]

Later in the same work he presents his next major difference with Freud's
(1911) theory of primary and secondary processes. He states:

The weakness of this [Freud's] theory of consciousness is manifest in the situation for which I have proposed the theory that alpha function, by proliferating alpha elements, is producing the contact barrier, an entity that separates elements so that those on one side are, and form, the unconscious. The theory of consciousness is weak, not false, because by amending it to state that the conscious and unconscious thus constantly produced together, THEY do function as if they were binocular therefore capable of correlation and self-regard... For these reasons...I find the theory of primary and secondary processes unsatisfactory. (p.54)

[What Bion was beginning to do was to challenge the wish-fulfilment hypothesis that Freud (1900) had assigned to the motive of dreams. Eventually, Freud's wish-fulfilment hypothesis was to end up in Column 2, the psi column, of Bion's (1977) famous Grid as the saturated element that attacks and challenges the truth that inheres in the emerging definitory hypothesis of Column 1.[2] The implications of this for psychoanalysis were to become so far-reaching that to this very day they have not been fully realised. Let me epitomise: for Bion the unconscious spews forth Absolute Truth, Ultimate Reality,[3] not wish-fulfiling drives primarily. Dreams mediate and facilitate the acceptance of Truth in transformations initiated by what Bion (1963) was to call 'alpha function' ('dream-work alpha', Bion 1991). Thus, he stood the psychic apparatus and the theory of the unconscious on its head. His formulation of the binocular complementarity and reciprocity between the unconscious and the conscious states was a radical revision of Freud's view of their being in adversarial conflict. Bion views them as differing partners (binary oppositions) situated in different vertices, each participating in the enterprise of mediating 'O' (beta elements, Absolute Truth, Ultimate Reality, noumena, things-in-themselves, godhead). In brief, by invoking the concept of the 'binocular perspective', Bion was able to transcend Freud's monocular vision of the conflict between Systems Ucs. and Cs. in favour of their being complementary binary oppositional functions responsive to 'O'. Bion was to do the same with Klein's (1946) paranoid-schizoid and depressive positions, i.e, reinterpret them as being cooperatively and complementarily dialectical in confronting and processing (transforming) 'O' (P-S←D).]

Citation from *Elements of Psycho-analysis*

In *Elements of Psycho-analysis* (1963) Bion continues to explicate his theory of the importance of the effect of alpha function on beta (β) elements to produce alpha (α) elements that become dream thoughts:

> Dream thoughts. These depend on the prior existence of α and β elements: otherwise they require no elaboration beyond that which they have received in classical psycho-analytic theory. They are communicated by the manifest content of the dream but remain latent unless the manifest content is translated into more sophisticated terms. (p.23)

[Beta (β) elements will replace Freud's drives as the irrupting repressed, and alpha (α) elements will become the acceptable-to-the-mind elements that constitute a transformation 'mental digestion' of the beta (β) elements to becomes dream thoughts and/or unconscious phantasies, the forerunners of memory[4] and of thought-about thoughts and feelings.]

Citation from *Attention and Interpretation*

Bion (1970) states the following:

> Dream-like memory is the memory of psychic reality and is the stuff of analysis... It may appear that this contradicts the psycho-analytic theory of dreams unless it is remembered that the dream is the evolution of O where O has evolved sufficiently to be represented by sensuous experience.[5] The sensuous elements of a psychotic dream do not represent anything. They are sensuous experience. (p.70)

And in a footnote to the last sentence and on the same page he states:

> The use of the sensuous experience to represent a psychic reality differentiates the neurotic dream and its symbolic quality from the psychotic dream. (p.70)

[I should like to select that portion of the citation that postulates that the dream is the evolution of 'O' where 'O' has evolved sufficiently to be represented by sensuous experience. I believe this is the nucleus of Bion's revision of the theory of dreams and dreaming. First, the dream is the impression that evolving 'O' makes on the subject's dream receptor (what/whom I term the 'dreamer who dreams the dream', also known as the 'ineffable subject of the unconscious' (Grotstein 2000)). The dream receptor employs alpha function to transform these sensory impressions of 'O''s evolutions into evolving alpha elements as dream thoughts. This idea implies that the dreaming function serves to intercept the absolute realness of relentlessly continuing (evolving) 'O', transform, not it, 'O', but one's sensory-emotional impressions (experiences) from 'O''s evolving intersections with oneself, and transforming it into myth (dream and/or unconscious phantasy) for further mental elaboration and processing (i.e. dream interpretation).]

Citations from *Cogitations*

He has already begun to differ from Freud's view of dreams:

> I suspect that Freud's displacement etc., is relevant; [but] he took up only the negative attitude, dreams are 'concealing' something, not the way in which the necessary dream is constructed. (Bion 1991, p.33)

[This citation represents yet another dimension of Bion's paradigm change. Whereas Freud considered dreams to be disguised wish-fulfilments of instinctual urges (a negative view), Bion positively valorises the dream and dreaming as fundamental participants in epistemology, i.e. the processing of 'O' (Absolute Truth, Ultimate Reality, beta elements, noumena, things-in-themselves, godhead) in order for transformations into 'K' (tolerable and practical knowledge) to occur. One might analogise this paradigm with the notion of the origin of fertile soil from the transforming effect of lichen on erupting lava.]

Later in this same work he states:

> ...[P]sychoanalytic use of the dream as a method by which the unconscious is made conscious is an employment in reverse of what is in nature the machinery that is employed in the transformation of the conscious into material suitable for storage in the unconscious. In other words, the dream-work we know is only a small aspect of dreaming proper – dreaming proper being a continuous process belonging to the waking life and in action all through the waking hours,[6] but not usually observable then except with the psychotic patient... At any rate the hypothesis that in an analytic session I can see the patient dream has proved to be very valuable especially with its counterpart of seeing the contrasting activity of hallucination.

> To return to the patient's fear of the Positions and the potential emergence at that stage of a murderous superego: the patient tries to cope with this by dreaming with the analyst – or does he just continue what he does all the time? He may then be so afraid that he produces an artifact that is not a

dream but a hallucination, and then can make no use of it because he can get no more from a hallucination than he could get milk from an imaginary breast... Or he may 'dream' (a) introjectively, (b) projectively. (pp.37–8)

[In differentiating 'dream-work' from 'dreaming proper,' Bion seems to be emphasising that the former is a part of the latter and that the latter, dreaming proper, occurs continuously through wakefulness and sleep. To this very day most people, even analysts, seem to believe that dreams occur only at night. Bion helps us realise that alpha functions continuously in order to help us process our ongoing impacts with 'O', not the drives per se. The concept of the reverse function of dreams relates to the two-way function of dreams, i.e., informatively revelatory and protectively repressive. I infer from Bion's reference to the 'murderous superego' that the latter is formed first by the projective identification of unprocessed 'O' into an unwilling object where it is then murderously hated in order to personalise it (with hate) and to try to destroy its dreadful effect, the result of which becomes the internalisation of a murderous superego, which is also suffused with dread, 'O'.]

> The Dream is an emotional event of which we usually only hear a report or have a memory, although as we shall see it is a matter of some doubt what we mean when we think, or say, we remember a dream. I wish now to extend the term, 'dream', to cover the kind of events that take place in an analysis of a schizophrenic – events that appear to me to merit the description, 'dreams'. One of the points I wish to discuss is related to the fact that the actual events of the session, as they are apparent to the analyst, are being 'dreamed' by the patient not in the sense that he believes that the events observed by him are the same as the events observed by the analyst (except for the fact that he believes them to be a part of a dream, and the analyst believes them to be a part of reality), but in the sense that these same events that are being perceived by the analyst are being perceived by the patient and treated to a process of being dreamed by him. That is, these events are having something done to them mentally, and that which is being done to them is what I call being dreamed–subjected to a process which I hope to describe in more detail. (p.39)

[That the dream is an emotional event suggests more than it states. One of Bion's most radical departures from Freud was his view that experience was essentially emotional, and that the unconscious contains unprocessed emotional or proto-emotional elements (beta elements). Thus, Bion's epistemology is primarily an epistemology of emotions. As for his comments about the schizophrenic analysand, it was my impression that Bion believed that his analysand was attempting to 'dream' (by day) the emotional events of the session in preparation for eventually, one hopes, being able to reflect upon them, as the analyst is already doing. In the meanwhile, the analysand experiences himself as being transitively 'dreamed' in the session, presumably by an internal object which is indistinguishable from the analyst. This phenomenon has much in common with Tausk's (1919) 'influencing machine'.]

In a later undated citation Bion (1956) presents his schematic outline of dreaming:

> Schematic presentation of dreaming
> Murderous superego: therefore avoidance of the depressive positions is achieved by not dreaming, or by dreaming with precautions, e.g., of being with the analyst or, like Y, only allowing the dream to develop when he knows someone is there; instead of quieting down when his mother arrives, his dream appears to become more vivid and worse. It also explains why X seems to cling so tenaciously to my badness in the session. (pp.36–42)

[I have elected not to include the clinical data to which these statements refer. I have already interpreted 'murderous superego' as the internalised unsuccessful container of beta elements, 'O'. 'Depressive positions' in the plural may either be recondite or a misprint in the original text. The main idea in the passage, however, seems to refer to the psychotic analysand's fear of dreaming because of the introjective consequences of dreaming and because of the dream companion, i.e., mother is dangerous, but psychoanalyst is tolerable, even as a murderous superego.]

First stage	
a. No dreams (in the ordinary sense of night-time phenomena).	b. Dreams suppressed and has hallucinations as a substitute.
	These hallucinations are excretory, projective.

Second stage	
a. No dreams.	b. Dreams suppressed but has hallucinations as a substitute. These are intended to be introjectory, but because of fear of the superego and, paradoxically, creating the superego by synthesis, it is not rewarding as the true dream would be, and in any case the hallucination cannot yield the free associations, etc. which are what makes a true dream yield its meaning. So: no free associations and no development of personality is possible. The patient cannot get sustenance from a hallucination.

Third stage	
a. Dreams reported. No free associations and not easily distinguishable from hallucinations – 'I was standing at the window as usual.' Dream seems to be excretory in function.	b. Confusion. Projective identification – splitting almost exclusively with 'dreaming the session'. That is to say, the session is dreamed; my interpretations and all other events of which he is aware, are not seen, listened to, heard in the ordinary way but are subjected to 'inaccessible-ization'. Thus: train stuck in tunnel – two chairs and a three-piece suite – a stool-chair. Mostly excretory to deal with the ego qualities of the interpretations by dispersal.

	Fourth Stage
a. Dreams, more frequent but lacking associations and mostly excretory – arm drops off when he gives a traffic signal, thus indicating uselessness of attempting to warn because parts of the body persist in wanting to be destructive. It lies on the grass – in a tantrum? – but there are no associations. Does the analyst know the meaning, or is it obvious?	b. Introjective and projective. The dream-work intended to convert material into a form where it is compact and can be stored – an important function because of memory. His mind being a kind of 'gut', mental storage seems to mean that the dream is a mental digestive process. The nature of the dream and its function vary according to stimuli. The weekend break seems always to lead to sessional dreaming – I think of the excretory kind, but in later stage perhaps more introjective and retentive.

[This outline-sequence seems to portray the analysand's progressive development from the use of evacuatory hallucinatory 'dreaming' ultimately to introjectively (and retentively) meaningful dreaming.]

> I think the fear of dreams must contribute to making the patient anxious to avoid the dream-work of the conscious state. Should it simply be introjection that is avoided? No: because according to me the process of introjection is carried out by the patient's 'dreaming' the current events. Introjection Dreaming, would be the formula. (p.43)

[This is a novel idea about dreams, one that differs from Freud's idea of wish-fulfilment. Bion is stating that dreaming introjects emotional reality so as to (alpha-) process ('alpha-bet(a)-ise') it for acceptance. It is an interesting idea that hallucination fails to improve the analysand because it yields no free associations, which are required for the dreaming to have meaning and therefore be able to sponsor emotional development. Bion also shows how the analysand 'dreams' away his experience during the session by evacuation rather than by acceptance (introjection).]

> Anxiety in the analyst is a sign that the analyst is refusing to 'dream' the patient's material: not (dream) = resist = not (introject). It may be worth considering, when a patient is resisting, whether the resistance bears characteristics relating it to phenomena Freud described as 'dream-work'. But Freud meant by dream-work that unconscious material, which would otherwise be perfectly comprehensible, was transformed into a dream, and

that the dream-work needed to be undone to make the now incomprehensible dream comprehensible... I mean that the conscious material has to be
subjected to dream-work to render it fit for storing, selection, and suitable
for transformation from paranoid-schizoid position to depressive position,
and that unconscious pre-verbal material has to be subjected to reciprocal
dream-work for the same purpose. Freud says Aristotle states that a dream
is the way the mind works in sleep: I say it is the way it works when
awake... Freud says the state of sleep represents a turning away from the
world, the real external world, and 'thus provides a necessary condition for
the development of a psychosis'. Is this why X talks of losing consciousness? It follows on dream-work which is intended to be destroyed, or has
been destroyed, as part of an attack on linking. (p.43)

[Of all Bion's contributions, this one, that of 'reciprocal dream-work' or 'par-
allel-processing', derived from his idea of 'container/contained', has had the
most far-reaching effect on psychoanalysts and psychotherapists around the
world. It is seldom realised that Bion is one of the fathers, if not the father, of
the intersubjective approach to psychoanalytic technique. His idea that the
psychoanalyst should 'dream the analysand' (by abandoning memory, desire,
understanding, and preconceptions – and all forms of imagery) corresponds
to its infantile precursor in which the mother, in a state of reverie, 'dreams her
infant'. This phenomenon seems to be congruent with Winnicott's (1956)
concept of primary maternal preoccupation.]

The following passages constitute Bion's summary of his conceptual-
isations of the links between dreaming and thinking:

The dream

The dream is the mechanism by which

(1) the ego links the sense data of the external experience with the
     associated conscious awareness of the sense impression;

(2) the stream of unconnected impressions and events are made
     suitable for storing in memory;

(3) these stored events are reviewed and one is chosen [the selected
     fact] which enables facts already 'known', i.e. stored, to be
     harmonized so that the relationship between them is established
     [constant conjunction] and the place of each element seen in its
     relationship to the whole;

(4) the interplay between paranoid-schizoid and depressive
     positions is made possible by a selected fact which is known as

'harmonizing or unifying fact' spatially, and the 'cause' temporally, or when time is an essential element in the relationship between the elements...

The dream, therefore, is the mechanism by which they come into operation,

(a) the social conscience, associated with splitting of the superego and retreat from the depressive position to the paranoid-schizoid position. This seems identical with the social guilt and true superego which can only come into operation with the Oedipus complex, but which I think is a highly persecutory superego which becomes more persecutory since it is split up. Each split itself becomes a complete superego and this leads to further splitting, the fragmentation becoming progressively more minute. This contributes to the state where dreams are 'invisible', wet, and being awake is 'dry'; (b) the individual superego, a murderous object, which becomes manifest if synthesis of the fragments of the paranoid-schizoid position is effected by dream-work bringing the depressive position into being...

Social and individual superego both contribute by their fearfulness to patients' need to make destructive attacks in dream mechanism. When this happens in the session, the patient will show fear that he is dead or has lost consciousness, because the dream is that which makes available, as part of the personality, both the events of external emotional reality and the events of internal pre-verbal psychic reality. If the dream-work capacity is destroyed, the patient feels dread which is peculiarly terrifying because it is nameless, and because the namelessness itself springs from the destruction of the patient's capacity for dream-work which is the mechanism respon- sible for naming. (pp.44–5)

[In these passages Bion is outlining the selection and prioritising aspects of the dream's epistemological functioning. When he speaks of 'the interplay between paranoid-schizoid and depressive positions', he is depicting their complementary function in harvesting the yield from sense impressions in order to relegate them to scales of relative importance on one hand and organise them into constant conjunctions on the other. Without the capacity for dream-work, the analysand plummets into nameless dread, 'O', which he can no longer make sense of (name).]

The domain of the dream

Into the domain of the dream flow the sense impressions [of emotional experience] associated with the coming into being of the reality principle and the pre-verbal impressions associated with the pleasure-pain principle.

None of these can be associated with consciousness, memory, recall, unconsciousness, repression, or suppression unless transformed by dream-work. The domain of the dream is the storehouse in which the transformed impressions are stored after they have been transformed. Dream-work is responsible for rendering pre-communicable material 'storable' and communicable; the same for stimuli and impressions derived from the contact of the personality with the external world. Contact with reality is not dependent on dream-work; accessibility to the personality of the material derived from this contact is dependent on dream-work. The failure of dream-work and the consequent lack of availability of experience of external or internal psychic reality gives rise to the peculiar state of the psychotic who seems to have a contact with reality but is able to make singularly little use of it either for learning by experience or for immediate consumption...

In this respect the dream seems to play a part in the mental life of the individual which is analogous to the digestive processes in the alimentary life of the individual. Why?...

The domain of the dream must be seen as containing an amorphous mass of unconnected and undifferentiated elements... In so far as dream-work is operative, the course of events in the vicissitudes of these elements can be seen to take different forms: visual, auditory, haptic, olfactory. (pp.45–6)

[When Bion speaks here of sense impressions associated with the reality principle and the pre-verbal impressions associated with the pleasure-pain principle, he may be referring to the functioning of the depressive position and the paranoid-schizoid principle respectively, thereby hinting that the function of the former deals with objective reality and the latter with the mythifying antecedents of epistemological rendering of sense data.]

Freud says, it is easy to see how the remarkable preference shown by the memory in dreams for indifferent, and consequently unnoticed, elements in waking experience is bound to lead people to overlook in general the dependence of dreams upon waking life and all events to make it difficult in any particular instance to prove that dependence...

My belief is that the dependence of waking life on dreams has been overlooked and is even more important. Waking life = ego activity, and in particular the play of logical thought on the synthesis of elements, i.e. particles characteristic of the paranoid-schizoid position. The function of the dream is to render these elements suitable for storage, and so to constitute the contents of, what we call memory. Waking life = ego activity

= logical operation. This in turn is essential for synthesis and communicability or publication... The way in which memory behaves in dreams is undoubtedly of the greatest importance for any theory of memory in general... In my idea above, the dream symbolization and dream-work is what makes memory possible. (p.47)

[The difference between Freud's and Bion's views here is striking. Freud states that dreams are dependent on waking life, and Bion states the opposite, which is consistent with his epistemological conception. Let me just single out a few of the items for discussion. One is the idea that the very act of dreaming is sponsored by the ego. Another is the epitome of Bion's notion of epistemology: as random sense data obtrude on the awareness of the individual's sensory apparatus, they are hierarchically sorted, processed, and selectively organised by the 'selected fact', which gives coherence to the data and allows for them to be linked together as constant conjunctions to become meaningful and non-meaningful memory. Another item, one where he transcends Klein, is to posit that, just as consciousness and unconsciousness exist in a joint, 'binocular' enterprise, so does the relationship between the paranoid-schizoid and depressive positions (P-S←D) vis à vis 'O'. Put another way, initial mythification as the first aspect of alpha functioning serves to 'dream' or 'phantasmalise' the sensory data of emotional experience. This initial process corresponds to Freud's primary process, which Bion includes under alpha function, along with secondary process, i.e. correlation and 'common sense'.]

Dreams

We close our most important sensory channels, our eyes, and try to protect the other senses from all other stimuli or from any modification of the stimuli acting upon them...

The sensory stimuli that reach us during sleep may very well become sources of dreams...

Then why is it that dreams we report, or have reported to us are so often in terms of 'visual images'?...

Is it not a 'modification of the stimuli' reaching us? And could this be something to do with the dream-work as an attempt to achieve 'common sense' as part of the synthesizing function of the dream? It may be an aspect of 'linking' one sense to another; the transformation of tactile stimuli into visual excretions as in hallucination. If this is so, it would fit in with Freud's idea that sleep is to be preserved... The hallucinated patient then would be

doing what I said he was doing when I described him as taking interpretation and evacuating it as far as possible away from himself by 'seeing' it, i.e.
visually evacuating it as a hallucination. If this is so, the dream proper may
be an attempt at visual and flatus-like evacuation. (pp.48–9)

[That dreaming can be understood as one of the operations of evacuative
projective identification is, I believe Bion would now say, not only a
propensity of the psychotic, but also of the 'psychotic' aspects of
non-psychotic individuals or maybe even of normal functioning altogether.]

One way of dealing with the problem of scientific evidence for dream
theories would be to restrict the search for data to experience shared by
analyst and patient, or at which analyst and patient are both present. Such
occasions might be all those on which the patient said he had a dream, or all
those on which there appear to be events taking place, e.g. the patient sits
up and looks around in a dazed way; the analyst, identifying himself with
the patient, feels that the experience the patient is having would be more
understandable if the patient were asleep and dreaming...

'More understandable.' Why? Because it is more appropriate to the facts as
the analyst sees them. But this means that if the analyst were feeling what
the patient seems to be feeling, then he, the analyst, would be disposed to
say, 'I must have been dreaming'. (p.51)

[The only way I can understand this passage is to think that Bion is reminding
us that every psychoanalytic session is a dream – and a shared dream at that.
This passage may also allude to Bion's mystical, nonlinear conception of
reverie.]

What do I mean by saying that the negro [a dream figure in Bion's dream] in
the dream was not a real person? Of course he was not. But I suppose that
while I was asleep and in that part of mind, if any, in which I am still asleep,
he must have been thought of as just a real person, a fact, what I have called
an 'undigested' fact. But now I regard him as an ideogram, and this means
that some fact has been 'digested' and that the visual image of the negro,
which I am now recalling, is a significant element in the process of (the
mental counterpart of) digestion. Are 'undigested facts' then used in the
process of 'digesting' other facts? Is their 'indigestibility' a quality that
renders them useful for this function, as if it were some kind of container
for an eroding liquid which must be able itself to resist the erosion by its
contents?...

On this basis there is always some 'undigested part' of a dream-product
('dream-product' is usually called the dream itself), although my point is

that if the person can dream, then he can 'digest' facts and so learn from experience. Obviously what is needed is to consider what 'digesting' facts consists of in detail. (p.52)

[This passage may in part refer to Freud's (1900, p.525) concept of the 'dream's navel', where the dream goes into the unknown. More important, however, is the presence of the 'digestive' functioning of dreaming.]

The Interpretation of Dreams

([1900a], *SE 4*, p.54)

Most of the criticisms are hostile and indicate the need in a waking state to disparage the dream. This is compatible with the α-theory that there is a failure of 'digestion mentally'. It would explain partly why the 'facts' and their ideational counterpart had not been digested if the rational conscious attitude was so hostile to the ideational counterpart of the stimulus, wherever in reality it originated. For such hostility would be likely to inhibit dream-work α, and in so far as the inhibition failed – for after all the patient has dreamed – this hostility now extends to the product of the dream-work. (p.56–7)

[This passage is obscure without its clinical referent, which Bion did not include, but here again he is continuing the idea of dream-work alpha as a mental 'digestion' of the random sense data of emotional experience.]

Logic and dreams

Logic is possibly that element by which it is hoped to establish coherence between elements that otherwise remain separate and persecutory, as in the paranoid-schizoid position. (p.57)

[This passage, obscure because of its brevity and lack of referents, which is also a portion of a 1959 entry in his notebook, reveals, in my opinion, an earlier notion in which he considered that the paranoid-schizoid position was the ultimate 'signified', i.e. danger. It would be only a few short years later (1965) when he would discover 'O' and then relegate P-S to one of the component features of dream-work.]

Dream-work-alpha

Under the title dream-work-alpha I propose to bring together a number of mental activities all of which are familiar to practising psychoanalysts, although they may not have previously associated them together in this way and may not indeed feel the need or value of associating them in the way I propose after they have familiarized themselves with what I am about to say. The title, 'dream-work', has already a meaning of great value. I wish to extend some of the ideas already associated with it and to limit others. It has seemed to me least likely to cause confusion if I group my ideas under a new title which indicates the affiliations of my ideas and yet makes clear that a distinction is being proposed from the theories already grouped under the term, 'dream-work'.

The main sources, other than the stimulations of psycho-analytical practice and historical affiliations of these grouped ideas, are three-fold.

(1)   Freud's *The Interpretation of Dreams* (1900a, *SE 4/5*) and especially the elaboration of his theories of dream-work.

(2)   Freud's paper, 'Two Principles of Mental Functioning' (1911b, *SE 12*) and his *New Introductory Lectures on Psycho-Analysis* (1933a, *SE 22*). Essential to this orientation are the views he expresses on narcissism and the future development of that concept in his paper, 'Instincts and their Vicissitudes' (1916c, *SE 4*).

(3)   Melanie Klein's theories of splitting, projective identification, and the paranoid-schizoid and depressive positions. In one very important respect I have made extensive use of her description of the difference of her views on guilt and superego formation...from those of Freud... (p.63)

[Bion is establishing his metatheory for a psychoanalytic epistemology (and ontology) by invoking Freud's theory of dream-work and the two principles of mental functioning (pleasure-unpleasure principle and the reality principle) and Klein's conceptions of splitting and projective identification, her ideas about the Positions, and her conception about the origins of the superego.]

[T]he true dream is felt as life-promoting, whereas the dream employed as a container for projective identification is felt to be an artefact, as deficient in life-promoting qualities as a hallucinated breast is felt to be deficient in food. But its very function as a container for the unwanted would make it suspect in any case...

The fact that the dream is being employed in an excretory function contributes to the patient's feeling that he is unable to dream or, rather, his thought is far less exact than the phrase, 'unable to dream', would suggest, and does nothing to decrease his feeling that he is lacking in an essential mental capacity...

So far this discussion suggests that a dream exists and that it is characterised by visual images; further, that the dream-work and its production can be employed for two dissimilar purposes. One is concerned with the transformation of stimuli received from the world of external reality and internal psychic reality so that they can be stored (memory) in a form making them accessible to recall (attention) and synthesis with each other...

The other purpose, with which I am here predominantly concerned, is the use of the visual images of the dream for purposes of control and ejection of unwanted (pleasure-pain-determined want) emotional experience. The visual image of the dream is then felt as a hallucinated – that is to say artificially produced – container intended to hold in, imprison, innoculate the emotional experience the personality feels too feeble to contain without danger of rupture, and so to serve as a vehicle for the evacuatory process. The dream itself is then felt to be an act of evacuation in much the same way as the visual hallucinations are felt to be a positive activant of expulsion to the eyes (see 'On Hallucinations', p.67). (p.67)

[In this series of citations Bion ingeniously distinguishes between two differing functions of the dream. We must remember that he earlier distinguished between the psychotic evacuatory (hallucinatory) 'dream' and the normal introjective dream. Here he seems to be saying that even amongst normal or neurotic individuals there is a propensity to use the dream as an evacuatory container for projective, instead of introjective, identification (acceptance).]

If one kind of patient feels he cannot dream, what does the patient feel – the kind that feels he can dream? I propose to limit the term, 'dream', to the phenomenon as it appears in the light of the common-sense view that we all have dreams, know they occur when we are asleep, and know what they are when we have them. This dream is popularly believed to be due to indigestion: I suggest that the belief expressed in 'in vino veritas', should be extended to expressions of popular common sense, at least in this instance. In short, I suggest that what is ordinarily reported as a dream should be regarded by us as a sign of indigestion, but not simply physical indigestion. Rather, it should be taken as a symptom of mental indigestion, or, to phrase it more exactly, as a sign – when a patient reports a dream to us and we are satisfied that he means by this what we all ordinarily understand by a dream – that there has been a failure of dream-work alpha. The failure may of course be due to precisely such causes as the use of visual imagery in the service of projective identification which I have just been describing, but there are other more common causes of failure of dream-work-alpha, and there are also degrees of frequency with which the patient resorts to the use of dream imagery in the service of projective identification. Investigation of the dream as a symptom of a failure of a dream-work-α means that we have to reconsider the series of hypotheses that I have grouped together under the heading of dream-work-α. The first cause of breakdown in capacity to dream is associated with the synthesizing function of α in relation to the superego. (pp.67–8)

[Bion would appear here to be confirming a point made by Freud, that the 'successful dream' does not get reported because the subject is unaware of having dreamed it, so 'successful' was it in keeping him asleep. Dream-work alpha would seem to belong to the 'silent service'. His reference to the superego is less clear. I infer that he is suggesting two hypotheses. First, a severe superego may attack and thereby cripple the dreaming activity of dream-work alpha. The second is that the very existence of the primitive superego represents a questionable, secondary default container for 'O', thus suggesting a defect in the containment capacity of the subject's dream-work alpha.]

Various forms of dream manifestation

1. Organic

   (a) The patient may be concussed – an unlikely contingency but one to be borne in mind in view of the patient's disturbed condition, and therefore the possibility that he has been in an accident.

   (b) He may be drunk.

   (c) He may have taken some other drug – cocaine, barbituates, etc.

2. Psychological

   (a) Alpha is in progress. That is to say, he is attempting to transform immediately current events in the room into assimilable form. This pre-supposes that his alpha capacity is rudimentary and is being expressed aloud presumably to get the analyst's help. But it may slide off into

   (b) Dreaming. This is the emergence of an activity which the patient dare not allow himself out of the analyst's presence through dread of the dream's manifest content, and in particular destroyed objects, un-alpha'd objects and superego. (1958, pp. 65–85)

[As I have earlier suggested, the very existence of destroyed and superego objects betokens a failure of the operation of dream-work alpha.]

(c)   An artificially contrived dream or a hallucinated dream – the latter must be distinguished from the hallucination. Without this distinction the inability to produce associations cannot be properly understood and there is blurring of the distinction between the process intended to evacuate (hallucination) and a process concerned with a need to introject. The artificially contrived dream sounds what it is; it is consciously fabricated, and that, I think, must be taken as the distinction from the hallucinated dream. The hallucinated dream is one produced under duress; the patient must dream, and it is the compulsion which leads to an uncontrolled hallucinated dream.

[The last sentence of this citation is the most meaningful in comprehending the distinction between a hallucination and a hallucinated dream. The latter represents a compromised attempt to dream (introjectively), whereas the former represents an inability to dream introjectively altogether.]

(d)   Hallucination: olfactory, auditory, visual. The function is evacuatory, and it is stimulated by immediate events. If the analyst knows the content of the hallucination, then he must see it as an immediate situation not transformed (digested) at all. Thus the patient starts up, pointing and saying, 'My wife, it's my wife! She's coming for me! Stop her!' This is a visual image – he is evacuating it through his eyes. It might be argued that this is how he sees me and that I must therefore be transformed mentally into an image of his dead wife. In fact it is a view that is plausible but untenable for reasons I shall give later. He does not in any true sense see me or have any other sensory perception of me. I remain an undigested fact because his very partial sensory awareness of my presence has acted as a stimulus to his projective mechanisms and he has ejected an old, undigested fact. I shall not for the moment consider the nature and origin of the visual image of his dead wife, which is here a fact undigested in the past, except to say that it is probably a past dream fragment which he did not originally digest, that it dates from a time when he could dream and that it therefore has great prognostic significance. Indeed it could be taken as a sign suggesting the possibility of psychoanalytic repair and cure because it indicated that there is something to repair. For the moment I want to consider only that, excluding any effect interpretation may have, the original undigested fact, the image of the dead wife, remains undigested; in addition there is a new undigested fact, namely my presence and intervention as the analyst. There is every reason to suppose – again excluding the effect any interpretation may have – that the new undigested fact, in addition to the old one, will at some future date reappear. (p.93–4)

[Bion is once again emphasising what amounts to a profound ontological as well as epistemological point – the need for the analysand to 'accept, introject, and process all experiences rather than evacuate them.]

17 October 1959

The Dream

The term 'dream', I shall always use for the phenomenon described by Freud under that term. The dream is an emotional experience that is developmentally unsuccessful in that it is an attempt to fulfil the functions which are incompatible; it is in the domain of the reality principle and the pleasure principle, and represents an attempt to satisfy both. That is to say, it is an attempt to achieve frustration evasion and frustration modification and fails in both. In so far as it is an attempt at modification of frustration, it requires an interpretation; as an attempt at frustration evasion, it has failed to satisfy because the wish-fulfilment element in it leaves the personality aware that the wish has not been fulfilled in reality. The dream thus occupies a conspicuous role in treatment; it contains, and is itself a manifestation of, painful stresses. But for this same reason its importance is less central amongst the processes involved in the process of smooth development; the crucial mechanisms are those associated with rendering the perceptions of experience fit for storage in the psyche, namely α, and for making these stored transformations of experience available again when the psyche needs them. The problem is, what are these crucial mechanisms? It may be that we can never know, that we can only postulate their existence in order to explain hypotheses that are capable of translation into verifiable data, and that we shall have to work with these postulates without assuming that corresponding realities will at some time be discovered. I regard α as a postulate of this nature...

α destruction

> One consequence is starvation of the psyche in its supply of reality. There is therefore nothing that can be opposed to phantasy. This is an additional reason for failure to wake up; there is not enough 'up' to wake up to... Two conditions need differentiation: (1) a feeling that he cannot dream; this is so strong that it inhibits realization that he is dreaming; (2) an actual inability to dream. The appearance of dreaming that the patient then presents can be due to phenomena that look alike but are actually different, according to whether they are associated with (1) or (2). If (1), then the disjointed elements are α elements that the patient cannot synthesize, e.g. through fear of superego, or hatred of reality, or dread of depression. If (2), then the disjointed elements are β elements. (pp.95–6)

[Once again Bion is affirming that the dream – and dreaming itself – and therefore dream-work alpha – serves two masters, the pleasure-unpleasure principle and the reality principle.]

> Consequently the patient...needs to restrict these attempts to sessions. Then, and only then, is he sure of the external aid that the presence of the analyst affords. It is this that leads to the events I have already described in which the patient strives to dream in the session. But, in the instance I am giving, the patient cannot dream. The combination of incapacity to dream with urgency imposed by psychic starvation gives rise to the phenomenon I have described as the hallucinated dream which affords no associations – associations being equated with sustenance. (p.98)

[What Bion seems to be alluding to here is that the psychotic patient can only, if at all, dream in the safety of the analyst's presence, yet this patient cannot dream even there but can only become aware of his inability to dream (process) his experiences. Consequently, he can only hallucinate (evacuate through the senses).]

> It may appear that I am suggesting that synthesis must be associated simply with a bringing together of the elements according to some known rule to form, say, a polynomial or a determinant. But we cannot assume such a restriction and exclude the bringing together of these elements in a quite different manner; for example, in such a way that would issue in a dream, or in some structure such as that suggested by Stendhal's description of a painting as, *de la morale construite*. Certainly with the psychotic personality there is a failure to dream, which seems to be parallel with an inability to achieve fully the depressive position. It may therefore be said that the

capacity to synthesize issues in two main events: (1) the logical construct, a mathematical formula, sentence, etc. and (2) a dream...

The inability to dream: I leave aside for the present the minute fragmentation etc. that may be associated with an inability, as I think, with dreams that are devoid of sense i.e. visual impression, auditory, olfactory, maybe tactile and taste impressions that are felt to be a kind of urination. I concentrate on the situation itself in which the patient has dreams devoid of sensory impressions, or all sense impressions and no dreams. If such a patient reports a dream, I suggest reporting a hallucination and that he always feels it to be a 'queer dream'. I suggest that an inability to dream is so serious that the patient is compelled to have a dream that is a counterpart, on the level of dream thinking, of the hallucinatory gratification experienced in waking life when true gratification is impossible...

Seen in this light, X's objection to noise may be his objection to a sense impression as well as to the thing his sense impression conveys to him. The deprivation of sense impression must then lead to an inability to dream and a need to hallucinate sense impressions as a substitute for the dream...

This failure to dream is felt to be such a grave disaster that the patient continues to hallucinate during the day, to hallucinate a dream, or so to manipulate facts that he is able to feel he is having a dream – which is the daylight counterpart of the night-time hallucination of a dream. But it is also the attempt to suck a dream out of an experience of reality or actuality. And in this respect the dream that yields no associations and the reality that yields no dreams are alike; they are similar to hallucinatory gratification. (pp.111–2)

[Bion seems to be saying that dreaming depends on the input of sense impressions, which seems to be compromised or absent in psychotics. It was Federn (1949) who postulated that in psychosis a decathexis of the ego boundaries occurs in which the 'true-self' (Winnicott 1960) aspect of the patient withdraws into an inner fortress, leaving behind its sense organs on the now abandoned ego boundary. Thus, another way of interpreting Bion's thesis is that the patient has lost contact with his sense organs and, as a consequence, with sense data, which however, does return to him/her as hallucinations, but those would be introjective hallucinations. Bion believes that hallucinations are evacuations. Perhaps we could reconcile the issue with the notion that the psychotic's reception of the hallucinations from the disowned ego boundary is equated with evacuative projective identification. That the psychotic patient has to 'suck a dream out of reality' is poignant testimony of the patient's keenly experienced need to find a dream, denoting that he is aware that he needs to – and cannot – dream!]

18 February 1960

α

The occasions when the patient expresses a number of feelings verbally – 'I am anxious, I don't know why', 'I am feeling a bit better, I don't know why', – may be an expression of an experience such as I suggest takes place when he has a dream. That is to say, he has an emotional experience on which dream-work-alpha is done so that the emotional experience can be made available, stored for use in consciousness. Ordinarily alpha operates to enable a conscious emotional experience to be stored in unconsciousness; it just occurs to me that this may be very like the function performed by logic in the elaboration of a scientific deductive system in which premises and derived hypotheses are so arranged that they follow each other...

But how is alpha related to logic? There are logical dreams, but on the whole they would seem to be rare. Yet the ordinary dream has a logic, it is narrativised. The patient today said he had had a dream, but in fact could only report disjointed fragments in a way not unlike the ordinary session. (He said, incidentally, that in twenty years' time a new patient might be cured by psychoanalysis in half the time that he is.)...

But what else can one say about the construction? Freud assumed that the interpretation, the latent content, was the origin of the dream, and that it had been worked on by the dream-work to produce the dream. I say that the origin is in emotional experience – perhaps even an experience that is emotional and nothing else – and that this is worked on (rationalized?) to produce the dream, the manifest content as we know it, and that it is the analyst who then does the interpretation to produce the so-called latent content. Then what validity or significance is to be attached to this product, the latent content? (p.135)

[Here Bion again is radically altering the psychoanalytic conception of the significant content of unconscious mental life generally and of the ultimate agency of dreaming particularly. The origin of dreams, he states, lies in emotional experience, i.e. the interaction between 'O' and the impression (impact) evolving 'O' makes on one's emotional make-up.]

VI Dream-work α

Psycho-analysts, and Freud in particular, have described how the dreamer compresses, distorts, displaces, and disguises the dream-thoughts in such a way that the manifest content of the dream bears little apparent resemblance to what he calls the latent content of the dream, namely that content which is revealed by interpretation. This transformation of dream-thought into manifest content is, Freud says, brought about by dream-work. I wish now to employ this term to describe a related but different series of phenomena. To avoid confusion with the concept already established in psycho-analytic usage, and to avoid inventing a term that introduces – by virtue of its penumbra of already existing associations – implications I would prefer to exclude, I propose for my purposes to modify Freud's term by calling it 'dream-work-alpha'. What I propose to designate by this term I shall now relate. (p.179)

[In this entry, undated but probably written in 1960, Bion is beginning to outline some of the main points in his new epistemological metatheory for psychoanalysis. He goes on to define dream-work alpha, alpha elements, and beta elements.]

Dream-work α

To what extent is myth-making an essential function of α? It may be that the sense impression has to be transformed to make it suitable material for dream-thought, but that it is the function of dream-thought to use the material put at its disposal by α, the units of dream-thoughts so to speak, in order to produce myths. Myths must be defined; they must be communicable and have some of the qualities of common sense – one might call them 'common non-sense'.

Dream-work and α

The episode of the rain storm has emerged at different times in fragments. Rain – without a raincoat – taking the only taxi – pneumonia feared for me – self in rain at my house. Then there was his account of the baby with a horn on its nose – some cowl on its head – his wife and blood – shambles. There was his dream of his other self. This was coherent and might be an account of what I had said to him in a session. If so, it is almost accurate, but I am his other self and it is called a dream.

What do I know about all this? Virtually nothing. It is hardly even true to say that I know he said it, because although I was present and heard him talking and saw him lying on the couch, there is little I can do to digest it. In other words, I do not know what took place – I *suspect*. The conditions do not exist for me to have the experience of knowing, but the conditions do exist for me to be suspicious. I can only pile one hypothesis on another. Taking the view that I need to be able to operate α, I find in fact, that I cannot. (pp.186–7)

[Bion seems to be using 'myth-making' as a synonym for 'phantasy-making' and includes it as one of the components of dream-work alpha. Once again, he includes myth-making, i.e, phantasying, as a component of dream-work alpha and thus of (emotional) thinking. In the case example cited, Bion seems to be struggling to find the alpha element cum selected fact that would give coherence to the manifest content of the session – in vain – because of the patient's splitting attacks.]

'Our mind…would be obliged to forget each of these details before examining the next because it would be incapable of taking in the whole,' as Poincaré describes the state preceding the discovery or selection of the harmonizing fact. Nor is it wholly satisfactory to postulate a state of mind akin to the depressive position unless it is made equally clear that it must not be *identical* with the emotional experience associated with the depressive position.

Freud has described the value of a state he calls benevolent neutrality, a kind of free-floating attention. Poincaré would appear to desiderate an absorption in logical mental processes that, if not in themselves mathematical, at least issue ultimately in mathematical formulation.

For convenience, I propose to call this state, which is neither the paranoid-schizoid position nor yet the depressive position but something of each, the Positions. I shall further suggest that the process of discovery or selection of the harmonizing fact or, I should prefer to regard it, its ideational counterpart cannot be initiated or maintained without the mobilization of the mental processes of dreaming.

It must not be supposed that I am setting this up in contrast with, or as an alternative to, what I conceive to be the logical or mathematical absorption that Poincaré had in mind; nor am I suggesting that the analyst should go to sleep. But I believe that the analyst may have to cultivate a capacity for dreaming while awake, and that this capacity must somehow be reconcilable with what we ordinarily conceive of as an ability for logical thought of the mathematical kind. (p.215)

[*Cogitations* is the only place where Bion mentions or elaborates his concept of dream-work alpha, and this was his private notebook – not meant for publication in his lifetime. As we know he publicly employed the term 'alpha function'. One wonders why 'dream-work alpha' never saw the light of day until the posthumous publication of *Cogitations*. If we conflate dream-work alpha with mythification, logic, and the Positions, we get a stereoscopic model in which dream-work alpha utilises a back-and-forth reversible inter-action between the paranoid-schizoid and depressive Positions (as the 'Positions') in order to achieve mythification of evolving 'O' so as to facilitate the mentalisation of emotional experience, which he seems to confirm in the following citation:]

> Nevertheless, there is no doubt that mathematicians have formed a method of recording and communicating their formulations which makes teaching of the formulations and their use assume an enviably uniform and stable discipline – at least to me who proposes that myth and dream should be regarded as corresponding to algebraic calculi and therefore as capable of yielding, after scrutiny, the tools that can interpret, through their suitability to represent a problem, the problem itself, and so open the way to its solution...

> I propose now the task of establishing the fundamental rules for the use of dream or myth. The first point is that all dreams have one interpretation and only one – namely, that alpha-elements are constantly conjoined. The second is that every dream has a corresponding realization, which it therefore represents. This realization may be of such insignificance or rarity that it is never observed to occur, although potentially it might do so. Sometimes it is observed, and its resemblance to the dream that represents it is so nearly conscious that the dreamer has an illusion that he expresses by saying he had a dream that came true. This usually means that the dreamer believes the facts of the realization were correctly foreshadowed in a dream in which the same or similar facts occurred in a similar narrative. This is an illusion in which the similarity that exists between an emotional experience (as it is recorded and stored through the agency of alpha-function) and an event (to the understanding of which the stored emotional experience is essential) has been transferred to what are believed to be two narratives. In fact, one narrative serves to mark the conjunction of alpha-elements required to store two different but related emotional experiences: one, that which was experienced in sleep or the waking state known in déjà vu phenomena; the other, that which was experienced in the course of actual events in the individual's life. Since the same dream would serve as the product of alpha-function operating on the two emotional experiences, it is believed that the supposed events of the narrative of the dream, and the events of the emotional experience to which the dream serves a function

analogous to that of algebraic calculus to empirical data, are the same. (p.230)

[The point Bion makes here is very subtle yet important. To me it can be understood in the following way. When we experience an emotional event, our dream-work alpha is in operation at the moment of the experience. The result of this process is the creation of alpha-elements suitable for dreaming (the emotional experience as latent content). Once formal dreaming occurs, the alpha-elements are then further processed by dream-work alpha into the manifest content of a dream. In certain circumstances, the two events, the day dream and the night dream, can become confused because they are both dreams.]

> We have now arrived at this position: the core of the dream is not the manifest content, but the emotional experience; the sense data pertaining to this emotional experience are worked on by α-function, so that they are transformed into material suitable for unconscious waking thought, the dream-thoughts, and equally suitable for conscious submission to common sense. Freud clearly thought that this material was equally suitable for more than correlation with and by common sense, and attempted to apply to it the methods of scientific investigation, as if what I am calling α-elements lent themselves to that kind of procedure. This is to assume that the α-elements can be used for purposes other than simple correlation – one of the most rudimentary of scientific procedures. The manifest content, as it would be called if we were discussing dreams in Freud's terms, is a statement that these α-elements are constantly conjoined; that being so, it is in every way analogous to the selected fact, which is to display the constant conjunction of elements characteristic of the paranoid-schizoid position, and it has the property of showing to be related. We shall have to consider later how the manifest content of a dream (a narrativised collection of visual images) and a mathematical formulation such as an algebraic calculus can come to be fulfilling an apparently identical function when they are in every other respect so different from each other. (p.233)

[Bion is affirming that emotional experience is the true core of the dream. Further, he asserts that the sense data of emotional experience are transformed by dream-work alpha both for waking thoughts and for formal dream thoughts. Finally, he is suggesting that there is a mathematical pattern to the constancy of conjunctions of the alpha-elements formed in the paranoid-schizoid position to warrant scientific validation.]

Conclusion

It is difficult to harness the awesome complexity of Bion's conception of dreams and dreaming. While still remaining loyal to the main ideas of Freud in that regard, he has extended Freud's conception of dreams and dreaming to newer dimensions. He distinguishes the dream as hallucination in the psychotic from the non-psychotic dream, which employs dream-work alpha to transform beta elements (unmentalised emotional experience) into alpha elements that are suitable for mental processing. Dream-work alpha constitutes a mythification of beta elements (evolving 'O') into myth-themes or dream-phantasy narratives utilising a dialectical interchange in the 'Positions' (P-S←D). Emotional experience must be worked on by alpha function in order to produce dream thoughts for memory and conscious reflection. Dreams represent the introjection of emotional reality.

Dream-work alpha (alpha function) differs from Freud's primary and secondary processes. Dream-work alpha is inherent, presumably, as a Kantian category (Grotstein 2000).

The Systems Ucs. and Cs. function binocularly, as do the 'Positions' (P-S ←D). Consequently both are involved in the epistemological processing of the sense data of emotions.

Psychotics suffer from defective alpha function; therefore they cannot dream and consequently cannot truly be either awake or asleep. The psychotic 'dream' is a hallucination that seeks to evacuate emotional pain into an object which thereupon becomes a persecutory superego laden with 'O' (Grotstein 2000).

A radically different picture of the unconscious emerges in terms of its binocular partnership with consciousness and with its content, emotional truths as garnered from 'O'.

One cannot think without dreaming because thoughts and thinking depend on the 'alpha-bet(a)-ization' of raw emotional truth (beta elements, 'O').

Dreams are continuous; they occur while we are awake as well as while we sleep.

Whereas dreams, particularly dream thoughts, constitute the ongoing caesura (contact barrier) between Systems Ucs. and Cs., and between the personality and 'O', the act of dreaming itself constitutes a 'grid' between the emotional receptors of the personality and 'O' for the formatting of experience (see Bion 1977; Grotstein 2000).

One of the other purposes of dream-work alpha is to create a protective barrier between Systems Ucs. and Cs. The establishment or the failure of the establishment of this contact barrier may be a deciding factor in mental health generally, but it may be a marker for analysability, that is where the analysand can appreciate the distinction between an internal and external world – to be able to recognise symbols and metaphor rather than be constrained by symbolic equations (Segal 1957, 1981). Implacable resistances, alexithymia, and primitively organised mental states may be a function of an inadequate barrier.

The analyst must dream the analysand and the analysand's 'O', as must the mother earlier. This idea, even though incompletely understood by most analysts and therapists, was the main launching pad for the postmodern concept of intersubjectivity (as 'container/contained'). In other words, reciprocal dream-work transpires between analyst and analysand. The contact barrier may also facilitate the subject's capacity to prioritise and abstract, correlate, and publicate his/her emotional feelings.

One also sees two Bions in these preceding passages. The early Bion pointed out that the psychotic was intolerant of psychic reality, i.e. he hated feeling and thinking. The later Bion becomes more charitable as he leaves the one-person model for the two-person model, i.e. container/contained, in which the operation of the analysand's mother's dream-work alpha is decisive for his/her emotional outcome.

References

Bion, W.R. (1961) *Experience in Groups*. London: Tavistock Publications.

Bion, W.R. (1961a) 'A psycho-analytic theory of thinking.' In *Second Thoughts: Selected Papers on Psychoanalysis*. London: Karnac Books.

Bion, W.R. (1962) *Learning From Experience*. London: Heinemann.

Bion, W.R. (1963) *Elements of Psycho-analysis*. London: Heinemann.

Bion, W.R. (1965) *Transformations*. London: Heinemann.

Bion, W.R. (1967) *Second Thoughts*. London: Heinemann.

Bion, W.R. (1970) *Attention and Interpretation*. London: Tavistock Publications.

Bion, W.R. (1977) *Two Papers: 'Grid' and 'Caesura'*. Edited by Francesca Bion. London: Karnac Books.

Bion, W.R. (1992) *Cogitations*. London: Karnac Books.

Blakeslee, S. (2000) 'Experts explore deep sleep and the making of memory.' *New York Times: Science Times 14*, November 2000, D2.

Federn, P. (1949) 'The ego in schizophrenia.' In Edoardo Weiss (ed) (1952) *Ego Psychology and the Psychoses*. New York: Basic Books.

Freud, S. (1900a) *The Interpretation of Dreams. Standard Edition 4*. London: Hogarth Press.

Freud, S. (1900b) *The Interpretation of Dreams. Standard Edition 5.* London: Hogarth Press.

Freud, S. (1911) *Formulations of the Two Principles of Mental Functioning. Standard Edition 12.* London: Hogarth Press.

Grotstein, J. (2000) *Who Is the Dreamer Who Dreams the Dream? A Study of Psychic Presences.* Hillsdale, NJ: Analytic Press.

Klein, M., Heimann, P., Isaacs, S. and Rivere, J. (1946) *Development of Psycho-Analysis.* London: Hogarth Press.

Segal, H. (1957) 'Notes on symbol formation.' In *International Journal of Psychoanalysis 38,* 391–7.

Segal, H. (1981) 'Notes on symbol formation.' In *The Work of Hanna Segal: A Kleinian Approach to Clinical Practice.* New York and London: Aronson.

Tausk, V. (1919) 'On the origin of the influencing machine in schizophrenia.' *Psychoanalystic Quarterly 2,* 519–56.

Winnicott, D.W. (1956) 'Primary maternal preoccupation.' In (1958) *Collected Papers: Through Paediatrics to Psycho-Analysis.* New York: Basic Books.

Winnicott, D.W. (1960) 'Ego distortion in terms of the true and false self.' In *The Maturational Processes and the Facilitating Environment: Studies in the Theory of Emotional Development.* New York: International Universities Press.

Endnotes

1. In *Transformation* (1965) and in *Attention and Interpretation* (1970) Bion introduced perhaps his most controversial concept, that of 'O', which he designated for the domain beyond the senses to grasp or understand. He analogised it with Kant's noumena and things-in-themselves and also with Absolute Truth, Ultimate Reality, and the godhead. It represented Bion's incursion into the meta-epistemological and mystical landscapes of psychoanalysis. In the psychoanalytic session 'O', in its evolving trajectory, has intersected emotionally with the analysand as the 'analytic object'.

2. I should state that this is my own opinion as I reflect on the implications of the extensions of Bion's conception. I have stated this opinion elsewhere (Grotstein 2000).

3. He is later to call this 'O' (Bion 1965, 1970).

4. To my knowledge, Bion was the first to implicate dreaming with the maintenance of memory, a finding that has only recently been confirmed by studies in empirical neuroscience (Blakeslee 1900).

5. The reader should bear in mind that when Bion employs the term 'sensuous experience' he means the emotional sensitivity to 'O'.

6. This idea, on which I have already commented, represents a radical innovation in terms of dream theory. One of its practical applications in technique is to regard every analytic session as constituting a dream in its own right.

CHAPTER 8

Extracts from *The Enchanted World of Sleep*[*]

Peretz Lavie[**]

Nathaniel Kleitman is, without doubt, the father of modern sleep research. The discovery which truly revolutionised sleep research, that of rapid eye movement (REM) sleep, was made in 1953, in Kleitman's laboratory, by a young doctoral student named Eugene Aserinsky. Like many other scientific discoveries, this was stumbled upon by chance, and there are several versions of the precise circumstances under which it was made. William Dement, Kleitman's disciple and successor, has provided us with an eyewitness account. Dement began his studies at the University of Chicago Medical School in 1951 and set his sights on specialising in psychiatry. Kleitman's lecture on sleep, which was given as part of a course on neurophysiology, changed his life. He went to see Kleitman and asked for a job in the sleep laboratory. At the time, Aserinsky was studying for his doctorate in physiology with Kleitman. Thus Dement, Aserinsky, and Kleitman formed the first research group in the field of sleep.

Kleitman attached great importance to the slow eye movements which accompany the process of falling asleep. As a great part of the cerebral cortex is committed to controlling eye movement, he theorised that there was a strong connection between the slow eye movements and the depth of sleep.

Consequently, he decided to examine whether slow eye movements appeared at any other times during sleep. In the spring of 1951, before Dement had joined the team, he authorised Aserinsky to conduct tests on the subject. To avoid having to spend many sleepless nights, Aserinsky began by observing infants, who also sleep during the day. In his initial observation, Aserinsky immediately saw that the infants' slow eye movements when falling asleep were replaced by rapid eye movements once they had fallen asleep, and that they were identical to eye movements during wakefulness. Once Aserinsky and Kleitman had succeeded in recording rapid eye movements in adults, they were convinced that the cause was either noise or a malfunction in the recording instruments. In order to ascertain that these were indeed true eye movements, Aserinsky asked observers to watch the eyes of the sleeping subjects closely while the recording instruments did their work. He wanted to be completely sure that the eyes did indeed move during sleep and thus eliminate the possibility of a technical fault. It quickly became clear that it was very easy to observe rapid eye movements through the eyelids of the sleeping subjects. (pp.19–20)

In a paper published in the journal *Science* in 1953, which became the cornerstone of modern sleep research, Aserinsky and Kleitman called this type of sleep REM sleep. REM sleep is also known today by several other names – 'dream sleep,' 'paradoxical sleep,' and 'active sleep' – but for convenience I shall use the term REM sleep to describe this type of sleep in humans, and paradoxical sleep when referring to animals. (p.21)

REM sleep

Approximately an hour and a half after falling asleep, the physiological changes which indicate the first appearance of REM sleep occur. The brain waves show characteristic variations: theta waves – this time without K-complexes or sleep spindles – and short bursts of alpha waves activity which, when appearing during sleep, indicate a high level of alertness. The brain waves in REM sleep are in fact almost completely identical to those in stage 1, which we have defined as half sleep or the transitional stage. We may therefore conclude that REM sleep is shallow and awakening from it is easy. But that is not the case, for REM sleep is deep, although under special conditions awakening from it can be very easy. The combination of electrical activity in the brain, which indicates shallow sleep, and deep sleep (from a subjective standpoint) has given this type of sleep one of its many names – paradoxical sleep. At the same time, the rapid eye movements which attracted the attention of Aserinsky appeared, thus making the discovery of REM sleep possible. (pp.21–2)

Sleep paralysis

Eye movements and brain waves are not the only indications of REM sleep. Other changes, no less bizarre, also occur. As I mentioned earlier, the skeletal muscles relax during the falling asleep stage and this relaxation reaches its peak in sleep stage 4, the stage of deepest sleep. There is a further change in muscle tonus during REM sleep: it disappears completely. In this type of sleep we are in fact in a condition of total muscular paralysis, and this, too, is a phenomenon caused by a spontaneous variation in brain activity. Just like the mechanism which inhibits nerve impulses sent from the sensory receptor to the cerebral cortex, there is a reverse inhibitory mechanism, from the brain to the muscles. This prevents the transmission of nerve impulses from the motor cerebral cortex, the areas connected with muscle control, to the spinal column, and it is these signals which change the characteristics of nerve cell activity in the spinal column and cause paralysis. Why, then, do we have rapid eye movement? Because the control of the eye muscles is not executed via the spinal column but through special nerve fibers protruding from the brain stem, and these fibers remain unaffected by the paralysis.

Some people appear to be fully aware of this motor paralysis which accompanies REM sleep, and it is by no means a pleasant experience. In these instances, the sleeper wakens to an acute sense of paralysis: he is unable to move his hands or feet, has difficulty in detecting his own respiratory movements, and therefore fears that he might not be breathing or even that he is choking. Only his eyes respond to his commands, as they comb the bedroom in panic, as though pleading for help. Most people describing these 'sleep paralysis' events recall a panic-stricken experience. As they try to call for help, they are unable to utter a sound, and the fear of choking is succinctly described as the 'fear of death' in its fullest sense. Although in most cases this is a one-time or rare event, in some instances it is a regular phenomenon, sometimes occurring several times a week. When the sleep of people suffering from this disorder is recorded, we find that the paralysis always occurs after waking from REM sleep. We can understand from this that the mechanism which inhibits the nerve signals on their way from the motor cerebral cortex to the spinal column is not removed after the sleeper has awakened, and thus the commands to the muscles continue to be inhibited during wakefulness. Even without outside intervention, an attack of sleep paralysis will subside on its own after a few minutes, but touching the paralyzed subject, or even calling his or her name, will immediately terminate it.

There is another outstanding example of muscle paralysis where people fall asleep as soon as their heads touch the pillow and immediately sink into REM sleep, without passing through any of the first four stages. These people can enter REM sleep directly while standing, sitting or even driving a car. The attack causes them to lose control of their muscles, which is potentially extremely dangerous. This disorder is called narcolepsy. (pp.23–5)

REM sleep: a window on the world of dreams

The discovery of REM sleep by Aserinsky and Kleitman in 1953, coupled with the fact that waking from this sleep stage is bound up with a clear and detailed report of a dream, allowed researchers, for the first time, to identify the moment of the 'dream.' It is not difficult to imagine the excitement that gripped those interested in dreams once it became clear that dreams did not occur at random throughout the night, but at a specific and easily identifiable stage of sleep. The discovery of REM sleep brought psychiatrists and psychologists much closer to the sources of the dream itself, so it was hardly surprising that the majority of sleep researchers who rushed to their laboratories in order to study what transpired during REM sleep were those whose main interest lay in dreams. They no longer had to rely on their patients' memories in order to learn about their dreams; by waking them up at the correct time they were able to hear the dreams first-hand.

The technique was extremely simple: all the researcher had to do was to remain alert throughout the night and observe the instruments recording the subject's brain waves, eye movements, and muscle tonus. At the precise moment that the recording sheet showed the characteristic configuration of REM sleep, the researcher had to rouse the patient. As we have already seen, this configuration is easily identifiable and almost unmistakable. Several minutes after the appearance of REM sleep, the researcher would open the bedroom door, quietly call the subject's name and, when he or she awoke, ask, 'Did you dream about anything?' It was only some years later, for reasons that will soon become apparent, that the question was revised to, 'Did anything cross your mind?' And indeed, this wait for the onset of REM sleep was usually not in vain. In 80 to 85 per cent of the cases, the subjects awakening from REM sleep were able to provide a clear and detailed report of their dream.

So if dreams occur during REM sleep, why are we unable to remember them every time we awaken from it? After the subject awakens from REM sleep, although the story of a dream is stored in a readily accessible memory bank, it remains there for a very short time. If we divert the subject's attention from the story of a dream or delay its telling, then the 'memory banks' close and traces of the dream will become blurred. In many cases, therefore, people awaken from sleep with a clear feeling that they have had a dream but are unable to remember anything about it. This also explains why it is easier to remember dreams after being awakened suddenly. When people wake up gradually over a few minutes, their attention may drift and the dream story rapidly fades.

The majority of studies conducted in sleep laboratories during the 1960s dealt with planned awakening from REM sleep in order to obtain dream reports. However, as more and more dreams were collated in the laboratory, it became clear that laboratory dreams were vastly different from those reported during treatment on the psychiatrist's couch. Laboratory dreams were much shorter, less 'strange,' and poorer in content than those reported in psychology and psychiatry literature. Most of them dealt with everyday matters, and a few included strange details which deviated from normal thinking while awake. The picture which was formed of the content of dreams showed that the majority were based upon the same images and events to which we are exposed in our everyday lives. People dream about subjects that are close to their hearts: lawyers dream about courtrooms, judges and criminals; doctors dream about operating rooms, hospital corridors and white-clad nurses; students dream about lecturers and examinations. It is therefore not surprising to find that those who dream about matters of paramount national and global concern are usually politicians! Fred Snyder, a veteran American sleep researcher, summed up his rich experience in the study of the contents of dreams thus: 'Our findings on the contents of dreams show that they are a true reflection of our waking lives.'

Some explained this phenomenon by the interrogation method used. The need to awaken the sleeper in the middle of REM sleep in order not to miss the dream is reminiscent of watching a movie to the middle without seeing the end. Others explained it thus: the spontaneously remembered dream is usually the last one of the night and is probably exceptional in comparison with those dreamed early in the night.

Is there, then, a difference between the dream reports received from the early REM period of the night and those of the later periods? It was indeed found that there is a development in dream character during the night, from one dream period to the next. Usually, after awakening from the first dream period, the report is brief, deals with the present, and in most cases lacks a plot or central characters. The reports become richer in detail and plot as awakening is effected from REM sleep late at night. Dream reports made in the early hours of the morning are richer in detail, central characters, and feelings, and compared with dreams from the first half of the night, they tend to deal more with the dreamer's early childhood. These dreams from the last hours of the night, prior to awakening, are those which are remembered spontaneously. (pp.66–8)

Dreams, thoughts, or hallucinations?

Not everyone agreed that dreams occur exclusively during REM sleep. Some claimed that this apparent relationship was a result of methodological error. When awakening from other sleep stages, subjects were unconsciously guided by the researchers to give a negative reply to the question 'Did you dream?' When people wake up and are asked this question, their replies will depend, among other things, on their conceptions of the term 'dream.' Although it is widely accepted that a dream is a kind of cognitive activity which takes place during sleep, the definition of this activity may vary radically from person to person. There are those for whom a dream is every cognitive activity which occurs during sleep, irrespective of its content. Others report on a dream only when the cognitive activity includes events deviating from day-to-day reality. It is probable that people who awaken from sleep stages other than REM sleep deny having 'dreamed' because the experience they underwent did not fit their conception of a dream.

David Foulkes, who worked first at the University of Chicago and then at the University of Wyoming, was the first to test this possibility scientifically. He reworded the question put to the subjects; instead of asking them, 'Did you dream?' he asked 'Did anything cross your mind before awakening?' Thus, the subject's reply was not limited to dreams. Indeed, Foulkes's studies and those of later researchers showed a far higher percentage of reports after awakening from sleep stages other than REM sleep, compared with the first laboratory studies, which had been confined to reports of actual visual dreams. When a comparison was made between reports of REM sleep and those of other sleep stages, it became clear that there was a vast difference in their character. Subjects who awakened from sleep other than REM sleep reported in most cases on their thoughts, fragments of thoughts, or fragments of ideas. These reports differed greatly from REM sleep reports, which are usually exemplified by the development of a plot and a plethora of details and feelings. For example, a student who spent a number of nights in the Technion Sleep Laboratory made the following report after awakening from sleep stage 2 at the beginning of the night: 'The thought of the math exam we had yesterday crossed my mind.' A completely identical subject appeared in the report made by another student who awoke from his third REM sleep: 'I dreamed that I was sitting in the Ullman Building studying math. I knew the lecturer but I was unable to identify any of the other people around me. My pocket calculator was on the desk and for some reason I tried to spread mayonnaise and ketchup on it just as you woke me.'

The preponderance of reports after waking up from stages of sleep other than REM was explained by some researchers as evidence that the stream of consciousness never ceases. The brain produces cognitive activity in all stages during sleep and wakefulness. The reason that reports after awakenings from REM sleep are richer in detail and plot than reports after waking up from stage 2, they claimed, is that retrieving the cognitive activities is dependent on cortical arousal. Higher levels of arousal, such as in REM sleep, are associated with more details being reported.

Another form of cognitive activity connected with transitional sleep, or sleep stage 1, is called 'hypnagogic hallucinations.' Duing the falling-asleep process, which is gradual and continues for several minutes, a great change occurs in the thought process. From the focused thought of wakefulness, thought becomes more and more associative and less focused until it becomes pictorial. The pictures may change rapidly, jumping from subject to subject and from one view to another. In many cases there is a clear continuity between the last sensory impressions experienced immediately before falling asleep and the contents of the hypnagogic hallucinations. As we shall see, these hallucinations can be altered by the use of external stimuli. (pp.69 – 71)

Remembering dreams – and forgetting them

There is a consensus which holds that the chance of a person awakening from REM sleep and remembering his or her dream is approximately 80 per cent. Nonetheless, not everyone has the same ability to remember dreams. There are those who are very good at it and remember their dreams every morning, while others are convinced that they did not dream at all because they are simply unable to remember even a single dream for months on end.

What causes these variations in the ability of people to remember dreams? As we have seen, remembering a dream is first and foremost conditional on the time of awakening from sleep. People who tend to wake up during REM sleep are more likely to remember their dreams than those who awaken from the other sleep stages. But the remembering of dreams also depends upon the depth of sleep. Those who sleep very deeply are less likely to remember their dreams than light sleepers, and in this context it is worthy of note that in our study of the dreams of sleep apnea sufferers, we found that they better remembered their dreams when they underwent repeated apneas than when they slept undisturbed as a result of successful treatment of their ailment. Their breathing disorder caused shallow sleep, and they were able to awaken from it more easily than after treatment, when their sleep became deeper and consequently their ability to remember their dreams diminished.

Memory is affected not only by the time we wake up in the morning and the depth of our sleep but also by our desire and readiness to remember dreams. People who underwent psychological treatment in the course of which they discussed their dreams suddenly discovered that they began to remember their dreams increasingly. Subjects who participated in studies in which dreams were collected reported that their very participation in the study increased their ability to remember. Therefore, the best advice I can give people who want to remember dreams is to get into bed after having a firm decision to do so! They should keep a notebook and pencil on their bedside table in order to record the story of their dream immediately after awakening, before the memory dissipates.

The ability to recall a dream is also related to its content. We tend to better remember dreams that are rich in content, unusual, strange, and which arouse both our interest and emotions. Those that are brief, trivial, and devoid of emotion tend to be swiftly forgotten. Just as we are able to encourage the remembering of dreams, we can also encourage the forgetting of them. By the use of autosuggestion, people who suffer from unpleasant dreams or nightmare can diminish the remembering of their dreams. In the cases of people who have undergone traumatic experiences, the 'erasing' of dreams can be so efficient that even awakening the sleeper from REM sleep does not improve recollection. (pp.80–81)

References

Lavie, P. (1996) *The Enchanted World of Sleep*. Translated by Anthony Berris. New Haven, CT: Yale University Press.

Acknowledgement

The editors would like to thank Dr Adi Gonen for his help in editing this chapter.

This extract is reproduced by kind permission of Yale University Press from Peretz Lavie's *The Enchanted World of Sleep* (1996), translated by Anthony Berris. New Haven, CT: Yale University Press.

CHAPTER 9

Fabiana's Dreams[*]

Claudio Neri

Dreams signal the essential moments in the search for identity. In the story of Fabiana, a patient in one of my therapeutic groups, three dreams had particular importance. These dreams (actually two dreams and a 'scenic representation') showed the state of the self and the progress in her healing process (Pines 1999). First of all, though, I want to present Fabiana.

Two changes

During a five-year period of participation in group therapy, Fabiana has managed to effect a number of changes. Two of these changes are particularly significant – change in her relationship with her family and her success in acquiring the ability to make decisions.

At the beginning of her analysis, Fabiana was 27 years old. She didn't get on well with her family at all. Her opposition extended to anything that could be connected with traditional values. For example, she refused, and radically opposed, the idea of a wedding or of having babies. Fabiana's opposition was nourished by fear. Fabiana was frightened of her family and particularly of her mother. The very thought of her mother coming, for a brief visit, from Sicily to Rome threw her into a state of confusion and fear. In

* This publication is an expansion upon a previous paper (Neri 2000) presented at the Australian Association of Group Psychotherapy (Sydney, 16 April 2000).

the presence of her mother, Fabiana would feel utterly inadequate, she would despise herself, and be unable to find any sense in what she was doing.

Now Fabiana visits on holiday the village where her family lives, and where she herself lived until she was 18, and draws a sense of protection and calm from it. Furthermore, she is content to be cooked for and taken care of by her mother.

Fabiana's opinion of her mother has changed. Fabiana says: 'Of course, my mother's way of thinking is very different from mine. But she has really done a lot considering the way in which she was brought up. Above all she has made a great effort to understand me, and continues to do so.' The second change is that she can now make decisions. Fabiana no longer lets situations influence her or accepts things as they are; on the contrary, she makes decisions. The acquisition of this ability has considerably increased her self-esteem. This achievement has also proved to be fundamental in setting up a new relationship with her family. Fabiana no longer considers meeting her mother or other relatives as being the cause of a sense of loss or nullification. She no longer finds it necessary to defend herself by resorting to strong opposition, isolation and flight. She now knows that she has the ability to choose and to carry on with her own life project.

Right to exist

The ability to develop a different relationship with her family also came from the experience of being part of this group. Taking part in a small therapeutic group is a global experience for its members. One participant explained this well in the following words: 'The group is a world for me as it is for the other members.' Thanks to this aspect, the small group stimulates an intense experience of belonging. This, in turn, is very important for the participants' sense of self, of being a person with a right to live and to occupy an affective space. Many patients have not experienced an adequate acknowledgement of this right in their family environment. Taking part in a therapeutic group gives them a second chance.

Liveliness: developing a soul

Over the years, some aspects of Fabiana's personality which had always been present but hidden and unexpressed, emerged. They have, in fact, come to life and acquired new depth and intensity. For example, Fabiana now pays attention to those around her. She has become enterprising. The loyalty to the clan she belongs to has changed into a loyalty which is associated with independent thought. The sense of belonging is now something different from submission or total consensus.

The process of 'liveliness' has been helped by the existence of different ways of thinking within the group compared to those of Fabiana's place of birth and also those of the social reject and rebellious youth movement she had joined when she moved to Rome.

People who emigrate to far-off countries face difficult conditions and find it hard to cope with customs, rules and ideas which are different from those they knew. They have to cope with powerful regressive forces. They may well become ill, become dissipated and feel lost. However, in certain conditions the emigration experience can be a real success. First of all, the person who changes country must be in fairly good health. Second, he should find a non-hostile and somewhat stimulating environment. Third, there should be some affinity between the person and the country where he is going to settle down. Given these three conditions, the person can often discover new and unexpected resources in himself. The new country – a new and unknown 'outside', when it is not empty or structureless – offers open space in which to collocate thoughts, desires and therefore aspects of one's self – that previously had no place in which to exist or were compressed and asphyxiated.

Something similar happened to Fabiana on entering the group. The small group is a place where different worlds meet – the worlds of the different members of the group. These worlds are all on the same level. Encountering different worlds has helped Fabiana to understand that different worlds exist within her, too. Hitherto undisclosed channels for communicating and undiscovered fields of action, have been revealed to her (Pines 2000).

The second element which has stimulated this liveliness in Fabiana, and caused the emergence of hidden aspects of her personality, is getting in contact with the experiences of other members of the group. People who take part in a small group – and among these, Fabiana – learn to see, when one of them speaks or relates, whether what is said has the characteristics of an experience or those of a dream or illusion. Furthermore, they are able to clear away repetitive and confusing flights of fantasy and to focus their interest on present and relevant elements. For example, the members of a group can say to one of the participants: 'Now stop talking about your parents! Tell us about what you are doing!'

Furthermore, the members of a group benefit from contact with life experiences. It's as if there was a pool of experiences from which one can draw out what he needs. A real life experience makes it possible to discover in the self and in the world around something that is enduring and that can be studied and cultivated. This gives a sense of being in a safer position.

The dream about the mouse-baby[1]

A well-known saying goes: 'If you want to find a friend, be yourself' – the question is what is your 'self'?

There have been three crucial moments in Fabiana's search for identity.

A dream she had during her third year of group analysis shows how Fabiana found the courage to take a look at herself.

> I was at work. Everyone knew that in a certain room there was a horrible monster. The monster was horrible – they said – because it fed on itself. I wanted to see it, at all costs. The door had been left ajar so I could see it. I thought the monster would be big, or even enormous, but surprisingly it was small. It was a child. It might have been three years old. The body was that of a child, but the head was that of a mouse. It was biting its arm. I had two conflicting feelings towards it – disgust and tenderness. I would have liked to take it home with me. Two colleagues, and friends of mine, were there with me. One said that I was very brave. The other said that I would not be able to cope with the task. I was doubtful: I was not afraid of the monster, but I didn't know how to feed it and bring it up.
>
> Immediately after the dream, I thought, that if someone has nothing to feed on, he feeds on himself.

The child in the dream is three years old. Fabiana's analysis had lasted the same length of time.

The head is that of a mouse. The mouse is biting its arm. When Fabiana started her therapy, she was on drugs almost every day, injecting herself with heroin. During the first years of group therapy she continued using drugs, though not as frequently as before. With the decrease in use of heroin, bulimia appeared. Fabiana often filled herself up with food and then vomited repeatedly. The mouse might quite possibly represent this hungry and violent aspect of Fabiana's personality.

I would like to underline another aspect of the dream. Before opening the door, Fabiana thought that the monster would be 'big, or even enormous'. When she finds the courage to look at it she realises it is small. I believe this difference in dimensions is because Fabiana looks at it from where she works, that is from inside the group. When she is alone, the monster-child is enormous, while, when she's together with her analyst and the other members of the group, it is small. It even elicits a sense of tenderness. Fabiana says she 'would have liked to take it home' with her. For the first time, Fabiana thinks of keeping 'her-self,' instead of getting rid of it.

Tamagotchi[2]

A second representation is offered by an object which she brings to a session a year later.

> The Tamagotchi is a red pendant of three centimetres, in the shape of a heart. Fabiana explains that on one of the two sides of the pendant there is a small rectangular panel – a monitor [or screen]. She points out that her Tamagotchi is not a puppy or kitten, but a baby dinosaur.
>
> The Tamagotchi-dinosaur weighs 70 kilos. It has to be nourished, cuddled, cleaned, put to bed. Whenever it needs something, it gives a warning signal by sending out a soft sound. If you don't take care of it, in an adequate and continuous way, the dinosaur dies.
>
> Till now, it hasn't been much of a hassle for her. Although, sometimes, it seems nothing satisfies the Tamagotchi, there is not much that needs doing, only what Fabiana described before. It is sufficient to try one thing after the other – feed, cuddle, clean it when it dirties itself, put it to bed – and see which one of these works.
>
> The Tamagotchi can be turned off. When Fabiana is at work, for example, she turns it off. Even now, before coming to the session, she has turned the switch off. While saying this, Fabiana takes the Tamagotchi off her belt and shows it to the other participants, but doesn't give it to them. Then, she turns the Tamagotchi on. The virtual dinosaur puppy gives a chirp. Fabiana rapidly presses some tiny buttons on the side of the monitor [screen]. She turns the Tamagotchi off and hangs it back on her belt.

In the dream about the monster, the hungry and violent aspects of Fabiana's personality were represented by the mouse, while now there is a dinosaur. Dinosaurs are very primitive animals, also often loved by children.

Fabiana's brief demonstration during the meeting shows a 'caring' side and a 'cared for' side. The 'caring' side is represented by Fabiana and the 'cared for' side by the Tamagotchi-dinosaur. This situation is quite similar to that of a little girl playing 'mummy' with a doll and identifying with the doll to whom she is being the mummy.

Through the Tamagotchi game, Fabiana shows her most urgent needs. The Tamagotchi cannot wait – if the answer to its needs is not immediate, it turns off and dies.

Birth[3]

The third crucial contribution to the emergence of her self is a dream related by Fabiana during her fifth year of analysis. It is a dream about birth and also a dream about separation, and it prepares for the moment in which Fabiana will finish her analysis.

> I was in the hospital where I work. Four of my female colleagues and just one man were there. Just as in the group, where there are four women and Roberto. I was about to give birth. My colleagues were standing round me, then they took me to a special room.
>
> Dr Neri was in that room, too. I asked him: 'Why are you here?' Dr Neri answered: 'I'm here to help with the birth.'
>
> I gave birth. The scene changed. I had had a baby girl. She was quite big: she must have been six years old. I was quite happy. Although I was present, I was dead. This made me sad, mainly because I would not be able to enjoy my baby.
>
> I thought: 'Who will take care of her?' I gave myself an answer: 'My colleagues will.' I was quite calm then. I looked for Dr Neri, but couldn't find him.

Fabiana gives birth to a baby. The presence of the analyst at the delivery confirms Fabiana's generative ability and indicates that he is the father figure for the baby girl.

Shortly after, though, the scene changes. The baby's mother dies. More precisely, although she is still present, the mother is dead. Fabiana's mother – according to what I was told by Fabiana, during our meetings before starting group analysis – suffered serious postnatal depression and was taken into care for six months. Her mother was hospitalised a second time some years later when Fabiana was still a child.

On waking, Fabiana – who identified herself with her depressed mother – is mistaken, and can no longer find the analyst. She gives the baby to her female colleagues.

A series of events in the following months allows us to reach a better understanding of who this 'dead mother', this 'mother who feels dead', really is. Above all, these events allow a more adequate understanding of what Fabiana thinks she could do about this aspect of her mother, which is present in her, too.

The 'birth' dream inaugurates a new phase of her analysis. During the months that follow the dream, Fabiana recuperates aspects of her 'drug addict' identity. During the group meetings, she talks a lot about heroin and what it was that led her to drugs. Furthermore, she tells us about male and female friends who used drugs.

Fabiana reclaims this aspect of her identity socially, too. Although she does not use drugs any more, she starts following a drug addict meeting service. She informs her colleagues at the hospital. She speaks about drugs with friends from home.

I remember that during our first meeting, before entering the group, Fabiana told me that she sometimes used heroin, adding that she used it to cure her depression. I said that heroin did not seem to me to be the correct medicine for depression, and maybe group therapy would be more useful.

Group work

In the first of the three images of herself that Fabiana brings to the attention of the group (the dream of the 'mouse-baby'), the group appears as a 'place of work'. In this dream, the group is also represented by the presence of two 'friends and colleagues'. They express different opinions on the possibility of Fabiana taking the mouse-baby home with her.

During the second representation, the other members of the group witness Fabiana's caring attitude towards the Tamagotchi.

In the last dream, the women in the group take care of the baby when the mother dies. The women in the group, that is, substitute for the depressed or absent mother and also substitute for the analyst, whom Fabiana cannot find.

However these images do not suffice to indicate how the group has worked through the contributions that Fabiana brought in (Friedman 1999). This work may be better explained through a brief clinical episode. I have chosen the episode in which group members speak of one of the Tamagotchi's attributes – the fact that it is a Tamagotchi-dinosaur.

Marcello: Dinosaurs are primitive animals that lived in a world that no longer exists.

Loredana: There are carnivorous and non-carnivorous dinosaurs.

Antonia: In certain conditions, all dinosaurs are carnivorous.

Analyst: I have read somewhere something similar about chimpanzees.

Antonia: What Dr Neri has said has made me think that he wants to show us evolution: from a world of dinosaurs to a world of chimpanzees.

Gabriella: The doorkeeper of my block, who comes from Sri Lanka, is very jealous. When he drinks, he goes crazy. Yesterday he beat up his girlfriend.

Loredana: Still, the girl might like the fact that he is jealous and beats her up.

Analyst: We, too, are authorised to make contact with violent passions. And even madness. We are an analysis group.

Fabiana: During one night in the past year, I went into a building which the Dutch government provides for homeless people, at a very cheap rent. In the middle of a large room, there was a man, sitting at a table, who was writing in a notebook. I spent the evening with some friends and then I went back to that room to sleep on a sofa. The man was still writing. The day after, when I woke up, he was still writing. I looked at the notebook and he was writing down all that happened in the room: 'A girl comes into the room, she goes out.' A Dutch friend of mine told me that he was out of his mind. He coped with his madness by writing. Every one of us has his own way of coping with his madness.

Analyst: It certainly is a case of madness, as Fabiana says, but I think that this homeless man is above all very lonely. What kind of aloneness does he suffer from? We may be lonely because someone we love or someone who we are used to having around us, is absent. However, there is a different kind of aloneness – cosmic aloneness. The aloneness of those who are alone because the world has disappeared.

Marcello and Loredana's comments on carnivorous animals recall a central theme of Fabiana's: 'What to eat? What to feed on?' Two years before, commenting on the dream of the mouse-baby who bites his arm, Fabiana said, 'I thought, that if someone has nothing to feed on, he feeds on himself.' Marcello and Loredana, when they talk about 'carnivorous dinosaurs', indicate that eating means facing up to the fantasy of attacking and eating other animals.

The analyst speaks about the passage from dinosaurs (very ancient animals) to chimpanzees (anthropoid apes). Antonia points out that this implies evolution. Gabriela continues with the same theme, but at a certain point she removes herself in a way from the equation. She attributes passions to people from Sri Lanka. Loredana puts herself at this level where relationship and strong feelings exist. She speaks about jealousy, passion, pleasure, identifying herself with the girlfriend of the doorkeeper. Gabriella notes that the violence of passions can make one lose control. Passion can lead to madness.

The analyst allows passion and being mad during sessions. Fabiana can then speak about a special kind of madness, which coincides with extreme loneliness. Maybe her mother and the analyst also feel alone in this way.

A characteristic of the therapeutic group

The group permits the expression and sharing of states of mind and extreme feelings – being hungry, feeling mad with jealousy, feeling boundlessly lonely. These states of mind can be expressed because the group is not only hunger, madness and solitude, but these elements included in the overall group feelings and structure. If it were only hunger, madness and solitude, it could not even be talked about.

The world of the group has not disappeared like that of the dinosaurs. The presence of the analyst and of the other members of the group gives hope that the feelings and states of mind expressed will be gathered up, will find meaning and be transformed. The ability to gather up, name, give a sense to and transform states of mind and feelings is an essential characteristic of the psychoanalytic group (Neri 1995).

Mental setting of the analyst

What gives this characteristic to the small psychotherapeutic group? I will take into consideration just one aspect of the question, the one that highlights the analyst's contribution.

The presence and mental setting of the analyst do not determine how the group works, however they define its peculiarities (Neri 1998a). The characteristics of the analyst's mental setting while working are:

- patience
- to be gratuitous (a non-utilitarian approach)
- non-sense
- reciprocity
- investment.

Patience

The first characteristic of an analyst's mental setting while working is patience. Ability to be patient does not come solely from technique. It is more a result of the development of certain aspects of the analyst's personality. This is what makes his own personal analysis essential.

Winnicott (1965) talks of 'keeping alive', underlining the importance of the analyst's ability to tolerate his patients' attacks, thereby keeping himself and his ability to be interested in their needs and requests alive. (See also Neri 1989)

Bion (1963) speaks in terms of an 'oscillation between patience and certainty'. Patience provides for preparation and is alternated with moments in which the analyst reaches the certainty of an idea, which he can then communicate to the group.

Corrao (1998, 1998a) takes issue with Bion's desire for certainty; he emphasises tolerance towards the uncertainty of results in analytic work. An ambition to 'construct' is more of an obstacle than of real help in analytic work. According to Corrao, uncertainty is not a coincidental element, on the contrary it is an integral part of analytical practice and method. The basic epistemological theory of psychoanalysis is founded on the principles of uncertainty, incompleteness and reversibility.

To be gratuitous (a non-utilitarian approach)

The second characteristic of the analyst's mental setting is being gratuitous. An effective analyst is one who is able to allow himself the pleasure of imagining and thinking, without having to cope with calculating how 'useful' and 'congruent' those thoughts may be. Marion Milner (1956) writes:

When we discover how to stop looking at the world with the limited and focalized attention of utilitarianism, and stop interfering and trying to use it for our own purposes, then...something very similar to a miracle can happen.

[When we abandon this utilitarian outlook we start to feel more in contact with the world.]

This is a state [of intimate relationship, which is a condition] which we have surely all experienced in certain moments of our childhood, but have often lost when the utilitarianism of adulthood takes over. (pp.178–9)

Non-sense

At first sight, this may appear to contradict what I said previously, when I said that the ability to give some sense is a characteristic of a psychoanalytic group. However, if there are no moments of 'non-sense', one will not be able to give more authentic sense to states of mind and feelings.

Non-sense is a condition free of propositions and with a 'just turning over' functioning of the mind. Images, emotions, thoughts and feelings emerge without any connection between themselves. An analyst should accept them without forming any hypothesis about the existence of a theme. Looking for a hidden theme, as the technique of free association suggests, would imply creating an organisation. On the contrary, the analyst and the group members need to experiment and live through the condition of lack of sense, becoming able to cope with the unknown.

Reciprocity

An analyst should put himself in the place of the group members and allow them to see the situation from his point of view. He should try to learn the language spoken by his patients and be happy if they learn his language.

Investment

The last aspect of the analyst's mental setting, which I wish to mention lies in his ability to invest his affect on people taking part in the analysis with him, on himself and on his work. Routine can cause the analyst to suffer from a sort of affect haemorrhage as psychoanalyst and psychotherapist. A supervisor's or a colleague's intervention, communicating esteem and showing him personal affection, will allow the analyst suffering from a process of impoverishment, to find new faith in himself and to recuperate his ability to understand and give treatment. This is why it is necessary to choose the professional group one belongs to, with great care, and from time to time, choose a new one. Making this choice does not necessarily mean that the first choice was a mistake. It does not even mean that the original group should be abandoned or erased. It really means adding something new, facing up to an experience of scientific and professional emigration and immigration.

References

Bion, W.R. (1963) *Elements of Psychoanalysis.* London: Karnac Books.

Corrao, F. (1998) *Orme I.* Milan: Cortina editore.

Corrao, F. (1998a) *Orme II.* Milan: Cortina editore.

Friedman, R. (1999) 'Dreamtelling as a request for containment and elaboration in group therapy.' *Funzione Gamma 1.*

Milner, M. (1956) 'The sense in nonsense (Freud and Blake's Job).' In M. Milner (1987) *The Suppressed Madness of Sane Men. Forty-four Years of Exploring Psychoanalysis.* London: Routledge.

Neri, C. (1987) 'Keeping Alive.' *Rivista di Psicoanalisi XXXV,* 4, 823–41.

Neri, C. (1997) 'Les passages de l'individu au groupe, du groupe à l'individu (le rêve du monstre).' *Revue de psychothérapie psychanalytique de groupe 28.*

Neri, C. (1998) *Group.* London: Jessica Kingsley Publishers.

Neri, C. (1998 [2000]) 'Tamagogi.' *Les cahiers du C.R.P.P.C. 1* (Hors Série), 54, 63.

Neri, C. (1998a) 'Eustokhìa e Sincronicità.' In G. Rugi and E. Gaburri (ed) *Il campo gruppale. L'istituzione, la mente del terapeuta e gli scenari del gruppo.* Rome: Borla.

Neri, C. (2000) 'Fabiana's change. How group psychotherapy works.' *Bulletin of the Australian Association of Group Psychotherapists 18,* 42–50.

Neri, C. (2001) 'Rire aux éclats. La sexualité dans le groupe.' In P. Privat and D. Quelin (ed) *La sexualité dans le groupe d'enfants.* Paris: Dunod.

Pines, M. (1999) 'Dreams: are they personal or social?' *Funzione Gamma 1.*

Pines, M. (2000) 'Bion, Foulkes, and empathy'. *Funzione Gamma 3.*

Winnicott, D.W. (1965) *Maturational Process and the Facilitating Environment.* New York: International Universities Press.

Endnotes

1.   This illustration has already been published in Neri 1997.

2.   This illustration has already been published in Neri 1998.

3.   This illustration has already been published in Neri 2001.

CHAPTER 10

The Dream in a Tavistock Group

Marion Solomon

The content of dreams has been looked at from diverse points of view. Psychoanalysis first regarded the manifest content of dreams as mere surface content: the goal was to free associate various parts of the dream to uncover unconscious material. The further development of psychoanalytic theory led to a shift in focus from patients' unconscious disclosures to the task of uncovering resistances and understanding transference in the analytic setting. This, in turn, lent greater significance to the manifest content of dreams.

> The manifest content, in spite of its characters of disguise and distortion of the latent dream thoughts, has gained significance in its own right, especially as a mirror of the transference situation. (Foulkes 1964, p.126)

Still, in individual work, the analysis of latent material is primary. The dream is a message sent by the individual's unconscious; it is a private matter shared with the therapist only after the establishment of a particular kind of relationship. Study of the latent content of an individual's dreams requires a complete focus on that individual. However, when the therapist is 'induced' to employ psychoanalytic forms of dream interpretation in a group setting, the group commonly indulges in rampant dream expression. Members offer a continuous stream of dreams for the therapist's analytic attention. Given the therapist's permission to analyze each other's dream material, the response is usually resistance. The analysis of dreams in group therapy requires an entirely different way of utilizing the material.

This chapter describes an intensive short-term analytic group experience based upon a Tavistock small group model. Specifically considered are some special features of group approaches to unconscious processes in the Tavistock short-term analytic group model, and the chapter further describes how dream material is treated within that model. An example is given of how dream material is understood in the Tavistock model in terms of manifest and latent dream content and in comparison with the content of dreams and the process of presentation. What emerges is an understanding of some of the universal unconscious dynamics that emerge in small groups.

Procedures

The typical small Tavistock study group consists of 12 members who meet for a specified time with the stated task of studying the group's overt and covert relational processes as they occur. Prior to participation, prospective members are asked to study carefully an application form that states clearly that the group is intended for mature adults capable of absorbing considerable stress. We have found that this short, straightforward application procedure minimizes misunderstandings and provides a set of integrated, unifying principles known to both members and staff.

Consultants

The staff in Tavistock groups are identified as consultants. At the outset of a group experience, a statement is made by the consultants about their purpose and position. Consultants are trained to strictly observe the limits of their defined function. During the group experience, the consultants must avoid actions or statements that do not facilitate learning or aid the group in its primary task. In observing this strict definition, consultants avoid eye contact with members, do not indulge in nurturing responses to individual members, rarely answer questions, and arrive and depart from meetings punctually, without unnecessary comments or social conversation. The task of the consultants is to facilitate the group's ongoing process only by objectively describing that process as it occurs.

The group's task

Each Tavistock group experience is focused on a specific primary task. For the small groups whose experiences form the basis of this paper, the primary task was 'to provide members with the opportunity to learn about the self in a group'. In working toward this goal, it is expected that group processes will also demonstrate something about the nature of personal and organisational authority, the distinction between authority and leadership, and the conscious and unconscious processes that govern the occurrence of these two phenomena in groups. Thus, members are expected to work toward the stated goal, to question the experience, and to understand and study the group's processes in the 'here and now' in pursuit of the goal. While some groups place understanding of individual dynamics in the foreground, with the group as background, this has not been the purpose of small Tavistock study groups.

Group process

Members of the group described in this book meet with two consultants for a series of one-and-a-half-hour experiential sessions, with breaks of one half-hour. The sessions occur consecutively, all day, over a weekend or several weekdays. Since the task of the group is to examine its own behaviour in the 'here and now', specifically as it relates to the primary task, the consultants attempt to explain group processes, especially unconscious ones, in simple everyday language. Individual members are perceived and commented upon by consultants only in terms of their role in the group; counter-transference reactions and interpretations relate to the entire group, not to individual members. Thus, in contrast to small therapy groups that emphasise individual dynamics, these groups study the overt and covert processes of the group as a whole. The final session is a one-and-a-half-hour discussion with participation of members and consultants.

Observations

Descent

At the beginning of the first session, members typically try various ways of coping with what is perceived as an anxiety-provoking situation. Introductions are made, often with discussions of personal background, followed by periods of silence and groping for structure and rules for procedure. A member will sometimes suggest an activity such as changing the room arrangement, moving the chairs closer together, or trying approaches used in other groups. There is then invariably a turning to the consultants for leadership, locating in one or both all authority to perform the work of the group. When this does not succeed, there ensues confusion, joint action to convince consultants to assume leadership, regression to dependence, rage, and a loss of feelings of competence possessed upon entering the group.

The frequency of mutual attacks, rejections, distortions, and accusations that then commonly occur is remarkable, as is the intensity of aggression. It usually emerges that it is precisely those individuals who try to resist the mounting atmosphere of paranoia and mutual recrimination, and who attempt to maintain some semblance of autonomy, who are attacked most aggressively. It is as if there were a general envy of people who maintain their sanity and individuality in stressful situations.

The extent to which sane, normally well-functioning people regress to infantile emotional states and behavioural responses often surprises members. We have observed, in a particularly regressed group, members fantasising with great glee how they would like to crack and empty the skull of one of the consultants, proceeding then to describe in detail how they would stomp on the brain until it was in bits and pieces. We have also watched members search for a scapegoat and then relax when one of the members offered himself as the 'resident crazy'. Often what is most frightening in such groups is the growing emergence in awareness of components of sadism and murderous hatred.

Rioch (1970) describes a typical Tavistock group experience:

> They tended to think that the increased uneasiness which they felt was intended by the consultant as a part of a manipulative plan. This is the beginning of the paranoia which is a frequent phenomenon in the conferences. The assumption is that if something happens, someone must have planned it – if not for a good reason, then for a bad one. Since people are reluctant to blame their discomfort on God, the 'management' must be responsible. The extent to which sane, 'normal' people engage in paranoid thinking of this kind is astonishing to themselves when they become aware of it. (pp.340–55)

When efforts to entice the consultants into a leadership role fail, the group members may select another member on whom they feel they can depend; or they might join together to sabotage and destroy the task of the group, fight with the consultants, flee in fantasy, or actually leave the group. At times they try to encourage pairing of two members in a symbolic sexual union to provide a messianic solution for the future, or all differences are negated and the group relaxes in a closed idealised unit providing thoughtless, problem-free bliss.

Deliverance

The behaviours described above occur repeatedly at the beginning of Tavistock group experiences. They are usually interspersed with attempts to perform real work – that is, experiencing and understanding group processes as they occur. Gradually, the group's resources of organisation and structure rise to the surface. This can be seen as a stage at which, with or without consultative help, regressive pulls have, at least temporarily, been overcome, and the cohesive selves of the participants have returned to adequate functioning. One by one, leaders, including the consultants, have been established, idealised, and found wanting. The group has been idealised and fantasised as both perfectly benevolent and totally malevolent. Ultimately, it is recognized that the group is simply a congregate of individuals with a common task. What has been idealized, feared, and depended upon is finally broken down.

Projections may be repossessed. One or two members may pull themselves out of the whirlpool of regression and respond to the group with re-emerging competence. Other members then follow. This re-establishment of the competence of members, in combination with their processing of the group's experience, leads to a renewed sense of learning and achievement.

The anatomy of change

In individual analysis and analytic psychotherapy the patient experiences periods of induced regression, disorganisation, and reorganisation. It is intended that the transference neurosis set this regression in motion, initiate the re-experiencing of relative arrest, induce examination of the repetition compulsion, and ultimately promote healthier adjustment. Foulkes (1964) describes transference as 'a compulsive repetition of the most relevant and unresolved conflict situations...still active...in the current life of the individual'(p.177).

The focus of attention in the Tavistock group is not on historical material in itself, the etiology of current problems, or the current life situation, but rather on the compulsion to 'replay' unresolved psychological issues in current life situations, particularly in the 'here and now' group situation. Hence, dependency, aggression, jealousy, power and sexuality are oft-repeated themes in Tavistock groups.

The psychological needs and maladjustments underlying the material presented in group sessions may seem related to 'real' events, but they actually arise from 'unconscious structures which are based on a combination of actual events, distorted memories of actual events, and the conscious and unconscious fantasies clustering about them' (Heath and Bacal 1968, p.23).

Linking of these 'compulsive replays' of unresolved issues with outside (i.e. life) reference points may occur, but this is not directed by the consultant. Rather, we have found that this is more effectively accomplished by the individual himself, or by the individual in concert with the group. When this linkage occurs, the group member may become conscious for the first time of some aspect of his own behaviour and may choose to take on a new role. The 'enlightened' group member then typically 'uses' the group to experience himself repeatedly in the new role, and to 'test' novel ways of interaction by receiving insights into how others experience his new role. When this happens, it is usually an event of great consequence for the individual.

Dreams: To interpret or not to interpret

It usually occurs that on the morning of the second or third day of a Tavistock group one or several members recount recent dreams. The themes of such dreams are often picked up (unconsciously) by other group members, and these themes then become the topics of group attention. Heath and Bacal (1968) call this unconsciously adopted dream material 'the common group tension' (p.23). We might also understand it as the common denominator of the dominant unconscious fantasies of all the group members. This characterisation will become more clear as I discuss the process of understanding and interpreting dream material in Tavistock groups.

When dreams are first mentioned in a Tavistock group, the consultant listens closely for the group message. Why is the group sending this message at this time? If the dream is not truly a group message, other members will not pick up on it. It is thus important that the consultant not respond immediately, regardless of how relevant the dream may appear. The group must be given the opportunity to either acknowledge or deny the importance of this dream message to its 'here and now' experience.

Example 1: The red flag of avoidance

The following example may further clarify my point. On the morning of the final day of a weekend group, a group member described a dream in which she was aware of walking in a strange neighbourhood. The farther she walked, the more she felt herself to be in danger. A large dark man was following her, and she felt that if he caught up with her he might rape and kill her. She went on to relate the dream's content to a fear of her father and a fear of men. When she finished, there was silence. Finally, another woman commented on a dream she had experienced the previous night. A young man, the youngest member of the group, then described a recurrent dream which he had experienced again the previous night. In this dream he finds himself in a dangerous situation, from which he savagely fights his way to safety, leaving behind torn bodies and limbs. Another member followed by saying she found all these dreams depressing, and that she would rather be out walking on the beach on such a beautiful Sunday morning. She added that she was determined to put all of the group's depressing activity out of her mind. At this point, I commented that the group had succeeded in 'getting rid of' Margaret (the first group member to describe her dream) so that they would not have to confront the issues of fear and murderousness and the danger she felt in this group. Not one person spoke to her or even looked at her since she related her dream. This interpretation seemed to enhance the group's conscious awareness, and led to an exploration of the competitiveness, aggressiveness, and enraged feelings lurking beneath the surface of the group's activity.

This example illustrates how, when a member's comments are ignored and avoided, the Tavistock group consultant should ask himself what reason the group has to 'destroy' this member or the material he or she has presented. When a member's comments *are* taken up by the group, the consultant must at first be equally questioning. Why has this material been presented and taken up by the group, and is it truly a part of the group's constructive work? Or does the group's focus on this new material represent a regression to a 'basic assumption', anti-work mode.

Example 2: The nurturing trap

In a dream described by a very successful elderly psychotherapist in a three-day Tavistock group, this woman remembered discovering a nest of tiny bluebirds unable yet to fly. The mother bird was not there, so she took the nest inside her home and fed the birds with an eye-dropper. Although her family was there, they did nothing to help. The group responded to the description of this dream with admiration for the woman's nurturing qualities. A warm glow of togetherness seemed to engulf the group. The consultant then interjected the interpretation that the group was seeking someone to take care of them and to replace the unfeeling and unnurturing consultant – a ploy to avoid their difficult work in the group.

Example 3: The conundrum of gender

In another Tavistock group, a man described a dream in which a benevolent parent cared for an injured son. This immediately provoked comments from the group about the male consultant. 'Lars seems softer today.' 'Yes, almost gentle.' 'Even his clothes seem more casual'. 'He is like the father in the dream.' The interpretation was offered that the male group members were feeling injured by conflict that had occurred between them and the females during the previous evening's session, and that they were now looking to Lars (the male consultant) as a benevolent maternal/paternal figure. They wanted to depend on him for nurturance and security.

This interpretation evoked general agreement and a further examination of childlike feelings among the group – the urge to seek some safe person to depend on. At that point I was seen as quite dangerous, particularly by the men, with the women members sometimes attempting to align themselves with me. Dreams of danger and injured children were repeatedly brought up by men in the group. Several dreams were mentioned in which Lars was perceived as a mothering figure and I as a quite stern masculine figure. I commented on the group's wish to give breasts to Lars, and their wish to give me a penis. Lars then commented that the women of the group seemed to be using the female consultant to castrate the men through her interpretation of the dreams. Regardless of the 'correctness' of these specific interpretations, the juxtaposition and entanglement of male and female roles was clearly a prominent aspect of the group's dream material.

Later in the same group, a man introduced what quickly became a group theme. He described a dream in which he was caring for a young child, and that this felt very good. But consciously he was puzzled because he had no children. A woman member commented that she had three nearly grown children, and that she did not like the thought of caring for young children again. Another woman in the group agreed, and there seemed to be a consensus abdication of the maternal role among the women of the group. I commented that the male member's dream indicated the group's wish that men could be nurturers and mothers. There then followed a number of emotional comments by several members of the group. The man whose dream had introduced this theme stated that he indeed wished he could bear a child, but since he could not he had hoped to be a parent through his wife. However, she had been unable to conceive, and this had been a great disappointment to him. Another male member commented that he loves children and wants more, but his wife does not want any more. He said he felt very deprived of someone young to nurture. The women of the group then reiterated their feelings of freedom and/or their lack of interest in having children.

At this point, a male group member who had been rather rigid until then said with considerable feeling that this discussion was really getting to him. He expressed his awareness of a great battle within himself: if he felt something in his groin about a woman, that was considered acceptable; but the same feeling about a man indicated there must be something wrong with him. He said he felt great confusion about this paradox, and as he spoke he fought to hide the tears welling up in his eyes. This disclosure was followed by a sharing of group feelings about Lars and I – our maleness and femaleness – and then by members sharing their feelings about the male and female aspects of themselves. After seven one-and-a-half-hour sessions within this group, this was a rather intense discussion with much personal disclosure. Lars commented that a box of paper tissues had become a symbol for this group, at that point.

Conclusion

These rather detailed examples have not been given to suggest that a deep expression of emotion is a goal of Tavistock groups. In fact, as suggested earlier, displays of emotion can be a technique used by individuals or the group as a whole to avoid difficult work. Important and meaningful content is just as likely to be found in sedate comments about death, in group members deciding to rearrange their chairs at anxious moments, or in calmly expressed dreams about Vietnam or the Holocaust.

What is important to remember in dealing with dreams in Tavistock groups is that the consultant strictly limits comment to the group theme. This means that, since the manifest content of dreams often constitutes the group theme, the consultant in turn must restrict comment to the manifest content of dream material expressed in the sessions. We have found that this restriction on the consultants' contribution coincides well with groups' central preoccupations with group equilibrium and with resolving difficulties in role assignment. And it is this designed coincidence between the consultant's technique and the members' motivation that seem best to result in movement and change.

References

Ezriel, H. (1956, 1951) 'Experimentation within the psycho-analytic session.' *British Journal of Philosophical Science 7*, 29–48; *8*, 342–47.

Foulkes, S.H. (1964) *Therapeutic Group Analysis.* New York: International Universities Press.

Freud, S. (1932) *New Introductory Lectures on Psycho-Analysis and Other Works. Standard Edition 22.* London: Hogarth Press.

Heath, E.S. and Bacal, A.H. (1968) 'A method of group psychotherapy at the Tavistock Clinic.' *International Journal of Group Psychotherapy 18*, 21–30.

Rioch, M. (1970) 'The Work of Wilfred Bion on Groups.' *Psychiatry 33*, 340–355.

CHAPTER 11

Self Psychology, Dreams and Group Psychotherapy[*]

Working in the Playspace

Martin S. Livingston

Freud (1914, p.154) used the term 'Spielraum', or playspace, as a metaphor for the analytic atmosphere that allows the unfolding of a transferential process. Meares (1990) suggests that this metaphor underlies the therapeutic process. He points out that implicit in the application of this conceptual imagery is an assumption that runs through from Freud to Kohut who directed our therapeutic efforts, for example, toward the 'growth of a healthy self' (Kohut 1984, p.70). That assumption is that 'certain kinds of mother–child interaction were necessary to the development of the self' (Meares 1990, p.70).

Play, in the sense of developing a spirit of freedom, curiosity, and exploration, is necessary to the 'growth of a healthy self'. It is very similar to the serious play that Winnicott (1953) described as occurring in an 'intermediate area of experience'. The present paper will present a self-psychological approach to working with dreams in group psychotherapy. It is an approach to working with dreams in the playspace created by an emphasis on safety

---

[*] Reprinted from *GROUP 25*, 1, with permission from Kluwer Academic Press.

and on the leader's empathic attunement to each group member's unique subjectivity.

Self psychologists, not unlike their classical brethren, have developed their conceptual understanding of psychoanalytic process and technique within the context of a dyadic relationship. This is particularly true in regard to working with dreams. The working through of dream material, especially the classical approach to dreams as the royal road to the patient's unconscious, requires safety and an attention to detail. The group setting does not seem to lend itself to an uninterrupted unfolding of the dreamer's process and an in-depth exploration of his or her associations to each dream element. The other members each have their own reactions to the material. Often these reactions are as much involved in an archaic process as is the original dream.

A self-psychological approach to dreams can lend itself extremely well to the furtherance of curative process in a group setting. Moreover, the very reactiveness of the other group members that may be considered to be a disruption of the process of dream analysis that might unfold in a one-to-one setting can also be seen as potentially of major value in deepening the therapeutic experience for the entire group, including the dreamer. Following a brief outline of the contributions of self psychology to working with dreams in the individual setting, this paper will consider the application of these ideas in psychotherapy groups. A group session will be presented in order to illustrate the usefulness of these concepts and to demonstrate one style in which a group leader can facilitate a group's working with dreams in the playspace.

Self psychology and dreams

The search for 'truth' and hidden meaning, often considered to be the spirit of psychoanalysis and psychoanalytic dream interpretation, is exciting and fascinating. This paper is *not* about dream interpretation in that sense. What I want to present here is a brief summary of a self-psychological approach to the *clinical use* of dreams. The major point of this summary is that dreams, and the analyst's responsiveness to them, provide an excellent opportunity for the development of a playful and metaphorical communication between analyst and patient that can enhance the curative process. In a previous paper (Livingston 1998) I gave a more extensive presentation of these ideas and some case examples applying them in a one-to-one setting.

A self-psychological approach to dreams stresses empathic attunement in an attempt to remain close to the patient's subjective experience (that is, to remain experience-near). Fosshage (1987) for example, states that 'The primary dream interpretive task from the vantage point of this model is to remain with, as closely as possible, the phenomenology of the dream; to understand the meanings of the particular images and experiences as they are presented in the dream itself' (p.31). By approaching dream images as an expression of affective reactions or thematic experiences (Stolorow 1978), rather than as the product of disguise, the self psychologist is enabled to sustain a stance of empathic immersion in the patient's experience of the dream and its connections to his or her sense of self.

As mentioned in the introduction to this article, the metaphorical play that I will illustrate with clinical material shortly has several similarities to a form of early childhood communication which Winnicott (1953) considered as taking place within an 'intermediate area of experience'. He described how a mother repeatedly fosters a special shared time with her child. It is an area between play and reality, between me and not me. In the metaphorical play with dream imagery that I am suggesting, the analyst, like Winnicott's 'mother', fosters a special shared time with his or her patient. Also, in a manner suggestive of an intermediate area of experience, judgements about 'logic' and 'reality' are suspended and playfulness and exploration are enhanced. Thus, working with dreams in this fashion may be seen as one particular way in which the analyst can provide an empathically attuned responsiveness which stays close to the patient's subjective experience. This serves to amplify and validate the affective communication contained within the dream and can be viewed as a self-object experience contributing to the facilitation of curative process.

Kohut understood many dreams in the traditional manner as the disguised representation of latent drives, wishes and conflicts. However, he (1977, p.109) also found that free associations to some dreams did not lead to meaningful hidden layers. He saw these dreams and their associative elaboration as attempts, through the use of imagery, both to express and to bind the nonverbal tensions of certain traumatic states (of overstimulation or self fragmentation). He considered this type of dream a 'self-state dream' in which the healthy sectors of a patient's psyche were reacting with anxiety to a disturbing change in the condition of the self.

Kohut considered the self-state dream as portraying, specifically, a fragmenting self. However, more recent writers include other dreams about the self and its experiences with self-objects. Greenberg (1987), for example, postulates 'that all dreams are self-state dreams, sometimes with evidence of failure (fragmentation), but other times with evidence of integration so that one can see the construction of new coping mechanisms, which is actually what structures are' (p.102). Ornstein (1987) takes a similar view. He sees all dreams as, in a broad sense, self-state dreams in that 'the dream is always about the self; that is, the dream always presents various aspects of self-experience to the dreamer's attention' (p.101).

We can now underline two essential aspects of a self-psychological approach to dreams, both stemming directly from Kohut's concept of the self-state dream. The first is that, as Fosshage (1987) points out, the need for an expert decoder no longer exists. He sees the therapist's role as an 'amplifier of images', which fits very nicely with the use of dreams to facilitate a curative process. In contrast to seeing dreams as preserving sleep through the disguising of forbidden or anxiety-arousing wishes, Fosshage (1983, 1988 and 1989) sees dreams as serving a synthetic or organising function 'in the development, regulation and restoration of psychic structure'. Because dreams are seen as serving this organising function, there is no 'theoretical necessity to posit the ubiquitous operation of disguise and transformation of latent into manifest content' (Fosshage 1983, p.652). The dream is the best possible expression of itself and not necessarily a disguise for something else. Thus, instead of being an authority on interpretation of hidden meanings, the analyst's interpretive activity now has the primary task of amplifying and elucidating the patterns of meanings manifested in the dream imagery.

The second essential aspect (which probably more than any other facet distinguishes a self-psychological approach) is also directly connected to Kohut's description of the self-state dream. Even when the thematic structure of a dream contains defensive elements and conflict, a self psychologist's guiding theoretical framework has a different focus than that of the classical analyst. Rather than observing the associative material in terms of interacting forces of id, ego and superego or infantile drives and prohibitions, the self psychologist's orienting principle (Tolpin 1983) is a focus upon the vicissitudes of the self. When conflict *is* involved, the essential conflicts are seen as being between self and self-objects. Dreams are still seen as a 'royal road'. However, self psychology has a different conception of what important experiences and ideas lie out of awareness than the classical analyst does. As Stolorow (1978) expresses it, dreams are seen as the 'royal road' to the individual's invariant organising principles and dominant leitmotivs which unconsciously pattern and thematise a person's subjective experiences of his or her self and self–self-object relationships.

Dreams are not seen as disguised material requiring interpretation to uncover the latent drives hidden beneath their content. However, the self psychologist's approach to dreams still is based on an interpretive process. The focus of this interpretive activity is on the working through of the self-object transferences and conflicts between self and self-objects.

The application of a self-psychological approach to dreams in group

A self-psychological approach to group psychotherapy with its stress on empathy and safety provides an ideal atmosphere to play creatively with dreams. Several writers have approached working with dreams from perspectives other than self psychology. Kieffer (1996), in her paper on the use of dream interpretation to resolve group developmental impasses, provides an extensive review of this literature. However, it is noteworthy that although there are many papers on a self-psychological approach to group psychotherapy and also many papers on dreams in group therapy, I could not find a single article focusing on working with dreams from a self-psychological perspective in group. The present paper will begin to address that void.

The analyst's experience-near responsiveness to each group member's subjective expressions sets a natural stage to facilitate the group's acceptance and exploration of dream material. Working with dreams in the manner suggested in this paper then carries over to the group's functioning in general and contributes to the deepening and illumination of affect and exploration of personal meaning.

As outlined above, self psychology views a dream as the best possible expression of a communication about the state of the self and its relationship to its self-objects. It does not see a dream as necessarily a disguise of hidden material that needs to be decoded and interpreted by an expert. This frees the group leader from the task of trying to obtain free associations and of uncovering and interpreting repressed content. It allows him to lead the group to work in the playspace created by a stress on safety and empathic attunement. Interestingly, one of the aspects of leadership calling for skill and sensitivity is setting a balance between what Bacal (1998) refers to as reactiveness and responsiveness. Patients in a group need to develop the capacity to be empathic and responsive towards each other. The leader sets an example of this attitude in his attempt to be sensitive to each patient's subjective experiences and especially to their vulnerability. He also often needs to interpret or explain a patient's needs and behaviour to the other group members. As these reactions become understandable to the group an empathic surround can be established. It is largely within this sense of a safe space that each patient's uniqueness and self-object needs can unfold. It is largely within the empathic bond established with the leader and among group members that an arrested development can be resumed.

At the same time though, in addition to twinship and attachment needs, patients also have a need to express and pursue their own individual self-delineation. Sometimes this runs counter to the group's need for respon-siveness and safety, as it did in their childhood families. In fact, it is when the original caretakers responded to the child's self-delineation unsupportively or even by withdrawing or becoming hostile that what Stolorow and his associates (Stolorow, Brandchaft and Atwood 1987) refer to as a 'funda-mental conflict' (p.52) is enduringly established. An organising principle is formed that assumes an inherent conflict between attachment needs and self-delineation. It is essential that the group leader be alert to this conflict and not encourage his group to always be responsive to each other at the expense of the expression of their own feelings and reactions. Reactiveness, as Bacal calls it, when a group member reacts from his or her own subjective position rather than from an empathic one, is equally important in a well functioning group. It must be encouraged and respected at the same time that another vulnerable patient may need support or protection. The balance between responsiveness and reactiveness is particularly crucial in regard to creating a playspace for processing dreams in group. The dreamer is in an open and vulnerable self-state and can easily be traumatised by wild interpre-tations or reactions. However, it is the other patients' 'reactiveness', their emotional and subjective responses, that is potentially most productive in deepening not only the dreamer's process, but the curative process in the entire group as well.

If a dream is met with an attitude of serious play and becomes the property of the whole group to work with, then exploration, curiosity and risk-taking are encouraged. Within this spirit of openness and shared vulner-ability, affect is amplified and personal meanings and organising principles are illuminated and explored.

Even within one school of analysis, there are many ways of working with dreams. As Bacal (1995) has expressed, 'Optimal responsiveness rests upon what might be called a theory of specificity, that the therapeutic process entails the operation of a complex, more or less unique, therapeutic system for each analyst-patient couple, in which the analyst's task is to discover and to provide what is therapeutic for that particular patient.' This means that there can be no one clear approach to dreams any more than to treatment as a whole. To some degree, even the same group of patients and the same leader must create their own style anew with each dream presented. With that limitation clearly in mind, I would like to present a clinical example of one style of working with dreams in the playspace.

On roaches and other hidden things: an illustration

The group in the session to be presented has been together for several years. There is a great deal of trust both with the therapist and between the members. It consists of three women and two men (one of whom was away that day) ranging in age from their early forties to mid-fifties. They work well together and tend to be both empathically responsive to each other and at times confronting. The session that I have chosen to present is an unusually useful one. It illustrates more than just the use of dreams in group. It also provides an example of the introduction of the idea of working with dreams to a group, as well as the early interventions of the leader in guiding the group's playing creatively with dream material.

A general atmosphere of openness and intimate sharing exists in this group, yet I was aware as I began to think about the present paper that dreams seemed to be saved for individual sessions. I decided that I would mention that in the group whenever I felt that it would fit in and not be too disruptive of the group's process. As it happened, the next session began with some social chatting and then settled down into a brief silence as is often character-istic of the group's style of centring and seeing what comes up. I chose to break the silence with my planned remark about the absence of dreams. Roz responded quickly. Laughing, she related that she didn't think that it would be all right to want that much focused attention. 'I didn't know that we could. I never bring dreams to group because I won't be able to stay with it long enough to get through to the feelings.' I told her that it is OK to want that kind of attention. The group laughed at the phrase 'OK to want'. Someone commented that she might well not get as much as she wanted, but then we can work with that like anything else. I added that one value in sharing a dream in the group and getting people's responses was that it might help us to deepen group members' understanding of each other.

Felicia, with some annoyance, asked, 'Why now? Why did you choose to bring this up at this point? I bet that I know.' I laughed because I sensed that she was right on target and annoyed at my need entering the situation. Tony interjected a question about whether or not it would be useful to talk about dreams and then added that it was nice to picture me thinking about the group between sessions and coming up with ideas to make things productive. Felicia persisted angrily, 'There is no way that I'll bring dreams to group. That's way too private and why did you bring it up anyway?' I decided to acknowledge my interest in writing about dreams at that point. She laughed. 'I knew it!' Her anger seemed to calm down as it was clear that I wasn't insisting on her sharing what she felt was too personal. Tony was disappointed. He felt that he was being given something and then it had been spoiled.

In the midst of working with these reactions to my intrusion in the process, Roz jumped in excitedly with a dream.

> There was a roach in the bathtub. It was getting bigger and bigger and then it escaped from the tub. Then there was a cat attacking it, but it still kept getting bigger and bigger. It was trying to get away. The cat got the shell and then the body of the bug began to stretch out away from the shell. It was getting away. I thought that it would die, but then I became afraid that the cat wouldn't be able to kill it. It was gross. The raw skin was gross and then it snapped free. It got away and got into my washing machine...into my clean clothes...into my whites. It was in my sweater sleeve. I tried to slam it dead...tried to smash it dead against the wall. Then the bug's head started to look like a kitten's head. There was spit flying, but it's not dying. I wanted to wake up to get out of there because the bug wouldn't die. The gross thing was the raw skin.

There was a pause while the group digested the dream and left some room to see if Roz would go further with it. I asked her if she had any thoughts about the dream. She responded that the ugliness under the shell was like a vulnerable and raw part. That it was getting into her clean stuff and that she was really trying to kill it. When she paused again, I asked the group if they had any reactions to the dream. I clarified that what would be useful was their emotional responses and reactions. I was not looking to figure out and interpret the dream at this point.

Tony said that he was uncomfortable listening to the dream, perhaps because Roz seemed removed in telling it. Roz responded that she was so disgusted with it. She wanted to keep it at arm's length. Marylin, with a little bit of embarrassment, said that it made her think of a penis. The way it stretched out and got bigger and the way it was spitting. Tony, still uncomfortable, reiterated that Roz was really detached from the dream, 'It is like she is telling a story.' I added that she treats the dream like a bug that she wants to keep at a distance. Then Roz responded, 'It is like I'm not responsible for the dream. No one will understand the horror. I think that I stay away from the horror because no one will understand if I really show the horror.'

Marylin very supportively told her, 'I would certainly be horrified.' Roz continued, 'It had to die and it wouldn't. It is like a part of my self. Some vulnerable piece of me.' Tony gently commented, 'That's what I thought.' Roz turned to him and slowed down, 'It is like you cut something. It is like being a chicken without a head.' 'What part of you do you think it is like?' Tony asked with interest. 'The needy part of me', Roz replied. 'But it had a kitten head', she added. Tony seemed to understand and reflected, 'Not a bug's head.' Felicia interjected, 'It was becoming a kitten, a cute kitten.' Then Tony said thoughtfully, 'It's transitioning. It's transforming to something.' Roz mulled these responses over and concluded, 'Well, it isn't cute yet!'

After a poignant silence, I asked the group, 'If this was your dream, what part of you would be the cut-off part?' For Felicia, it was clearly her fear; then she added, 'Also the hate part of me.' For Marylin, it was the sense of helplessness. She also felt strongly that she would feel compassion for the helpless creature that was being hurt. Roz was struck by this and her own awareness that she didn't feel any identification with the bug at all. 'I feel no compassion for it. It had no expression…no appealing expression.' Marylin, again identifying somewhat with the creature and appreciating its value, retorted, 'No expression, just a stubborn survival.'

At this point Tony concluded that this was a positive dream.

> We are all transforming. My life is transforming. It feels awkward. I can feel others' core issues as they respond to the dream and I wonder what mine are. I have been feeling the absence of my father. It was Fathers' Day last Sunday and I didn't feel like honouring my father. I felt that I am the father now and I didn't want to acknowledge him.

Marylin was upset with this idea and talked about how her son neglected both Fathers' Day and his father's sixtieth birthday. She and Tony each explored what this neglect meant to them. For her it was failing to acknowledge a 'good' father, while for him it brought out his longing for more engagement with his father and his father's inability to respond to this need. He also talked about how he needs to experience me as actively engaged in the group and is upset if I am relatively passive at times. I noted this and connected it to his disappointment with my not having brought in the idea of working with dreams after actively considering the group's needs. Tony responded, 'I have been getting what I need with other men now...and here in the group. That's why I am angry when Marty is not "strong and active". This is the first time that I am really feeling the absence.' Roz smiled and remarked, 'I guess that you have a core issue.'

The group continued in a lively manner. Content centred around Marylin's struggle with food and exercise and her stubborn refusal to give up trying, even though it is very difficult for her. Felicia was increasingly quiet and seemed to be withdrawing. When someone commented on this she acknowledged that she was having trouble from the beginning of the session.

> I want to be connected to you guys. I feel like I am with you in what you have been talking about, but somehow I am not really here. It has to do with a memory that I had on a job this afternoon. I was at a job site and I went to the bathroom in the basement of the building. It was dirty and smelly. It reminded me of playing in an abandoned bathroom as a kid. It smelled like kids going and peeing and doing dirty things. I remembered feeling scared, but interested.

'Did something happen?' I asked gently. Felicia felt angry at being asked. It was the same anger she felt when I asked about dreams. 'I had a horrible dream', she said, 'and I don't want to bring it into group. It was very sexual and it could have been you in the dream.' I asked if the dream and her wish not to talk about it was connected to the fear and hate part of her that she had associated to Roz's bug.

> Yeah! Without going into detail. I thought that it was you...and that Frank [her husband] was in the room watching. It was my boss Arty in the dream, but I remember thinking it could be Marty. Frank came in and I was on my stomach. I was trying to pull the wool over Frank's eyes and he was going along with it.

I reflected, 'You were upset that Frank didn't see.' 'I was really sexual and alive', she responded, 'And I was very angry that Frank wasn't saying "What are you doing?" It was very confusing. I was afraid to tell the dream. It feels shameful that I have such thoughts.' Roz, trying to be helpful, pointed out, 'I don't feel responsible for my dreams.' 'I do', Felicia responded, 'that I could have that emotion.' Tentatively I added, 'And you felt hurt that Frank didn't set some limit for you?' Felicia continued painfully, 'It is like Frank is my mother and she is not seeing! It was my fault for hiding something.'

Marylin spoke firmly, yet with tenderness, at this point. 'You weren't hiding anything. It wasn't your fault. She just didn't see.' Felicia calmed down a little and explained, 'I felt powerful. I could make her not see. I wanted Frank to go along and I was angry that he did. Just like I am sometimes angry that he seems not to notice me enough as a woman and at the same time I am often angry when he initiates sex...when he wants something from me.' Marylin reflected with a great deal of attunement, 'You were glad that he didn't interrupt you. You didn't want to stop, but you needed your mother to limit you. I am feeling very protective about the part of you that thinks that you stopped your mother from protecting you. You weren't that powerful!' Appreciatively, Felicia agrees, 'That's right, because I could easily feel guilty about that.' Roz is also very supportive of Felicia as a little girl needing protection. 'If it was my daughter, no one could keep me from seeing.' Felicia took a deep breath at this point and sighed. 'I feel more here now...more present.' Marylin continued as the group was ending, 'I feel bad when a little girl takes too much responsibility.' Felicia concluded, 'She should have stopped us.' Marylin added one further thought, 'Also, we don't expect to be protected.' As Felicia got up to leave she commented, 'I felt very confused. I'm OK now.'

Discussion and conclusion

The first thing to note as we look at this session is that there was no attempt at completeness or interpretation in the classical sense. Many aspects of both dreams were not delved into or pursued. In individual sessions both dreamers would have had more opportunity to stay with their own associative flow and to uncover more material. For example, Felicia's anger at her husband for not showing more sexual attention to her came out more significantly in her individual session the next day. Also, her ambivalent feelings about the therapist's responsiveness and about her relationship with her father were explored more deeply in later sessions (both individual and group). The value of working with dreams in group is not the opportunity for completeness and an orderly working through. The value that we can see clearly is in the aliveness and deepening of group process.

While the group did not stay overtly focused on the dreamers, the dream material added an aliveness and stimulation that led several members to become open and vulnerable. In fact, Felicia's experience and dream might well have been withheld totally without the playspace that was created in working with Roz's dream. Felicia alluded to the issues of shame and secrecy that kept her in many ways hidden early in the group when the idea of working with dreams was suggested. She then also responded to Roz's dream as touching on parts of her self that were connected to fear and hate. As is typical of my style in working in the playspace with dreams, I did not focus on this information at first. I went back to it later at a particular moment when Felicia seemed more open to going further. As Shapiro (1995) has emphasised, the timing of analytic interventions is enhanced by paying particular attention to the degree and quality of affect. This is equally important, as Harwood (1998) points out, in a group setting. While Felicia's fear was quite evident at the beginning of the session, the quality of her affect was more self-protective than open. At the later point I sensed a shift in the quality of her involvement and the availability of her affect. A recent paper (Livingston 1999) includes a more detailed discussion of timing in relation to affect shifts and vulnerability. At the point in the session that I sensed Felicia's readiness to explore further, I simply inquired if her previously expressed fear was connected to her hesitation about sharing her dream. It was a simple intervention on the surface, but it subtly made the connection between Felicia's deep yet unexpressed reaction to Roz's dream, her hesitation in the here and now and her childhood fears centring around her mother's seeming to ignore the Oedipal triangle yet perhaps being danger-ously angry or damaged. Interventions like this one are often not at all thought out. They arise spontaneously in the playspace if the leader is free and involved.

Another aspect of the leader's facilitation of the process was my clearly asking for reactions, emotional and subjective reactions, not for experi-ence-distant guesses about what the dream might mean subconsciously to the dreamer. I did this by example in the way I work with most material and I spe-cifically clarified that I was not looking to figure out and interpret the dream. I told the group quite directly that what I thought would be valuable was their emotional responses and reactions.

Another key intervention was asking the group, 'If this was your dream, what part of you would be the cut-off part?' I look for ways to include the group in the dream; ways to make the dream a group property. This particular one is especially self-psychological in that it leads to an exploration of self-states, including Felicia's frightened self-state.

Throughout this work in the playspace, there is a balancing of reactiveness and responsiveness. In this session the group finds that balance nicely by itself. However, it is not always that easy and it is the responsibility of the leader to return to a balance in this regard when necessary. Tony's reaction to Roz's dream is a constructive expression of reactiveness. He is gentle and aware that Roz might feel attacked or criticised, but the thrust of his expression is his own reaction and not an attempt to be attuned. This turns out to be quite valuable both to him and to Roz who realises a few things about her style of presentation that apply to far more than the presentation of the dream. It leads her to take the risk of bringing in a feeling that she fears no one will understand: her feeling of horror. This then becomes part of deepening the group's process.

In contrast to Tony's reaction, the women's response to Felicia's dream becomes a significant provision. Their responsiveness contrasts sharply with her transferential expectation that she will be either ignored or punished. The group was protective and warmly responsive. The power of such group responsiveness to ameliorate shame and guilt and to further a healing process is part of what makes group psychotherapy such a valuable addition to individual work.

What we have seen in this paper is one leadership style within a self-psychological approach to working with dreams in group psychotherapy. It stresses an empathic attunement, the creation of safety, and an experience-near playful relationship. 'Playful' is not used lightly here. It is used in the spirit of Winnicott's intermediate space where a mother suspends questions of what is real or not real and what is me and what is not. Freud's analogy to a playspace forms a metaphor for the creation of a such a special atmosphere in a group, or for that matter in individual work as well, that encourages exploration, risk-taking, and vulnerability. Working with dreams in this playspace deepens the curative process, not only for the dreamer, but for the entire group.

References

Bacal, H. (1995) 'Beyond empathy.' Presented to the Association for Psychoanalytic Self-psychology, New York.

Bacal, H. (1998) 'Notes on optimal responsiveness in the group process.' In I. Harwood and M. Pines (ed) *Self Experiences in Group: Intersubjective and Self-psychological Pathways to Human Understanding.* London: Jessica Kingsley Publishers.

Fosshage, J. (1983) 'The psychological function of dreams: A revised psychoanalytic perspective.' *Psychoanalysis and Contemporary Thought 6,* 4, 641–69.

Fosshage, J. (1987) 'New vistas in dream interpretation.' In M. Glucksman and S. Warner (ed) *Dreams in New Perspective: The Royal Road Revisited.* New York: Human Sciences.

Fosshage, J. (1988) 'Dream interpretation revisited.' In A. Goldberg (ed) *Progress in Self-psychology. Volume 3.* Hillsdale NJ: Analytic Press.

Fosshage, J. (1989) 'The developmental function of dreaming mentation.' In A. Goldberg (ed) *Progress in Self-psychology. Volume 5.* Hillsdale, NJ: Analytic Press.

Freud, S. (1914) *Remembering, repeating, and working through. Standard Edition 12.* London: Hogarth Press, 1958.

Greenberg, R. (1987) 'Self-psychology and dreams: The merging of differences.' *Psychiatric Journal of Ottawa 12*, 2, 98–102.

Harwood, I. (1998) 'Can group analysis/psychotherapy provide a wide angle lens for self-psychology?' In I. Harwood and M. Pines (eds) *Self Experiences in Group: Intersubjective and self-psychological pathways to human understanding.* London: Jessica Kingsley Publishers.

Kieffer, C. (1996) 'Using dream interpretation to resolve group developmental impasses.' *Group 20*, 4, 273–85.

Kohut, H. (1977) *The Restoration of the Self.* New York: International University Press.

Kohut, H. (1984) *How Does Analysis Cure?* Chicago: University of Chicago Press.

Livingston, M. (1998) 'Dreams, the understanding-explaining sequence, and the facilitation of curative process.' In A. Goldberg (ed) *Progress in Self-psychology,. Volume 14.* Hillsdale, NJ: Analytic Press.

Livingston, M. (1999) 'Vulnerability, tenderness, and the experience of self-object relationship: A self-psychological view of deepening curative process in group psychotherapy.' *International Journal of Group Psychotherapy 49*, 1, 1–21.

Meares, R. (1990) 'The fragile spielraum: An approach to transmuting internalization'. In A. Goldberg (ed) *Progress in Self-psychology. Volume 6.* Hillsdale, NJ: Analytic Press.

Ornstein, P. (1987) 'On self-state dreams in the psychoanalytic treatment process.' In A. Rothstein (ed) *The Interpretation of Dreams in Clinical Work.* Madison, CT: International University Press.

Shapiro, S. (1995) *Talking with Patients: A Self-Psychological View.* New Jersey: Aronson.

Stolorow, R. (1978) 'Themes in dreams: A brief contribution to therapeutic technique.' *International Journal of Psychoanalysis 53*, 473–5.

Stolorow, R., Brandchaft, B. and Atwood, G. (1987) *Psychoanalytic Treatment: An Intersubjective Position.* Hillsdale, NJ: Analytic Press.

Tolpin, P. (1983) 'Self-psychology and the interpretation of dreams.' In A. Goldberg (ed) *The Future of Psychoanalysis.* New York: International University Press.

Winnicott, D. (1953) 'Transitional objects and transitional phenomena: A study of the first not-me possession.' *International Journal of Psychoanalysis 43*, 89–97.

CHAPTER 12

Discussion of Martin Livingston's Working Playspace

Irene Harwood

It is both a pleasure and a burden to discuss Dr Martin Livingston's chapter on 'Self Psychology, Dreams and Group Psychotherapy: Working in the Playspace'. It was a pleasure to read, to agree with, and to enjoy saying, 'I agree, I agree'. It was a burden because it is difficult to find something to disagree with or to justify citing masses of additional relevant clinical material. I can easily picture the safe working playspace Marty provides for his patients. It is clear that he not only allows, but celebrates when his patients come up with what Winnicott called 'creative gestures'.

I found little to disagree with theoretically; I will merely emphasise what I consider theoretically essential when working from the perspective of the psychology of the self.

By now, Kohut's self psychology has expanded to embrace the theory of intersubjectivity. Group analysts and therapists who work from that perspective are informed not only by the work of American theorists (notably Stolorow, Brandchaft and Atwood, 1987) but also by the work of theorists and philosophers writing about intersubjectivity in the rest of the world. Accordingly, the group conductor pays attention to every single group member's subjectivity, his or her own, and to how all of these individual subjectivities influence each other and the entire group. Fosshage's theoretical paper (1993) listening from the empathic mode as well as from the other-centered mode has been spelled out and applied in detail to listening and responding by the group conductor in a previous publication (Harwood

1996, pp.167–171). In listening to a dream in group, one would consider parts and details of the dream in many different ways: from the dreamer's perspective, each member's perspective, and the group conductor's perspective. At the same time, the group conductor can toss up each consideration into the transitional space as one would playfully toss up a balloon. Everyone has free rein to bounce around the possibilities of the dream with no immediate thought to concretising its meanings – which would deflate the balloon. Thus, I agree with Dr Livingston that dream interpretation from the perspective of the psychology of the self is not about searching for the objective or 'hidden truth' in the dream. Instead, this playful process in the intermediate space of the group involves our curiosity about the possible meanings of the metaphor that the dreamer's unconscious brings to us and therefore brings us closer to the dreamer's subjective experiences about self and others. So let us dream up how many ways we can count the possibilities.

First, from the perspective of the psychology of the self, one would not insist or interpret that the dream always says something about the group, any particular member, or the group conductor, or how the dreamer experienced the last session. The group conductor stays as experience-near to the details of the material and how it is brought out by the dreamer and how the other members associate to it. As Dr Livingston writes, the dream is used as a metaphor and can be seen as many different metaphors that the group members can play with and consider. It could also be considered as what Lichtenberg (1989) calls the 'model scene' – an important thematic affective experience in the dreamer's life that has taken on metaphorical meaning.

On the other hand, having said this, acting as a group conductor I would always consider whether the dreamer is unconsciously communicating something about the group, a group member, or the conductor, or how the last group session was experienced. Whether I will wonder out loud about any of those thoughts depends on the associations of the dreamer, the other members, and my own as the dream is redreamed by the group members.

Second, I listen to the associations of the group members to see what they evoke for them, as Roz's dream did for Felicia in Dr Livingston's group. I also consider whether what a member may interpret for the dreamer may be closer to an insight about the dreamer or closer to a projection of his or her own. In the latter situation, I double-check my own take against other group members' subjectivities. I notice what I have come up with versus what other members have, and wonder what may be personal to me and what could be an additional contribution. I decide to share it depending on how experience-near or productive it may be for the dreamer or another member who offered associations.

Third, when I first listen to a dream, I allow whatever associations of my own to come up. I try to notice what has come up for me and also what has not, as much as I can be aware of the latter. My listening and working with associations to a dream in group, and then my further musings about them, differ little from how I listen to a dream in an individual hour. After paying attention to my associations, I ask myself if this is (a) a self-state dream (from traumatic to cohesive), (b) a transference dream to the group conductor, a member, or the group, (c) a dream trying to resolve a problem the dreamer encountered, e.g. solving a mathematical problem or writing a paper, (d) a dream about another current important relationship in the dreamer's life, (e) a dream saying what stage of development the dreamer is dealing with, e.g. revisiting birth, wish fulfilment of a potential in the future, a regression to an earlier sibling rivalry, or an earlier unresolved trauma, (f) an implicit or explicit memory the dreamer may be accessing, (g) a dream providing further information about the early internalizations of multiple extended experiences. The latter are subjective positive and traumatising experiences (Harwood 1986, 1993); they are not considered to be accurate memories of what early caretakers were like and of what are called internal objects in other theoretical frameworks. I also ask myself how the internalizations of early subjective experiences further inform about the present or past self-states of the dreamer, about the early important people in the dreamer's life, and if and how the internalizations of multiple extended experiences relate to anyone else in the group.

None of the above questions are mutually exclusive, nor can answers exist for all of them in considering a dream. All the same, I enjoy playing with the many possibilities. Fosshage (1987) suggested that the analyst acts as an amplifier of images. What the group analyst adds about the dream depends on what appears to be experience-near to the dreamer as well as to the other members of the group; however, I would not refrain from adding a possible interpretation, as Dr Livingston states, in a spirit of freedom, curiosity and exploration when I feel it is relevant, can be informative and growth-producing, but for whatever reason it was not brought up by the dreamer or by another group member.

I fully concur with Dr Livingston when he cites Stolorow's dictum (1978) that at the end of the royal road of dream interpretation from the perspective of the self lies an individual's 'organizing principles which unconsciously pattern and thematize the person's subjective experiences of his or her self and self-selfobject relationships', and in this particular case, the relationships in group as well.

Dr Livingston introduces his own subjectivity into his group by voicing his need for material for a dream chapter. At the same time, his honest direct response to his patient in admitting that need is both disarming and productive. Such forthrightness provided the sort of healing experience that can benefit those of our patients who have experienced their parents' dishonest denial of their own self-interest. Dr Livingston admitted his subjective need while not negating his belief that working with dreams could also be productive for the group members. His admission, I am quite sure, was experienced as healing or ameliorative to parental crazy-making statements in the past, such as 'it is only for your own good'.

I also appreciate Dr Livingston's focus on Bacal's (1991) responsiveness and reactiveness in the group process, and his explication of how it is often in the reactiveness of the other group members that lies the possibility of deepening not only the dreamer's process, but the process of the group members as well. I like how Dr Livingston asks for emotional responses and reactions to Roz's dream from the other members, rather than having them interpret the dream, for Roz, thus keeping it experience-near for all. The reader will notice by Tony's comments that interpretations occur nevertheless.

Before I venture to play with my understandings of Roz's dream in light of some of the concepts I described above, I want to attest that I do so without context. I do not know the patient nor the group members as Dr Livingston does. Though I am theoretically musing, I cannot pretend I have the answers, but am only offering another subjective take on the clinical material I read. The group conductor should know best what is most experience-near and relevant to the patient and to the group.

Roz's dream of the roach (bug) and the cat in the bathtub could be guessed at as an early traumatic experience with early significant others possibly stored in implicit memory. Roz's comment that she did not feel any identification with the bug at all suggests that this is not likely a self-state dream, though in it she indeed feels vulnerable and unprotected. Group members identify that she seems (still) to be detached and removed from the (affective aspects of) the dream. Therefore, it is important to stay experience-near to the dream material for Roz and not venture into theorising or speculating out loud about what might have happened to her earlier with significant others.

While everyone is exploring Roz's dream and their own reactions, it is interesting that what may be split-off and detached for Roz stirs up traumatic memories and associations for Felicia. Her further associations may suggest that Felicia may have been activated by the possible split-off aspects of Roz's dream – how the (mother) cat may not have fully seen what the (cock) roach-bug was doing in Felicia's early life. Often the dreamer can work with the dream only up to a certain point, but the unconscious is surprised by the disguise in the metaphor in the dream and may open up other members in their own associations regarding their own experiences. Thus, Roz's dream allowed Felicia to delve deeper and let her protective stance slip away, since someone else's dream provided a greater margin of safety than would directly bringing up her own material. Therefore, what may still appear as experience-distant for the dreamer may allow, through the playfulness in the group dream process, a more experience-near engagement for another group member.

I strongly agree with Dr Livingston's conclusion that group dream associations in a safe playful workspace further deepen self and group understandings while on the unconscious 'royal' yellow brick road of discovery.

References

Bacal, H. (1991) 'Reactiveness and responsiveness in the group therapeutic process.' In S. Tuttman and C.T. Madison (ed) *Psychoanalytic Group Theory and Therapy: Essays in Honor of Saul Scheidlinger*. New York: International Universities Press.

Fosshage, J. (1987) 'New vistas in dream interpretation.' In M. Glucksman and S. Warner. (eds) *Dreams in New Perspective: The Royal Road Revisited*. New York: Human Sciences.

Fosshage, J. (1993) 'Countertransference: The Analyst's Experience of the Analysand.' Presented at the 16th Annual Conference on the Psychology of the Self. Toronto, Canada.

Harwood, I. (1986) 'The need for optimal, available selfobject caretakers: Moving toward extended selfobject experiences.' *Group Analysis 19*, 291–302.

Harwood, I. (1993) 'Examining Early Childhood Multiple Cross-Cultural Extended Selfobject and Traumatic Experiences and Creating Optimum Treatment Environments.' Presented at the 16th Annual Conference on the Psychology of the Self. Toronto, Canada. In I. Harwood and M. Pines (1998) (eds) *Self Experiences in Groups: Intersubjective and Self Psychological Pathways to Human Understanding*. London: Jessica Kingsley Publishers.

Harwood, I. (1996) 'Can group analysis/psychotherapy provide a wide angle lens for self psychology?' In I. Harwood and M. Pines (1998) (eds) *Self Experiences in Groups:*

Intersubjective and Self Psychological Pathways to Human Understanding. London: Jessica Kingsley Publishers.

Lichtenberg, J. (1989) *Psychoanalysis and Motivation.* Hillsdale, NJ: Analytic Press.

Stolorow, R.D. (1978) 'Themes in dreams: A brief contribution to therapeutic technique.' *International Journal of Psychoanalysis 53*, 473–75.

Stolorow, R.D., Brandchaft, B. and Atwood, G.E. (1987) *Psychoanalytic Treatment: An Intersubjective Approach.* Hillsdale, NJ: Analytic Press.

CHAPTER 13

Reflections on Dreams

Their Implications for Groups

Salomon Resnik

Introduction

Dreaming is a way of thinking, but a highly complex one; it is a particular kind of experience in space and time, governed by what Freud called the 'primary process' – that is to say, a very primitive experience that takes place in the unconscious. Freud's book on dreams was published in 1900 to coincide with the mourning process he had to go through over the recent death of his father. Like everybody else, he was unable to work through certain things consciously, so he 'closed his eyes' to reality and had a dream. He tells us that the night before his father's funeral he dreamt of a printed notice or poster, like those that forbid people to smoke; in fact it read either 'You are requested to close your eyes' or 'You are requested to close an eye' (Freud 1900, 317–318). In an earlier version, reported in a Letter to Fliess (2 November 1896;[1] Freud 1954, p.171), Freud remembered the dream differently – the poster read 'close your eyes'. I would say that for Freud as for all of us, it was difficult to 'open his eyes' to such an intensely painful reality as his father's death. He loved his father, but was also very afraid of him. In the dream, Freud tries to face up to his ambivalence towards such an important figure. In the dream, that 'fundamental way of thinking', the process of mourning appears as a conflict: ambivalence and feelings of loss were something that Freud as dreamer wanted both to 'see' and not to see at the same time.

A dream is part of a complex series of themes which the spectator looks at with a mixture of curiosity and fear. Dreaming is not entirely split off from daily life. The multiplicity of daily life experiences becomes part of the dream world, as we shall see later.

One can imagine that in former times, among the Ancient Greeks of Delphi for example, dreaming and reporting dreams were part of a psychodramatic experience. In *Die Traumdeutung*, Freud speaks of the relationship between theatre and dreams. The roles in the oneiric scene are played by 'Darsteller' (actors) known to the patient – they are products of his or her own imagination. The dream 'producer', a special function of the ego, 'knows' which actor should play each particular role. The theatrical representation ('Darstellung') is a realisation in oneiric code of a particular forbidden desire, according to Freud. Other authors have different points of view concerning the 'cause' or reason for constructing a dream. I personally believe that we always dream, because it is part of life to do so, but there are levels at which the depth of the dream process is far away from the dreaming mind and perhaps from any kind of recording. This is interpreted physiologically by some authors as an inability to dream.

The same thing happens in psychosis, where psychoanalysts such as H. Rosenfeld and W.R. Bion (together with many of my teachers) often speak of this inability. Like Freud, I believe that dreams and psychosis are very close to each other. In fact, I would say that psychotics dream all the time, but they cannot 'wake up' and tell us that they are almost asleep. In my experience with psychotic patients in individual analysis and in groups, I have more and more come to think that delusional patients who hallucinate all the time and are in some way aware of the fact (Bion's hallucinosis, 1970) will accept the opinion that they are living in a dreaming state. Therefore, as in a 'dream screen', oneiric hallucinations are difficult to differentiate from daydreaming hallucinations. In my own book on dreams (Resnik 1987), I suggest that the dream screen is more three-dimensional than was at first thought, a kind of theatrical screen with the added rhythm of film-making. Bertram Lewin and Fairbairn spoke of dreams as a series of short films. I find that psychotic patients are often unable to watch films because it is too difficult to differentiate them from hallucinations; such patients tend to look on the projector as a 'machine for fabricating hallucinations'. A schizophrenic patient of mine went to the theatre and to the cinema after spending four years entirely locked up in his own home. He said to me 'I quite like the theatre, because the actors are alive; but in a film I cannot differentiate what is on the screen from my own hallucinations.'

Die Traumdeutung is without doubt one of the most important contributions by Freud to the field of psychoanalysis, to the understanding of the psychotic way of functioning of the mind, and to our cultural heritage in general. In the first edition, the discussion of symbolism was limited to a few pages; but in the second, several pages on sexual symbolism were inserted at the end of the section on 'typical dreams' in Chapter 5.

Given that Freud's book on dreams is very complex, my particular aim in this chapter is to explore the history and meaning of dream interpretation and its implications for a deeper understanding of the language of the unconscious in groups. In my own book on dreams (Resnik 1987), I suggest that the dream screen is more three-dimensional than was at first thought, a kind of theatrical screen with the added rhythm of film-making. Bertram Lewin and Fairbairn spoke of dreams as a series of short films. What I mean by that phrase is the manner in which the account of a dream in a psychoanalytic session is already – as Freud and some of his followers pointed out – a transference phenomenon. The patient is reporting his dream to other people – the psychoanalyst and the other members of the group – and is therefore also talking about the analytic session.

I always find the first chapter of Freud's book fascinating – the one in which he speaks of the scientific literature dealing with the question of dreams. There we can see how the oneiromants interpreted dreams in different civilisations and at different epochs.

Freud refers to Aristotle's two works on dreams *De divinatione per somnum* and *De somnis* (both published in translation in 1935). In them, Aristotle stresses that dreams are not sent by the gods – they are 'daemonic'. That statement requires some clarification, particularly as to the term 'daemon' ('daimon', in Greek) – a protective or sometimes criticising spirit (hence, with superego functions), a divinity, a sort of imp who can be inspiring. Cicero was influenced by the ideas of Posidonius. Posidonius's doctrine of dreams states: 'in dreams the spirit is most immediately awake and becomes the eye of the soul'. Demonology and angelology were very much concerned with the interpretation of dreams, mainly in the final period of Greek culture and early Roman times. The term 'daemon' also has the meaning of genius or guardian angel, or what in fairy tales would be called pucks and pixies – the same kind of idea as in Shakespeare's *Midsummer Night's Dream*. So there is the idea of the divine together with something playful, childlike and malicious – in fact, just as children can be. When we come to Socrates, dreaming becomes a sort of illumination, an archaic infantile illuminating fantasy. Speaking of his childhood, Socrates wrote: 'Daemon is a voice which goes back to my first years of life, it talks to me in such a way that it takes me away from any other thoughts and preoccupations. It invites me to concentrate all my attention on this inner inspiring dialogue.' This inner genie makes its way in an insistent manner into Socrates's mental space, asking him to interplay with it in his mind. It becomes, I suggest, a self-criticising voice or a critical superego shadow which tries to communicate positively or 'negatively' some of its intuitions. Socrates sometimes felt his soul to be inspired and he was guided in his poetic intuitions by these important creatures.

Freud spoke about dreams as a playful dramatised experience, such as children have. Melanie Klein (1940), exploring the primitive levels of the child's mind, discovered that infantile narcissism like the magic way of thinking and playing has a very important role in the waking and dreaming states of unconscious fantasy. Decoding the unconscious messages of the mind in child analysis is a very important step in the search for the meaning of *fantasien*, dreaming and hallucinating in general.

In my book on dreams (Resnik 1987), I mention the first dream of a child just 18 months old, who told me in the playroom at the London Institute of Psychoanalysis: 'You know, I saw you yesterday.' I asked if he was sure; he answered 'yes' and took my hand. He led me towards one corner of the room, put my hand into the wash-basin and turned on the tap. He used my hand as a tool (a transitional object) to gather up objects from under the water: small bits of wood, dolls, bits of card. The game was to put my hand into the water under his guidance and fish out the 'unconscious' objects. When I asked where he had seen all that previously, he answered: 'In my room, at night.' The little boy spoke of other children and made noises with his mouth, a noise like an explosion, 'Bang' (Resnik 1987, pp.26–7). This event became equated with fishing under the waters of consciousness for bits and pieces of a complex, multiple, fragmented reality. According to this view, the analyst-oneiromant behaves like an archaeologist: discovering fragments of a disintegrated or not yet integrated language which when they are brought together translate into an archaic-present language. That language is made up of the bits and pieces of a catastrophic experience (the explosive 'Bang') that children can undergo either in normal or in abnormal states in early childhood in the way that Klein described (the mourning process would be one such example).

This archaeological linguistic approach interested the ancient philosophers who studied the interpretation of dreams. For example, Plato (*Timaeus* 90a) and Xenocrates believed in the study of dreams as a way of decoding certain transcendental messages of spiritual life. For Aristotle, it is not only the spiritual life but also messages from the life of the body that are symbolised in dreams, so that the latter can be used as premonitions and warnings (Resnik 1987). Herbert Silberer (1917), often mentioned by Freud in his book, made an important contribution to our understanding of the multiplicity of factors at play in dreams. He was particularly concerned – as I am – by the functional aspects or categories of dreaming. The functional aspect of dreams concerns not only the material or contents of the act of thinking (oneiric thinking), but also with the way in which the *Darsteller* come on to the oneiric stage – do the actors walk, run, fly? Are they immobilised and petrified? Joyful? Sad? Disunited, fragmented into a complex of bits and pieces? Silberer puts the accent on thinking in the dream, and on the acting and body language as part of the message it contains. Not only people but matter of any kind, transparent or opaque, circles floating in the air, prisoners, geometrical figures – all have some special meaning. This way of reflecting on dreams is very close to pre-Socratic and Socratic thinking – Plato, like Heraclites, spoke of dreams being a fundamental Logos.

For Freud, there existed a set of 'grammatical' rules governing the language of dreams. For instance, displacement, condensation and dramatisation are part of that language, but they are not sufficient to account for the whole of the oneiric world. The dream is also a living re-creation of infantile expressions of a playful theatricality of the mind in its confrontation with adult everyday life (this was particularly the case with the little boy I mentioned above).

Dreaming is also a way of remembering. Time exists in dreams, as does space. The dream memory has to do with past unconscious experiences, stimulated and aroused by present circumstances (daily and nightly residues). Time in dreams may also involve a way of remembering that corresponds to Aristotle's idea in his book *On Divination*, where he poses the question of the premonitory meaning of dreams. This idea certainly plays a role in Bion's view of a 'memoir of the future'.

Aristotle believed in a written oneiric code related to the future, which he called anticipatory dreams. Psychic mechanisms such as condensation (*Verdichtung*) and displacement (*Verschiebung*) should be understood as the master craftsmen of mental functioning, the artist-artisans of the mind.

Indeed Freud uses the image of the actor or personage of the dream as *Schauspieler,* thereby expressing the idea of play.[2] In such role-playing on the dream stage, there is a vivid picture of a time which is simultaneously past, present and future – and none of these. This links up in some way with Husserl's view (1893–1917) that 'time is always presence'.

Clinical aspects

To illustrate these remarks on dreaming and psychosis, I would like to compare aspects of group analysis with neurotic and psychotic patients, and I shall mention briefly, in my conclusion, some of these as they appear in the individual analysis of a schizophrenic.

Dreams in group analysis with neurotic patients

In a group of highly intelligent adult neurotic patients (three women and three men), Stephen, 45, who is very much in conflict with an idealised and persecutory father figure, dreamt of a Soviet (as it then was) submarine made of lead and somewhat square-shaped – 'like this room', he said. Gorbachev, present in the dream, said, 'There's going to be a war, perhaps a cold war, and we need this submarine to defend ourselves.' All the members of the group became very involved with the dream, and Betty, a 35-year-old university lecturer in education, said, 'We are all inside the submarine.' In fact, psycho-analysing, as in the case of the little boy I mentioned in London, is a way of getting under the surface of the water – but with care, as another female patient pointed out, since we might come across other dangerous creatures or enemies. Stephen associated Gorbachev with the fact that my own name is of Russian origin – but in 'Gorba-chev' there is the idea of 'chief'. One of Stephen's problems in the group was to face his father as the 'chief' of the family incarnated by me as psychoanalyst, the powerful, admired and hated 'chief' of the group-family, whom the group needed in order to be helped but also was to be competed with – hence the danger of the war/power struggle. Larry, a very intelligent young doctor, said, 'I'm thinking about the cold war, lead is cold.' 'In fact,' he added, 'I was always afraid of my own father and his cold hurtful remarks.'

Garry, another member of the group, a musician, hardly ever says anything. He never misses a session, but he stands aloof – he keeps his distance and is sometimes 'cold'. After a short but very tense silence, several members began to talk of 'injustice' and how they felt resentful against their parents – and especially the 'chief' of the family who didn't understand them. In the transference situation this was an implicit reference to my capacity to understand them. 'This is a very difficult topic,' said Joyce, a woman of around 50, who often says she feels misunderstood by her mother (who sent her away to boarding school when she was an adolescent). She sees herself as very unhappy and unable to experience 'joy' in life. When she began in the group three years before, she had a terrible dream in which she was burying people in a cemetery. These were people she liked, so she could not understand why she was doing this. What emerged from her associations and later sessions was the fact that she was repressing her own feelings of joy and love: she was also inhibiting her hopes and desires. To love and to be loved are precious things, and I felt that the group was carefully facing up to these themes in the transference. Are parents cold? Are analysts cold? Sometimes. But at the same time, I gathered they were repressing and holding back their own warm feelings; they were showing themselves to be rather formal and cold, before being able to test adequately the relationship with otherness. Joyce was burying her own feelings of love and hate, though she was afraid to make this public in the group; her history justified in part (from her point of view) her position.

One day, she discovered her father was not her mother's husband, but a lover with whom she had been having an affair. She understood – or perhaps misunderstood – that she needed to keep 'cool' and become 'leaden' when faced with the man who was not in fact her father. She had to become a tomb, in order to keep the secret buried inside herself. The problem was that in many of her emotional relationships in life she found it difficult to exhume her own feelings. In fact, in the mourning process, one loses not only an object but also the relationship one had with the object – and hence part of oneself.[3] In this session, she reported a dream in which she was looking at herself in a lead-backed mirror, which did not distort her image very much. She felt that the members of the group were in some way lead-backed mirrors who sometimes distorted her image but now they could see her as she was and from different angles. I believe that this 'mirroring' experience (Foulkes 1964, p.110; Pines 1998, p.41) was a very useful one. Individual analysis in general proposes only one point of view; the group, by its very nature, suggests different perspectives. The group multiplicity reflects projections in different ways, depending on the manner in which each member can return the projections. One of the benefits of group analysis is to give a container for 'dissemination' and, if this works well as a matrix (Foulkes), the participants can tolerate and send back unbearable feelings and thoughts (Bion's 'reverie', 1962). It is also the opportunity as compared with the classic individual model for each participant to represent a point of view (every mirror has its own nature and capacity for refraction and reflection); in groups there are not only two points of view (patient and analyst) but several vertices (Bion 1970), and this enriches the fieldwork and makes it much more complex.

At that point in the session, Joyce felt that some of the 'returned'/ 'reflected' projections were quite warm and not dead feelings. Her inner world was not necessarily a cemetery, but a place that inwardly – under the surface – was becoming more alive. The problem is to come back to life and be able to deal with the unavoidable problems from which neurotic and psychotic patients try hard to escape. Joyce had been for many years cold and resentful towards the parents who had hidden her origins from her, thereby placing on her shoulders such a heavy load. How could she overcome her resentfulness and begin to understand why she became an inner metallic being, leaden and cold? The cemetery dream seemed to join up with Stephen's dream of the Soviet submarine and the war that was going on down in the depths. How could they break free of their past? Garry was very disappointed – he knew that his mother had wanted a girl instead of a boy, and he himself had transvestite fantasies of the mother's beloved girl-child. But the father? The 'Gorba-chief' or head of the family was loved, admired and hated at the same time, as I was in my position as chief or leader of the group.

In my counter-transference, I felt that underneath – in the underwater currents of the session – a tense kind of love was very strong between us. One of my characteristics as analyst is that I ask when I do not understand; but I do know that very old unconscious misconceptions (Money-Kyrle 1968) are based on the mind's distortions that give rise to what he calls mental illness. Meltzer (1981) agrees that mental illness is the result of unconscious moral conflict; he believes in the importance of the mother–infant relationship. I would add that misconceptions, mis-deceptions, and misunderstandings in general are not only in the mother but also in the child, the family and the social environment. I insist on the importance of misunderstanding and mis-conception (deception) in the analytical setting, both the classic two-person one, and with groups and institutions. The unconscious level of this kind of feeling has to be understood in terms of One and the Other: child/society, patient/analyst or institution. Misunderstandings are usually twofold – a kind of divided understanding that has never been elucidated. We analysts should be able to deal with our own narcissistic profession, to tolerate and make use of our misunderstandings – our mutual misunderstandings and misconceptions with our patients – in order to deal with their unconscious repetition (Freud 1920) in the transference.[4]

In the following session Larry reported a dream in which he was going to a place near Vladivostok, called Rosni (not Resnik!). It was of course very cold in Siberia, so that the 'cold war' was still going on in the group. In the dream, paratroopers were attacking people in a very violent and unjust way – this was a cruel and 'boiling' attack. Through Larry's dream, the group was still in a state of war, love and hate with me as the father figure – and with the group as a whole as a maternal figure made up of brothers and sisters (siblings are pieces of the basic maternal body). In time, the very warm feelings in addition to open hostility came to the fore; we were able to work through some very old unconscious misunderstandings thanks to this group analysis.

Dreams in a group of psychotics

In 1997 I began in Venice a group of chronic psychotic patients, having as observers the director of the hospital in which some of the patients were recovering and one of the doctors. Mr V. a 35-year-old lawyer, very cold, said of himself that he was 'a big frozen mountain' that he projected into the landscape somewhere in Italy or the Himalayas. Indeed, he had travelled alone in the Himalayas for two weeks in order to discover what he called 'his secret' – the secret of everlasting time. When I saw him alone for the first time, he presented me with a book about the unexplored aspects of mountains on which no human being had ever set foot – there was only snow and glaciers. His body was very unbending. It was only after some personal work with me at first, followed by group therapy, with the cooperation of one of the doctors, that he was able to thaw out.

During the session I will now describe, he was sitting on my right, very thin and pathetic with an enigmatic smile; he was looking at me and the two observers with curiosity. There was also Richard, a composer of music, who suffered from splitting processes with paranoid feelings; he had a history of periods of depression with several suicide attempts. Eleanor, a young, rather pretty girl but very inflexible, was a schizophrenic. She had once thrown herself from a second-floor window. She had been recovering for the past six months. In the session, she sat exploring her hands, and said, 'I have the same hands as my mother, who suffered from rheumatism. My mother feels useless – she is a painter, but she cannot work any more.' She added, 'I think there is something distorted in my anatomy.' Then Mr V. (the 'frozen' man) put his hand on his heart and said, 'My heart is beating. I feel myself moved.' Richard said the same, touching his own heart. I felt that very warm but distorted feelings were emerging within the group. Laura, another member, a university professor but quite psychotic (she had had several relapses), spoke about her self-destructiveness – for instance, how she used to burn her hand (and sometimes her face or her genitals) with cigarettes; the places that, according to her, her father used to examine when she was a little girl. She said, 'Eleanor is looking at how her blood circulates – it is distorted and not flowing properly.' She went on: 'My mother died of a tumour somewhere between her heart and lungs, with a lot of bleeding.' I took up the common denominator of the group concerning coldness, lack of life, paralysis of the 'circulation' of life and the fear that suddenly, as with Mr V. the frozen feelings could thaw out and an uncontrollable circulation of feelings could emerge in a bleeding way, as in a kind of haemorrhage. Then Mr V. stated, 'My time was immobilized for a long time, like a grey concrete wall made out of crystals.' 'Maybe the wall can break?' I asked. He said he admired the Himalayas because they resisted the passage of time, but he was afraid to go on exploring by himself, so he decided to come back down to earth.

Eleanor spoke of the fear she experienced when she saw the film *Mississippi Burning*; she became the spokesperson for the group – when feelings begin to circulate after a long time of hibernation, the danger is either a flood or the emergence of burning feelings.

In the following session, Mr V. reported a dream in which there were different musical instruments. He wanted to set up an orchestra with a broken cello, a violin with no strings and a harmonium. As he recounted this dream, the other members were delighted as they imagined themselves trying to create an orchestra. Richard, the composer, spoke about Schoenberg and Alban Berg, who were able to use ostensibly discordant tones in order to discover new harmonies. Richard was of course talking about the discordant notes in the group; perhaps also about the fact that Mr V. was taking into his dream-mind the broken elements of different catastrophic experiences as a result of which the mind as a mental instrument needed to be repaired.

The harmonium was related to the need for harmony in order to be able to work together and to orchestrate our work, and perhaps to discover the inner logic of the harmony of broken mental instruments trying to make sound in spite of their handicapped situation.

If schizophrenia has to do with split personality (Bleuler 1911) and with dissonance in the mind (the *folie discordante* described by Chaslin[5] in 1912), perhaps the task of the therapeutic aspect of the group. I felt that Mr V.'s dream demanded of me and of the observers a very great responsibility; perhaps, with reference to Bion, the idea was how to make the best of a bad job. I would say that the job was not bad but difficult, and that the patients were helping us a lot. In accord and dissonance there are two contrasting positions: accepting the opportunity to be repaired, or breaking the strings (the links) between inner and outer worlds.

The group had an interesting and eventful development over three years; some of the patients benefited greatly. The analysis of dreams in psychotic patients confronted us with a dilemma: are psychotics able to dream from time to time? I recall Bion telling me that a very deeply psychotic patient can behave in the same session in both a psychotic and a neurotic way, and therefore cooperate with the analyst in a very restorative way.

When a patient is on a less psychotic level, he can bring dream material to the group; when such patients are very psychotic, they are 'dreaming' or hallucinating all the time and they cannot wake up. The difference between Bion and me is that I believe that it is not only that they cannot differentiate between dreaming and being awake, I would say they are 'asleep' throughout their life, they are dreaming all the time and find it difficult to wake up. It is not possible to ask a patient if he or she has hallucinations; but if we think of him or her as being asleep all the time, then we can accept that he or she sees and hears things. Hence hallucinations become hallucinosis; this is a phenomenon of which he or she is aware – if we have the right instruments and if we can properly orchestrate something that requires reconstruction and restoration.

Discussion and conclusion

My aim in this chapter is to give a particular living picture of my clinical experience with individuals and with groups as to the importance of dream interpretation in the transference situation. Freud's book on dreams inspired my own *The Theatre of the Dream* (Resnik 1987). I believe that the investigation of primary processes through dreams is one of the royal roads (as Freud put it) for getting in touch with the deepest levels of the human mind, groups and society.

My own analysis with Herbert Rosenfeld gave me to understand the importance of the dramatisation of the dream in the transference situation –

where it becomes a true theatre in which the actors or *Darsteller* play out the various roles for the dreamer. According to Freud, the dreamer is both stage-manager and playwright of the dream. The dream in itself is a group theatrical experience. Simone, a schizophrenic patient I see every day in Paris, made use of his house and his body as a bunker. This patient was hallucinating all the time and, as I mentioned at the beginning of the chapter, he felt very disturbed when he went to the cinema for the first time in many years. He thought that his own hallucinations were mixed with the normal cinematographic ones. He is now waking up from his hallucinatory dream world and can watch television without being too afraid. He told me that he prefers the theatre, because there are real three-dimensional people; he himself used to live in a flat, two-dimensional world like a cinema screen or a dream-screen (Lewin 1946 and 1948). The common element between groups of neurotics and groups of psychotics arises when they become able to see that they are dreaming; they then become able to be less asleep in their daily life (in deep melancholic depression or chronic schizophrenia).

References

Bion, W.R. (1962) 'A Theory of Thinking.' *International Journal of Psycho-Analysis 43*, 415.

Bion, W.R. (1967) *Second Thoughts. Selected Papers on Psycho-Analysis.* London: Heinemann. Reprinted London: Karnac Books, 1984.

Bion, W.R. (1970) *Attention and Interpretation.* London: Tavistock Publications. Reprinted London: Karnac Books, 1993.

Bleuler, E. (1911) *Dementia Praecox or the Group of Schizophrenias.* Translated by J. Zinkin. New York: International Universities.

Chaslin, P. (1912) *Eléments de sémiologie et Clinique Mentales.* Paris: Asselin et Houzeau.

Freud, S. (1900) *The Interpretation of Dreams. Standard Edition 4/5.* London: Hogarth Press.

Freud, S. (1917 (1915)) *Mourning and Melancholia. Standard Edition 14.* London: Hogarth Press.

Freud, S. (1920) *Beyond the Pleasure Principle. Standard Edition 18.* London: Hogarth Press.

Freud, S. (1954) *Beyond the Pleasure Principle. Standard Edition 18.* London: Hogarth Press.

Freud, S. (1954) *The Origins of Psycho-Analysis.* London: Imago.

Foulkes, S.H. (1964) *Therapeutic Group Analysis.* London: Allen & Unwin.

Husserl, E. (1893–1917) *On the Phenomenology of Consciousness of Internal Time.* Translated by J.S. Churchill (1966). Bloomington, IN: Indiana University Press

Klein, M. (1940) 'Mourning and its Relation to Manic-Depressive States.' In M. Klein (1975) *Love, Guilt and Reparation. The Writings of Melanie Klein.* Volume 1. London: Hogarth. Reprinted London: Karnac Books, 1992.

Lewin, B. (1946) 'Sleep, the mouth and the dream screen'. *Psychoanalytic Quarterly 15.*

Lewin, B. (1948) 'Interferences from the dream screen.' *International Journal of Psychoanalysis 29.*

Meltzer, D. (1981) 'Does Money-Kyrle's concept of misconception have any unique descriptive power?' *Bulletin of the British Psycho-Analytical Society 8*, 14–22.

Money-Kyrle, R. (1968) 'Cognitive Development.' In D. Meltzer (ed) *The Collected Papers of Roger Money-Kyrle.* StrathTay (Perthshire): Clunie Press, 1978.

Pines, M. (1998) *Circular Reflections: Selected Papers on Group Analysis and Psychoanalysis.* London: Jessica Kingsley Publishers.

Resnik, S. (1987) *The Theatre of the Dream.* London: Tavistock. [A second edition is in preparation.]

Silberer, H. (1917) *Hidden Symbolism of Alchemy and the Occult Arts.* New York: Dover Publications, 1971. [Freud knew of Silberer's papers, published from 1909 onwards – see Standard Edition Vol.24]

Endnotes

1. Note that this is Letter 50, dated 2 November 1896, and not – as the Standard Edition claims (Volume 4, p.317, note) – Letter 60, dated 28 April 1897.

2. I am indebted to Riccardo Steiner for drawing my attention to this functional artistic side of dream-making as 'masters of the dream'.

3. In Freud's *Mourning and Melancholia* (1915), he speaks of the identification of the ego with the abandoned object: 'the shadow of the object fell upon the ego...as though it were an object, the forsaken object. In this way an object-loss is transformed into an ego-loss' (1917 (1915) p.249). Following Melanie Klein's understanding of the process, I would suggest that what is lost is not only the object but also the relationship *with* the object. In order to work through and overcome normal and pathological depression in such a case, the individual has to recover his or her own shadow (the shadow of the subject). Sometimes, in order to avoid mental pain or overwhelming guilt, people will tend to bury their own feelings of love and hate (ambivalence) with the object.

4. In many of my more recent papers I discuss this aspect. Professor Pietro Bria of Rome and I intend to write a book on *Shared Unconscious Misunderstandings*; the Italian word expresses this beautifully, *Fraintendimento*.

5. Eugen Bleuler (1911(1950) p.6) states that Philippe Chaslin, with his contemporary Séglas, was particularly concerned with catatonia and other such processes. In his 1912 book, Chaslin mentions the fact that he was already using the term 'folie discordante' and dissonant mimicry before the term schizophrenia began to be used (the current term up until that point was *dementia praecox*). Bleuler seems to have been helped by Chaslin's concepts of discordance or dissonance and disharmony. These concepts completed Bleuler's concept of *Spaltung* (splitting).

CHAPTER 14

Dreaming and Acting

Stefania Marielli [*]

I would like to focus on the different aspects of action that are involved in dreaming. Tolstoy's short story *The Kreutzer Sonata* describes a situation that could help to illustrate this theme. The story tells of a murder that matures in the protagonist's mind while listening to Beethoven's *Kreutzer Sonata*. Much debate ensued for many years in literary and musical circles about whether Tolstoy attributed to Beethoven's music a propensity to commit crime, or whether the story with its highly suggestive and subjective theme required a musical context, an appropriate expressionist background, to help convey links between the events, predictions, and a rich and singular profoundness. The description of the preparation of the crime, expressed by the enveloping musical theme, can be interpreted in two different ways: (a) a moral or psychopathological act of responsibility, (b) evidence that a personal catastrophe has come about that needs to be communicated. Accordingly, depending on which interpretation is considered, different levels of the perception of the events and different metaphors can be seen. Or is it a question of two facets of the same event?

Here I would refer to the musical setting created by this great Russian writer to show how a dream is linked to an action. I believe a dream, and in particular a group dream, contains elements that are not purely symbolic (see Tagliacozzo 1993). The dream has specific characteristics for the dreamer or for the group that make possible the representation of an action, or a type of

[*] English translation by Deberah Catts Petrini.

action. The group and the group dream, if we take Tolstoy's story, are made up not only of the *Sonata* and the main character, but include the thoughts and the characters created by him (e.g. the victim).

In exploring the different aspects of action in the group, J. C. Rouchy (1998) describes the act of starting a group by an analyst as an action that is rich in phantasms from the past (Abraham and Torok 1978), the characteristics of which will emerge from the newly founded setting. Also R. Kaës referring to the 'unconscious alliances' in the group setting, describes the foundation of the institutional group as an act of primary violence that creates the necessary field for the therapy and the individuals who are conditioned by the unconscious. This primary scene goes to form a fantasy that is forever present in the future of the institutional group (Kaës 2000).

The dual-faced dream: the witness

Sometimes dreams that carry out a special function can be observed in a group. These dreams reveal fantasies to do with its foundation or with later transitions. This type of dream seems to form part of a collective rite rather than evoke a representation according to the alpha function present in the individual mind, as Bion points out, or the gamma function present in the group mind (Corrao 1981). These dreams that take the group back to its earliest traditions and help to complete the transition towards a new period of change and a new identity could be described as dual-faced dreams. On one hand, the function of the dream is the representation that is directed towards the 'body' of the group and its most profound state, the place where the tradition is seen as a matrix or the primary scene exists.

On the other hand we have a situation where the dream's function is to portray and communicate with the outside. Both sides possess an active quality to them that more symbolic dreams don't have. The active or acting function is a causative element and tends to overshadow or elude the symbolic activity. It emerges with ease in the group due to its polysemous and multidimensional features, the simultaneity of its representations, and the need to construct and communicate common objects. The different phases of group events that appear to be ritual or inclined towards a collective 'action' (especially if they are represented by dreams) are not always empty of evolutive and emotive ideas or opposed to recognition; rather, they often indicate that change requires an extensive and ritualised scene to come about, a space that is explicitly dramatic, to enable coalescent and profound contents to fully articulate themselves.

In the group, I have observed that one or more witnesses sharing the experience of an event or confession is of immense importance in reorganising and giving new meanings to processes that otherwise would be slower and much more difficult. Consequently the dream assumes major significance when it is experienced as a collective rite or 'action' in the presence of witnesses.

I have also noted that these 'active' dreams, though maintaining a formal tie with the objects chosen for the representation, contain eccentric images and colours and frenetic movements, giving rise to unpredictable and enigmatic ideas.

The dream, the body

I would like to consider a sequence of oneiric events observed during a precise space of time. When the group dreams, different forms of 'acting' take place that are typical of that group in certain well-defined moments. It is as if it was driven or stimulated to act for different reasons, the most important of which is to exist, to be worthy of existing and to be capable of continuing.

I have often noted in the individual analysis that a patient dreams for the pleasure of exercising a function that is used for representing and communicating, and not simply for organising and communicating affective and mental contents. This vicarious function of dreaming is irreplaceable and is sought after for various reasons, the most common of which is to communicate physiological activities (for instance, urinating, perspiring, etc.). It is a representation of secretory characteristics and produces iconic aspects. The result of this type of dream could be complicated and difficult, but it manages to direct the contact and the experience towards the inner self (and above all towards the inner body). It facilitates a flow of linking elements in order to increase the consistency, the competence, and the cohesion of the different nuclei of the self – and in particular the corporeal self and its possibilities to be represented by the mind. I had a patient in therapy who seemed hysterical (as described by Freud); she had a split consciousness, and freely used schizoid defences. I found buried deep in her a nucleus of anorexia around which she had developed a long experience of attacks of panic and claustrophobia. (Ferrari (1994) states that the anorexic-bulimic syndrome as a somatisation in adolescents is part of a claustro/agoraphobic structure or organisation.)

These attacks, treated unsatisfactorily and without effect in the past, had left the patient in a situation fluctuating between somatic and psychic states.

The attacks affected her cardiopulmonary system, but it was a state where she felt really alive with a newly found capacity to communicate; all this had been denied to her in her childhood, where she had withdrawn onto her own 'private stage'.

Gradually I was able to grasp, in the long, theatrical and repetitive dreams that periodically appeared, a feature that represented 'panic attacks', thus enabling the dreamer to express conversations, feelings, and projected and introjected elements that she had experienced at the time of the schism. In my opinion, these 'panic attack dreams' were not represented symbolically to be shared with the analyst: their principal function was to reassure the dreamer that she existed, that she was not lacking in consistency and that she possessed a capacity of corporeal production, safely deposited at the analyst's rooms or with the analyst in person. This production seems to have origin in a precocious 'internal theatre' where the main characters referred to the negated body and its sensations, its functions and above all to its solitude. Dreaming, likened to a panic attack, only more contained and communicative, gave the patient a germinal solidity with the capacity to produce a sort of protective skin to defend herself from the analyst's words that often disturbed her. Moreover, this patient suffered from sporadic periods of deafness (she had suffered from otitis in childhood) that she used accordingly to vary her hearing on different planes and her corporeal and somatic presence in relation to the bond that she had with the analyst.

Returning to the dream in the group and the type of dream that can occur there, I believe that the aspect of the dream that could be likened to an action (or somatic action) goes to form a secret level in the oneiric plot, but it also could be the principal element of communication and behaviour in the group. Whatever the case, this aspect will return again and again until its specificity has been recognised, facilitating its transformation.

Drama and plot in the anorexic and bulimic group

In a group of young women all suffering from anorexic and bulimic disorders, in its fourth year of activity it was announced that a man would be joining in a short while. He did not suffer from the same symptomatology that characterised the group, although there were some aspects in his personality that were similar to the rest of the group. He was slightly older (over 30) and had had an individual experience with the group's analyst for some months prior to his entering the group (something the other participants had not done).

The dreams that I will refer to occurred in a period that lasted from the time I announced the arrival of the new participant until the entry of the group into a depressive elaboration three months later, requiring a difficult and painful working through, but at the same time structuring a new experiential field.

During this period the male presence was elaborated by the group as an attack against feminine identity and identity in general, resulting in a return to themes and moments in life which had been impossible to individuate before. Successively a sexual reaction emerged, fecundity and enthusiasm prevailed. Ultimately all the members of the group, including the young man, waged an attack against the possibility of having children, bringing to light mourning that possessed strong narcissistic characteristics.

The session following the announcement of the arrival of Giorgio, three patients had dreams to tell. These dreams were elaborated by the group, but it was clear from the start that their full meaning would gradually emerge in the future through successive elaboration, thus becoming milestones in the 'new situation' created in the group.

Sabina narrates that at an appointment at the gynaecologist's he found two *sarchiaponi* in her uterus, and it was necessary to remove them. The group worked around the sensation it had of being similar to a uterus that generated unwelcome babies, and intruding foreigners. And it recalled events of abortions and suicides, in particular of Sabina, rejected daughter of an unhappy marriage. At this point, Maria, the youngest of the group and fairly new (she had attended only three sessions) intervenes with the second dream.

She narrates that she was close to a baby's crib, and a dog was biting her head and hurting her. She noticed if she rocked her head backwards, the pain diminished and the dog was no longer a serious menace. The group interpreted that Maria was feeling threatened by the illness 'in her head', that she was in doubt whether to accept her presence in the group and that she had difficulty in accepting the new arrival. Perhaps it was better to go back, she wouldn't feel pain in her head. The rocking of her head backwards was interpreted as a retrogression (in the psychoanalytic process).

Giovanella responds on a different level. The threat that is burdening her is expressed in a dream that reveals the fear of not being able to use her usual defences any more. She has to do a locum, but when she arrives at the ward she is missing her identity card; she has to go home and get it, and then return.

This dream brings to light an old theme of Giovanella's regarding the decision to become a doctor. She tells of her father's frequent epileptic attacks when she was little. Then she unveils the fear of assuming the identity of a doctor that she does not feel is her own; she has a secret fantasy of taking over the analyst's role in conducting the therapy of the group, just like at home when she took over from her mother who she thought inadequate and whose time was fully taken up by her sick husband. The new arrival impelled her to reorganise her thoughts and feelings and to come to grips with her obesity and her femininity.

The following session Sabina recounts another dream about the gynaecologist. He located a Kalashnikov in her uterus, removed it, and treated her with gauze. At this point an affinity emerges between Sabina's dream and Maria who dreamt of the crib in danger. What the two shared was the experience of being undesired, aborted children. Maria tells us how she was born thanks to a policeman. He arrived in the operating theatre when her mother was about to have an illegal abortion. Afterwards she changed her mind and decided to have the child.

At this point, the group recognised the problem of the two unwanted and unjustly attacked children, and started to activate regenerating functions, expressed by the missing doctor's identity card that was promptly found (Giovanella's dream). But at the same time there was much bewilderment as to the risk of returning to this terrible situation, expressed by Maria's wish not to feel pain in the head any more (the dog biting her next to the crib). In my opinion, (a return to) the nuclear condition of anorexia and bulimia has to do with the anguish of the narcotic states of the mind. Narcotised with food seems to be the best and most possible way for the individual to endure the emptiness and loss experienced from early childhood.

The group recognises the treating of the wounds, and confidence begins to emerge; the figure of the policeman who saved Maria's life and her mother who ultimately desired the baby were appreciated. Also the figure of Giorgio started to acquire features that were sometimes magic (he was seen as a 'saviour' of the group) but closely controlled by the group; his identity was accepted (the ID card), and space was made for him to fit in.

Some weeks later, Sabina dreams she is giving birth and it is necessary to empty her bowels. She gets ready for this. The birth doesn't come about in the dream. Later on Sabina dreams that she gives birth to a beautiful baby. And after, Giorgio dreams that he calls his workmen to remove his belongings from his old girlfriend's house and take them to his new place.

During this whole period that lasted 12 weeks, the group fought to overcome a fear of dispersion and loss, and it became acquainted with the experience of hate, falseness and dependence. It strived to preserve a conscience that was capable of recognition and team spirit. Lastly, it learnt to recognise and accept the narcissistic anguish as a source of elaboration.

Two different points of view

At this point I would like to introduce some general considerations. Primarily, I noticed that importance was given to the manifest contents that were in dreams: for instance, the group reconstructed the dream regarding the hostility to the foreign body in the uterus, and the dramatic events leading to abortions and suicides, were also reconstructed.

In particular, in the first dream, the *sarchiapone* was seen as a very unfamiliar intruder, because it was an expression of a television culture belonging to the analyst and Sabina's parents (who were both actors), and not experienced directly by the dreamer. This fact seemed to point to a false self existing in Sabina, she willingly participated in film dubbing, and played small parts in films as a child. In addition, the word *sarchiapone* was not only imaginary but was created in an ambiguous situation between two persons who did not want to reveal their real identity, so they concealed themselves behind an indulgent verbal exchange, in a game of mounting reciprocal seduction, to hide their ignorance and incomprehension. Giorgio was seen as a sort of judge to whom facts were to be confessed and who had to be informed of all the essential information about the group.

Ethnic war was symbolised by the Russian machine gun, used in the war in Yugoslavia, the fear of being aborted was linked to the group's 'gynaeco-logical' notion of the dream, and the healing of the group was symbolised by the 'gynaecological medication' of the group's 'womb'. These elements associated with the injury of the self, the experience of being enclosed in a tight capsule, and with the annulment of the self, all became aspects of extremely violent but necessary communication. Necessary because tied to a theme that the group had been experiencing for a long time, torn between the anxiety of aggressive narcissism and the capacity to accept the distinc-tion, the diversity and the creation of something new. The group learnt to examine the different levels the dream had to offer.

In the end, when the scene of giving birth seemed to have been explored sufficiently, the group was able to face the idea of a transformation of its own corporeal image, expressed by the filling and emptying of its intestine, its digestive tract and its reproductive and sexual organs. During that period the group reminded me of children who collect stickers, swapping the doubles among themselves after school. The participants learnt to face the repetitive experiences that exist within the group, compared to the private and more corporeal experiences of the family where the games seem exclusive and unrepeatable. Information, memories, contacts, emotions, language, affects, experiences and thoughts were exchanged and 'swapped'. It was as if the discovery of the corporeal level of the dream along with its function and language was an occasion whereby the group developed a sort of tactile sense, the participants finally got to know each other, to confuse or distinguish each other, and to feel capable of existing.

On concluding the different points of view, I believe if these dreams were treated from a symbolic point of view and an objectivisation of the images with the relative sentiments that are linked to them was taken into account, I would have seen the aggressiveness directed towards new members of the group as an impediment to the creation of a common space even though it appeared as if there was a cosy atmosphere and a sense of solidarity. Perhaps having ideas and memories in common stimulated the group to be competitive on a narcissistic plane, and the emphasis on associations led to a false situation. Probably the extraneousness or the detachment provided form and contents to the common experience.

On the other hand, one could see that the group was not expressing a symbolic communication but was giving form to an overstimulation with predominantly somatic characteristics, as a response to the acting-out of the analyst who introduced the mysterious man, which in turn gave rise to acting-out that was deeply imbedded in the foundation of the group and in the stories of each of its members.

The dream, the corporeal self

I believe the function of the dream is to go straight to the inner self. Lichtenberg (1996) and Fosshage (1987) studied the dream in this light, seeing it as a way of providing the self with cohesion and vitality. When Sabina dreamed she did so in the name of the group, her intention being to give value and at the same time assure the group's specific characteristics of a long-lasting identity: relation with the body, the transgenerational family, and the political and cultural society are gathered in an enlarged group-space where their permanence is made possible. The temporal and semantic evolution of the corporeal and gynaecological repetitive dream provided the group with a longitudinal dimension, and a scansion that was constant. Moreover, it gave it a transformative signification that enabled the group to bear the 'wound' inflicted by the analyst (which almost caused a break up of the group).

At this point the discourse on the function of dreams could be widened to include other aspects to do with the therapeutic approach adopted in the group – for instance the possibility that acting-out aspects can develop and be transformed not only within the setting (Novelletto 1986). In his paper on the lacking of dreams and mythopoeia in the group, L. Zerbi Schwartz (1999) declares that the cause for this can be found wherever it is a question of absence, and she gives some examples:

- The physical absence of the therapist from the session.

- The absence of contents in the therapist's mind which she believes is caused by the tendency of the group to develop acting-out aspects.

- Behaviour e.g. arriving late, different actions, etc.

- The loss of active functions, like dreaming for instance.

The intermingling of these highly characterised elements with other active elements in the analytic process of groups is almost impossible to sort out without radically changing perspective. The perspective I use in this paper developed through many experiences of working in almost always homogeneous groups, composed of somatically or psychosomatically ill patients. It consists of an attempt to draw together or connect different levels of hearing and involvement, to favour the emerging of what Bion (1992) calls protomental elements (undifferentiated mental and somatic elements) in the analytic process of groups. The group dream is the most important way to get close to this state of 'confusion and distinction'. It provides us with paths to explore the fantasmic representation of somatic events that a group or an individual may have. Its appearance in the transference or in the group 'field' (as described by Neri 1998) can make possible the bringing together, or breaking apart of constellations of elements and functions of the body and the mind. So that when these elements become more comprehensible and shared by all, they can be utilised to resolve the pathological constraint, contributing to a process of responsibility and knowledge. In fact the construction of a field of elements that follow an illness (whether those elements didn't exist before the illness or whether they were hidden or damaged) cannot provide a sequential explanation for the reasons for that illness, but can tune them in onto a sequentiality that transforms them into experience. And so life and the dreams of the individual person and of the group go 'hand in hand', even when the dream is entrusted with the expression of the illness and its need to express itself, and even when life is in danger.

References

Abraham, N. and Torok, M. (1978) *L' écorce et le noyau.* Paris: Aubier Flammarion.

Bion, W.R. (1987) *Clinical Seminars and Four Papers.* London: Karnac Books.

Bion, W.R. (1992) *Cogitations.* London: Karnac Books.

Corrao, F. (1981) 'Struttura poliadica e funzione gamma.' *Gruppo e Funzione Analitica II*, 2.

Ferrari, A.B. (1994) *Adolescenza la seconda sfida.* Rome: Borla.

Fosshage, J. (1987) 'A revised psychoanalytic approach.' In J. Fosshage and C. Low. (ed) *Dream Interpretation: A Comparative Study.* Costa Mesa, CA: PMA Publications.

Kaës, R. (2000) *Le alleanze inconsce.* Lecture given at the faculty of Psychology, University of Rome. Published in *Funzione Gamma:* www.funzionegamma.edu

Lichtenberg, J.D. (1996) *The Clinical Exchange, Techniques Derived from Self and Motivational Systems.* Hillsdale, NJ: Analytic Press.

Neri, C. (1998) *Group.* London: Jessica Kingsley Publishers.

Novelletto, A. (1986) 'Clinical seminar at Italian Society for Psychoanalytic Psychotherapy.' In S. Marinelli (2000) *Sentire.* Rome: Borla.

Rouchy, J.C. (1998) *Le group, espace analytique.* Rome: Borla, 2000.

Tagliacozzo, R. (1993) An interview by S. Marinelli. *Metaxù 16.*

Zerbi Schwartz, L. (1999) 'Traumatic representations associated with separation. Acting as dreams that cannot be dreamed.' *Funzione Gamma 2.*

Endnotes

1. *Sarchiapone* derives from a television gag in the 1960s: two men on a train start up a conversation, one completely invents a word, the word *sarchiapone*, while the other pretends he understands its meaning and a hilarious conversation follows. Neither the word, its meaning or the object referred to exist.

CHAPTER 15

The Complementarity of Social Dreaming and Therapeutic Dreaming

W. Gordon Lawrence and Hanna Biran

The therapeutic dream and the social dream do not contradict each other. In this chapter we shall try to show the differences between these two types of dreams and point to their complementarity.

Dreaming and social dreaming

Dream-work and dreaming are indications of both the essence and absence of our human experience. Ever since humans had language they presumably were able to tell each other their dreams. Indeed the link between dreaming and language was indicated by E. F. Sharpe some sixty years ago who said that through the process of 'revealing the unknown implicit in the known' one can experience the growth of language. In particular, there is a growth 'of diction which has its roots in the infinite as well as the poetic'. The poet and the dreamer have the same task, which is to convey experience through language that is 'simple, sensuous and passionate (Milton)' (Sharpe 1937, p.18). Simile, metaphor and all the other figures of speech are essential to convey the dreamer's struggle in the immanent world of the day-to-day to give a sense of being in the transcendent world of the night. These figures of speech are ways whereby in common discourse we convey our sense of the infinite.

Furthermore, as Paul Lippmann expressed it, when dreaming we enter into a cultural experience when the culture's ways are being developed, tested, explored and reinforced in the deepest privacy of the dream (Lippmann 1998). Using the theory of quantum physics, it can be said that every atom of our body and mind contains at the sub-atomic level both waves and particles simultaneously. Every elemental event in neurophysiology is related to other elemental events as entities in the cosmos at large through waves and particles. Waves periodically collapse, coalesce or configure as particles. When it is in this form, it becomes a piece of information, a fragment of knowing, a shared experience of the infinite. We can have the working hypothesis that dream-work, which is continuous for 24–7–365 throughout our lives, is a wave function. When a dream emerges from the 'black hole of the psyche', to use Montague Ullman's evocative phrase (1975), it is a particle.

These ideas come after Freud's monumental discovery that dreams influence our daily life. Freud asked his publisher to issue his *The Interpretation of Dreams* in 1900. He knew the significance of his work. Not only did he show that dreams were at the core of our psychic life but that they also lay at the heart of our cultural tradition. Since then dreaming has become part of the repertoire of psychoanalysts, Jungian analytic psychologists, gestalt therapists and psychodrama. The flaw in Freud's thinking about dreaming was that he, and his immediate followers, concentrated on the content of the conversation between analyst and analysand, which led him into the decipherment of the latent embedded in the manifest content. They never saw that this conversation between analyst and analysand was a semiotic act and that, therefore, it was the process of the encounter that mattered. The encounter is composed of signs, signals, signifiers and symbols. It is about communication and about metacommunication, i.e. communication about communication.

Social dreaming concentrates on the dream and not the dreamer. The latter is the work of therapeutic dreaming. Our working hypothesis is that social dreaming and therapeutic dreaming are in a state of complementarity. Each has its domain, each its methodology. Whereas therapeutic dreaming has Oedipal concerns as its focus, social dreaming has the work of expanding the meaning of sphinx, i.e. thinking, knowing, arriving at consciousness, and scientific knowledge. Bion in his introduction to *Experiences in Groups* (1961) indicated this distinction. Whereas therapeutic dreaming focuses on the egocentricity of the analysand, social dreaming keeps the sociocentric concerns of the participants in mind.

Social dreaming has a short history but belongs to a tradition probably as old as humanity itself. The process of the discovery of social dreaming has been well enough rehearsed (Lawrence 1998), but the key evidence that led to the formulation of social dreaming was gathered through a reading of Charlotte Beradt's *The Third Reich of Dreams* (1968). Charlotte Beradt collected during the Third Reich dreams of Jewish citizens in Germany. Through a network of doctors, whom she asked to elicit dreams in the course of their diagnoses of patients, she was able to piece together the dreams that they were dreaming but could not give voice to. What emerges is a horrific story. People dreamt of the fate that was to befall them. While in daily life they thought they could resist, their dreams told them otherwise. This was clear example that dreaming and dreams can voice concerns of a social nature. The dreamers dreamt dreams that were way beyond narcissistic concerns and were speaking to what was happening to them socially in the culture of the society.

Social dreaming takes place in a matrix. The purpose, or primary task, offered to the participants in the matrix is: to associate to one's own and others' dreams as they are made available to the matrix so as to make links and find connections. Usually the matrix opens with one of the 'takers' of the matrix introducing the task and his/her colleagues. Participants are invited to offer their dreams. This dream sharing happens quickly and, after a time, someone will give associations and make links.

The idea of 'free association', that Freud introduced, is essential to the work of the matrix. Free association is the most subversive of activities and disrupts the consensual, rational, finite, logical reality to which most people subscribe. As such, it is always expanding the space of the possible. Dreaming is always introducing the dreamer to the tension between consciousness and the unconscious, the known and the unknown or the finite and the infinite. We are conscious of the infinite as a mental space that contains all that has ever been thought and ever will be thought in the cosmos. All thinking begins from a 'no-thought', from an absence. As human beings we make thought present from first recognising that it is not there.

The idea that people could dream 'socially' was first put forward at the first Social Dreaming Programme held at the Tavistock Institute in 1982. There were no dreams that were clearly personal. This was a startling, but nevertheless anticipated, discovery. It was found in the first programme that the idea of having the social dreamers convene in a matrix was a fortuitous insight, which was made by a then colleague Patricia Daniel. 'Matrix' is a place out of which something grows but it also refers to the network of 'all individual mental processes' (Foulkes and Anthony 1957, p.26). There is a sense of the most primordial of communication including feelings and nonverbal cues. The thinking was that if the social dreamers were convened in a group, the work would be obfuscated by the penumbra of associations to the concept of 'group'. It was felt that dreaming and dreams were to be the currency of the matrix and not the relationships of the participants. The value of this fortuitous intuition became clear when issues of transference and counter-transference were voiced. The reasoning was that if transference issues were addressed directly in the here and now of the matrix, the dreaming would be robbed of this material. In actuality, once transference issues are voiced in a dream any participant can point to them. It is not the transference to the takers of the matrix that is important but rather to authority figures in-the-mind that are given flesh in the dreams. ('Takers' was chosen as the name for the convenors of the matrix in preference to 'consultants'.)

The differences between the two forms of dreaming

As has been implied, in a social dreaming matrix (SDM) dream follows dream and association. A therapeutic group (TG) is usually small, about ten people, and is led by one or two therapists. The SDM may include as many as 40 people, and be led by one to four takers.

We may distinguish clearly between the therapeutic dream and the social dream by adopting Bion's term 'reversible perspective' (Bion 1963, pp.54–9). When Bion looks at a certain material, he emphasises that the materials of the mind, the group, the organisation and so on, are by nature three-dimensional, and there is no possibility of viewing them in their entirety. Every picture has its background; every centre has its margins; every text has its context. These pictures are not static, but rather are in constant motion. In fact, we, as viewers, choose the picture. We can always reverse the perspective, changing the figure for the ground and vice versa.

The TG would look at the dream mainly from the perspective of Oedipus, attempting to decipher the dream's components as shedding light on the personal drama of the dreamer. In the SDM we would look at the dream mainly from the perspective of the sphinx, as telling something about society, culture, humanity and the world in which we live. Still, one perspective does not rule out the other. In the TG Oedipus is the figure and the sphinx is the ground. In the SDM sphinx is the figure and Oedipus is the ground. What was the context in the therapeutic group becomes the text in the SDM.

The existence of the reversible perspective allows us an infinite play with diverse pictures. Thus we may look at the world not as a dichotomy, but as being in complementarity, constantly developing. In order to clarify the distinction, we may add that through the shifting of the focus from Oedipus to sphinx, the therapeutic dream and the social dream complement each other. To set out the distinctions:

The therapeutic dream (TG)	*The social dream (SDM)*
The dreamer is in the centre	The dream is in the centre
The individual aspect	The social aspect
Profound exploration of the past	Looking to the future
Dramatising the personal biography	Facing life as a tragedy
Oedipus	Sphinx
Egocentric	Sociocentric
Finite	Infinite

In order to demonstrate the different perspectives, we shall introduce a dream that was told in the SDM during the International Association for Group Psychotherapy (IAGP) convention in Jerusalem, August 2000. The dreamer was an observant Jewish woman, who lives in a settlement in the Occupied Territories. Once the peace process is complete, it is possible that the residents of the settlements will have to leave their homes and move to communities inside Israel. The dreamer said it was the first time she had such a dream, and that she woke up from it in terror. This was the dream as she narrated it:

> I'm driving my car on the way to visit my two sons who live near Haifa. I'm driving up a hill. On the way I meet my two other children who live elsewhere. I realize my family is scattered in different places around the country. I'm telling my two sons: don't keep on going because we will not reach Haifa. The Sabbath is about to begin and I will not ride the car on the Sabbath. My children show me a caravan near the road, and I decide to

spend the Sabbath there. The children ease my mind, telling me everything's fine. But I keep thinking how come two of my children are here and
two are there? I'm asking myself where am I, what happened to my home,
why am I not at home? I woke up with the question: Where is our home?

Had this dream been told in a TG, the focus of the discussion would have
been the dreamer's private life, her relations with her family members, or the
experience of being uprooted from her permanent home as part of her
personal history. The therapist would have explored what is fragile in her
inner world at the moment, and how she is preparing for the changes in her
life. The therapeutic thinking would have revolved around strengthening her
ego for the sake of facing the expected changes, and so on.

The social dream looks at the same material from a different perspective.
The participants introduced their free associations regarding the images in
the dream. The material which appeared in the associations had to do with
the human experience of uprooting, the fear of losing a home, the fear of a
family breaking up, human life being transient and unstable. The dream
brought up other dreams which had to do with family, generations, roots,
belonging, security, emigration, movement from place to place, unexpected
changes in a familiar scenery, refugees, survival and so on. The individual's
dream is no longer a private property, but rather turns into a representation of
human fate, the unknown, the insecure. The context of the dreamer's life
becomes the text of the matrix.

Discussing the dream again following the SDM we discovered that
additional perspectives are reflected in it. The dream is like one piece of a
jigsaw puzzle containing a multidimensional world. In fact, there are at least
three additional ways for looking at the social strata of the dream:

1. If we focus on the perspective of the sphinx, we may find a message
    for the future in the caravan scene. The dream is saying something
    about things still outside our field of vision. It is saying something
    about the changing, evolving world, about what will become. For
    example, living in a caravan may hint at transience, at a world of
    easy mobility, even at the nature of surfing the Internet. It seems
    that the human psyche will have to adapt to more and more
    impermanent situations, which will span shorter periods of time.
    There is something in this dream which stops the familiar and
    stable life routines, and although the change is experienced as
    catastrophic, it also contains some message for a future way of life,

for a world which will have fewer roots and more exposure to temporary structures.

2.   Another way of using the reversal perspective is to look at the dreamer as saying something that is going to happen to the Jewish settlers, something that raises alarm and concern in her society. But paradoxically, at the same time, this dream also recalls what happened in reality to the Palestinian people. It is like a mirror image pointing at the fate of the refugees who left their land and spent long years in camps and in temporary houses. The dreamer dreams that which had already happened to the other people: the breaking up of families, the exile from the land, and so on. If we look at this dream as shedding light on one half of the picture, while the other half remains in the dark, we may experience also some of the human tragedy of the other. It seems that this is a good example for the multidimensional aspect of the dream. We may not perceive all the dimensions, all the perspectives, but only a small part of the infinity reflected in the dream.

3.   There is a third perspective where a pattern can be seen to the dreams in a matrix, but usually seen with hindsight. This is the metacommunication of the dreams, i.e. communication about communication. Currently, in October 2000, the events in Israel are terrifying because for the first time the Jewish Israeli population is being attacked by the Arab Israeli population, and Jewish Israelis are seen as retaliating with much more sophisticated weapons. This means that the Arabs who live in the cities and villages of Israel and who have Israeli citizenship are now joining in spirit the Palestinians who live in the Territories. Former neighbours and places are becoming hostile and threatening, so 'Where is home?'

Working with the Israel Defence Forces (IDF) on the day before the SDM in Jerusalem, a short SDM was convened. Three vignettes of dreams were recalled. (a) 'I came back to the neighbourhood of my childhood. I visited the places in which I played and had fun with my friends. But in my dream there was no fun. I felt terrified. The familiar place was not familiar any longer.' (b) 'I visited my grandmother's home, a kind of visit that I like very much, but when I was inside her house a group of people tried to enter the house and hurt us. We hid. We were very frightened and we had been waiting for an opportunity to escape.' (c) 'I'm running and running and running but my feet stay in the same place and I'm making no progress. I feel my feet are petrified. A group of strangers follows me. They are going to kill me.'

We have not seen the significance of these dreams until now when the horrendous events in Israel have occurred. We ask ourselves if the Israelis of the IDF were dreaming events before they actually happened.

While the SDM was taking place in Jerusalem, there was an extraordinary exhibition of the work of Chihuly in the Tower of David. Chihuly is a glass-blower of enormous ingenuity. The whole of the Tower of David was devoted to his work. The Tower had been transformed into a wonderland of glass trees, monumental works of sculpture and smaller artefacts of stunning beauty. Multicoloured spears of glass flourished on terraces, glass balls were tucked into spaces in the Tower. Because it was all made of glass, the feeling was that it could all be smashed and so the exhibition was of a fragile, transient beauty.

Now, a few weeks after this event, Israelis and Palestinians are fighting around this ancient area of Jerusalem while their leaders are being cajoled by the Western powers to make peace. At its simplest, the issue is about 'Where is home?' The experiences of SDM point to the dreadful fact that no amount of rational argument will bring lasting peace until the primordial fears and anxieties expressed in dreams are addressed.

During the same seminar we held for organisational consultants in the IDF a day before the SDM in Jerusalem, one of the consultants narrated a dream in which he was playing a bizarre game. In the dream one of his eyes was made of plastic or rubber, and he would take it out, play with it and put it back in. This dream is connected by association to one eye which sees and another which lacks the visual function. It is a story about the limitation of vision, about the half of the picture that remains in the dark. This dream has also a therapeutic value. Had it been told at a therapeutic group, the group would have engaged with the Oedipal aspect of punishment and castration, with the parts of the dreamer's life which he cannot see at this moment, with the nature of the pain which in the dream he turned into play, and so on.

Simultaneously, from the perspective of the sphinx, the dream is telling something about the limitations of organisational consultancy. The sphinx may be warning the consultant against the sin of hubris, reminding him of the limitations of his vision and of the parts in him which are blind. From the point of view of the sphinx, we should explore the relations and ties between the consultants on the one hand, and the IDF as a system on the other. From a systemic point of view it should be assumed that there are parts in the system which attack the consultant's vision, devaluate the role of the consultant and turn the consulting eye into an artificial and useless organ.

Therapeutic dreaming and social dreaming as two different states of mind

People who are accustomed to clinical thinking, and who throughout their life underwent training, schooling and socialisation to become therapists, sometimes find it difficult to enter the world of social dreaming. They tend to confuse the SDM with group relation or group therapy. They enter the space of the social dream equipped with the tools of therapists. Occasionally this equipment becomes a burden, like an armour which makes it difficult for them to free-float in a different world. This causes misunderstandings, resistance and difficulty in assuming the role of a member in the SDM. A certain amount of forgetting that which is known is required in order to enter the SDM, because the known prevents us from seeing the unknown.

In order to play, in the Winnicottian sense, in the SDM, to be a curious voyager and an open-minded explorer in it, one has to enter a non-therapeutic state of mind, to free oneself of the therapeutic thinking, entering a mode of thinking devoid of concepts or theoretical models. While as therapists we are required to interpret, in the world of the SDM the focus is on associations rather than on interpretations. It is not easy to enter the state of mind of a child who explores the world for the first time, or of the voyager who discovers new lands, especially for experienced and knowledgeable therapists and psychoanalysts.

The same tools that are essential at the clinic may block the way to the social dreaming. At the clinic, a substantial part of the time is dedicated to diagnosis. We want to apply names to things. We wish to be accurate, and have a very narrow margin for error. We view the patients close up and try to place in front of them a mirror which will reflect their lives. The aim is to focus the picture in order to determine the direction in the therapeutic work. Also as patients we wish for clarity, wanting to understand ourselves better and more clearly.

In the SDM we enter a different kind of voyage. Every dream is a clear picture that goes out of focus by the introduction of the next dream. We do not wish to collect all the elements and discover one central meaning. On the contrary: the dreams are like elements which scatter through space, creating a dynamic collage. The dream is not given a name or a definition, but is sent to float in an open, infinite space. Each participant floats his or her dream in the

SDM space. The floating dream collides with other dreams. Free associations create links between the dreams, creating new meanings. The floated dream returns to the dreamer through somebody else's dream.

It is a different kind of dialogue. While in the therapeutic dialogue the wish is to maintain a sequence, to react in a continuous and sequential way, the dialogue at the SDM is of a synchronous nature. A person may narrate a dream and meet with no response. But after his dream has been floating through the SDM space for a while it vibrates through other dreams, returning in a different guise or on a different path. The dialogue takes place among the dreams, while the free associations serve as a kind of chain, stringing the dreams.

In the TG, dreams are explored in a protected environment. Free associations by the group's members are used at the therapeutic group too, but these associations are used in the service of the ego of the dreamer. Their aim is to shed light on the dreamer's life. The exploration would strive to focus on family history and biography.

A certain capacity for getting lost is required in the SDM. One has to leave one's familiar home and environment, and depart from any protective figures. This is an experience both wonderful and frightening. It can be creative and intriguing, but also brings one close to the fear of going mad, of losing one's sanity. An internal freedom is required in order to contain the fear and to manoeuvre in the infinite world of dreams.

In the SDM in Jerusalem, which lasted for four days, it was possible to discern the gradual build-up of the freedom to meet with the cosmic experience. In the first stages, much attention was given to the burdening connotation of Jerusalem. Later, attention was given to names: names of figures known from the past, names with historical connotations. The history of the religions and the holy sites was also dealt with, as well as meetings with families and previous generations. Gradually more dreams started to emerge, concerning surprising changes in familiar sceneries, multidimensional perspective, the ability to float, to hover, to stand alone facing nature.

The capacity to dream, to remember dreams and to narrate them is connected with the ability to lose control. In the SDM, an even greater capacity for losing control is required. Neither the participants nor the SDM takers have any control over the nature of dreams, their length, the pace of their emergence and so on. There has to be a willingness to absorb what is possible, to not remember everything, to not know everything and to not wish to understand everything. There has to be an ability to pick up what one meets along the way. This is the kind of trip taken by the accidental tourist, who is a passer-by through the infinite space of dreams. It is a state of mind similar to that of *Alice in Alice's Adventures in Wonderland*. Alice is constantly being surprised. Her adventures trespass all the boundaries of logic. In order to enter Wonderland she has to leave her familiar home and enter a new world, where perspectives and rhythms constantly change from one minute to the next. The book's great strength has to do with its ability to surprise, as well as introduce well-known objects into unexpected contexts.

In the TG, the dreamer has a sense of ownership or possession over his or her dream. The dream always sheds light on aspects that exist in the group, but first and foremost it belongs to the dreamer and to his inner world. The SDM invites the participants to deposit their dreams in the matrix or donate them to it. The matrix is not owned by anyone, and it exists while constantly changing.

In some of the dreams and the associations on the dreams at the SDM in Jerusalem it was possible to discern the wish to leave a personal mark, to own the dream privately or to feel that the dream is a private territory or personal property. This tendency was diametrical to the other tendency, which also appeared: the tendency to let go, to recognise necessary losses as well as our mortal personal existence.

The difficulty to let go of a personal dream in favour of the matrix reflects also the context in which the SDM was taking place within the tragic aspect symbolised by Jerusalem. It is a place where war over territory had caused much suffering, and the wish for ownership continues to cause violence and bloodshed. At the place where the wish for ownership dominates, there is no thinking, no dialogue and no transformation.

In this sense the SDM itself is a link between the individual's world and the social unconscious. Through the matrix it is possible to view the social context and the ways by which this context can oppress, limit or generally influence the individual's life. In the transfer from therapeutic dreaming to social dreaming a change must occur in the state of mind of the participant. It is necessary to let go of the need to probe deeply with each dreamer, of the wish to be in the centre, of the need to be a patient as well as of the need to be a therapist. This kind of transfer requires a different kind of partnership, and a different kind of alliance than the therapeutic alliance.

The paradox

In our contemporary world it is no longer possible to separate clearly disciplines and methodologies. Therefore, the boundaries between what is therapeutic and what is social are blurred. It is important to remember that two different applications of the world of dreams are discussed here, but also that interrelations and mutual influences between the therapeutic dream and the social dream are unavoidable. At the therapeutic group it is possible to find many elements of learning and growth which are free of the connotation of clinical pain. At the SDM it is possible to find elements of personal pain and unsolved personal dilemmas.

We may say, then, that we live in a socio-therapeutic world. Paradoxically, participation at an SDM may have a therapeutic effect. For example, when an individual is too closely locked within his or her personal drama, their psyche is not being aired and it meets again and again with the same elements. Such a person is sentenced to repetition compulsion. He or she might suffocate in a kind of mental prison containing materials which turn poisonous and destructive. At the SDM there is freedom from delving into the biographical details, allowing an exit from the self and a return on a different path. Since the SDM is an open system, a person may make contact with the world which is beyond the individual. The contact with the outside may lead to creativity and growth. The SDM constitutes a bridge, allowing access to the tragic position (Symington 1986) and to the transcendent position (Grotstein 1997). These are both spiritual positions which offer further reconciliation, greater tranquility and more freedom. Grotstein speaks of the ability to be an 'orphan of the real', which is a state similar to 'becoming O' (Bion 1970). It is a position in which a person gets to be one's own son, reaching an internal freedom, free of authoritative figures and pressures of the establishment. There emerged in the Jerusalem SDM a dream about snorkelling, followed by a participant's association who said a fish does not see the water. Another participant responded by saying that we don't see the air. Human fate determines that we shall always have blind spots, even regarding that which is obvious.

It seems that the SDM has a therapeutic value, even if it does not have a therapeutic aim. The richness of perspectives, dimensions and associations helps the individual to let go of control, of being in the centre, of ownership. The meeting with the SDM helps with recognising the fact that human thinking is constantly in the state of becoming and that this process is infinite.

If we look at Bion's ideas on dreaming through the metaphor of the cosmos, it would seem that there exist layer upon layer of beta elements, still waiting to be transformed into alpha functions, allowing further and further developments of thinking. These hypotheses Bion suggested that others could fill out with the evidence. Alpha functions operate on the sense impressions and the emotions but beta elements are undigested facts and remain so. If the alpha functions can be transformed into elements, they are available for thinking. If not, they become beta elements.

Howard Bloom (2000) ties down these hypotheses in a quite brilliant way. He writes of the global brain. Using evidence from a wide range of disciplines he convinces us that every living being in the cosmos is in communication with each other. He points to living beings using the information that is stored in the universe. Humans are no exception. Bion intuited this idea of information in the universe and showed how it could become thought. If, as Bion (1967, p.165) says, there are thoughts in search of a thinker, so we can argue that there are dreams in search of a dreamer. Although they are personal, subjective experiences which are dreamt, when voiced they can be of a social nature as well as a personal one.

References

Beradt, C. (1968) *The Third Reich of Dreams*. Chicago: Quadrangle Books.

Bion, W.R. (1961) *Experiences in Groups*. London: Tavistock Publications.

Bion, W.R. (1963) *Elements of Psychoanalysis*. London: Karnac Books, 1989.

Bion, W.R. (1967) *Second Thoughts*. London: Maresfield Reprints.

Bion, W.R. (1970) *Attention and Interpretation*. London: Tavistock Publications.

Bloom, H. (2000) *Global Brain*. New York: Wiley & Sons.

Foulkes, S.H. and Anthony, E.J. (1957) *Group Psychotherapy: The Psycho-analytic Approach*. Harmondsworth: Penguin; London: Karnac Books, 1984.

Freud, S. (1900) *The Interpretation of Dreams*. Oxford: Oxford University Press, 1999.

Grotstein, J. (1997) 'Bion's Transformation in O and the Concept of the Transcendent Position.' Lecture at Bion's Centenary Conference, Turin.

Lawrence, W.G. (1998) *Social Dreaming @ Work*. London: Karnac Books.

Lippmann, P. (1998) 'On the private and social nature of dreams.' *Contemporary Psychoanalysis 34*, 2, 195–221.

Sharpe, E.F. (1937) *Dream Analysis*. London: Hogarth Press.

Symington, N. (1986) *The Analytic Experience*. New York: St. Martin's Press.

Ullman, M. (1975) 'The transformation process in dreams.' *The American Academy of Psychoanalysis 19*, 2, 8–10.

CHAPTER 16

The Oneirodrama Group

The Therapeutic and the Supervisory Process of a Dream Drama Group

Ioannis K. Tsegos and Marianna Tseberlidou

Keep your dreams to yourself in case one cold night the psychoanalysts seize power.

Stanislav Jerzy Lec (1909–1966)

In this chapter we describe the procedures of conducting and also of supervising the work of a dream drama (oneirodrama) group taking place within a therapeutic community milieu, in the premises of the Open Psychotherapy Centre (OPC).[1] Besides the descriptions a short account is provided regarding the way we approach the nature of dreaming and also the way we use the dream in psychotherapy, which seeks recreation rather than insight. The same approach is applied for the supervisory procedure where the apprentice (student) is confronted as a vehicle (carrier) of an original material which has been used already with a more or less creative approach; this material the supervision group is going to treat, again, with a recreational method in order to promote learning through creative forms. In other words this approach is not so much scientific as artistic in intent. It is worth noting that the oneirodrama group, the supervising groups, the therapeutic communities and all the training activities of the OPC are conducted within a group and are group-analytic.

The identity of the oneirodrama group

The oneirodrama group was started in February 1993 by Marianna Tseberlidou within the context of the fortnightly psychotherapeutic community. Since then the membership of the group and also the coordinating staff have changed quite a lot, as is customary with all the community's groups. The conductor is an experienced member of the staff or an experienced student and the co-conductors (one or two) are students. There is also a continuous mobility in this group, as with all the sociodynamic groups, in order to give more students the opportunity for clinical experience. In the nine years of the group, four conductors have run the group and about nine students have participated as co-conductors. As regards patients, about 35 people have participated covering almost the whole range of diagnostic categories with a prevalence of psychotics and borderlines. Entrance into the group comes about after a suggestion of the staff or after a patient's initiative; there are no specific criteria apart from the availability of space.

The group meets every second Friday of the month, from 4.30 to 6.00 pm. Sexual relationships and violence are not allowed among the members nor meeting outside the Centre's premises. The content of each session is of course confidential as it belongs to the group and to its members; consistency and punctuality are required. Work is allowed to tail off over four sessions.

The main characteristics of this group are the enactment of the content of dreams and a playful attitude towards them. The session begins with a short general discussion about the group and a reporting of dreams followed by an agreement regarding the one that will be acted through. The dreamer decides his or her role in the enactment which may be different from the one he had in the dream, and does the casting among the members, if they are willing, as it is not necessary for all the members of the group to participate. The story may be enacted more or less following the narration, or small or large changes may be made in advance. There may even be spontaneous changes during the enactment according to actors' inspirations.

The actors go to the usual part of the room, where the imaginary stage is, following the group analytic psychodrama procedure (Papadakis 1984) (see Figure 1). After the acting through is completed, the group sits down again in a circle and discusses the action on the stage, the actors' and the audience's feelings, and their difficulties or distress.

People who do not remember their dreams or hesitate to reveal them can participate through playing into others' dreams. If no dream is offered by the

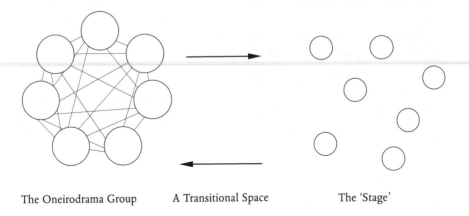

The Oneirodrama Group   A Transitional Space   The 'Stage'

Figure 1 The interchange between group process and stage action (After Papadakis, 1984)

members, the group therapist or the co-therapist may provide a dream of his or her own.

Interpretations of dreams are rarely offered in the group, as it is the feelings that take most of the attention. These may be related to the content of the dream or may emerge during or after the enactment, and they may be related to the group's life or to relationships of the dreamer or the actors, either among themselves or with people outside the group.

This group is a specific application of the group analytic psychodrama, with the same contract, structure and boundaries but with a content coming mainly from the world of dreams. The oneirodrama group, like the group analytic psychodrama, does not use a double or auxiliary ego; it is a kind of free verbal sculpting of a dream theme by the group as narrated by the dreamer.

Warming up

At the beginning of the session the free-floating discussion and the narration of the member's dream usually bring up memories or feelings of similar dreams from the other members and the therapists. The dreams of the previous two weeks remembered by each member are offered to the group in order to choose the ones to be acted.

The chosen dream is briefly narrated again by the dreamer who temporarily becomes the stage manager and decides whether the dream should have the same ending or plot, who is going to play whom or what (persons, objects or animals), who will be the protagonist (if the dreamer prefers to be in the audience). Not infrequently the plot of the dream may change even during the action. Occasionally members may refuse the role assigned to them by the manager and sometimes the group may urge the therapist to become protagonist, when they feel that the specific role would have a crucial impact on the dreamer's attitude towards therapy; nevertheless no one is obliged to act against his/her will.

Enactment

Actors go to the specific area of the room denoted as the stage, while the audience sits in a semicircle. If the therapists are not acting in the dream, they may help the dreamer with the initial arrangements, if needed, define the duration of enactment in case that another performance is going to take place and then they join the rest of the audience. Dreams requiring a large cast can be enacted without audience. Occasionally, though infrequently, a member of the audience may participate spontaneously during the enactment, even acting a self-invented role, provided that he/she announces the role. The scenario and the roles do not always follow the dreamer's narration; they also depend on the actors' feelings, attitudes or inspirations.

Return to the group

Discussion follows the enactment and usually the first to talk is the stage manager and the actors. They express their feelings, difficulties and needs, and explain to the others what urged them to alter the scenario or the role, or what impulse made them go onto the stage. They also ask the stage manager if they performed according to the dream. The audience contributes to the discussion with their own observations, thoughts and feelings. Without using the term, the group is always aware if catharsis occurred through the performance; if not, they ask for a new enactment of the same dream, using role reversal, a different protagonist or new actors. As an example we refer to a member's dream. In her dream, her mentally ill mother had again made, for the umpteenth time, a suicide attempt, and she was informed by phone, in the middle of the night, that this time her mother's attempt was successful. When she went to see the body she was surrounded by all her relatives. During the enactment of the last part when the relatives are around, a member of the audience comes on stage, announcing that she is a doctor and insisting that the mother is not dead. Though all the actors, including the protagonist, tried to persuade her about the fatal fact, she was so persistent that the actors ended the performance with the mother alive!

The whole group was very angry with this sudden change of the scenario. When the performance was discussed later, the 'doctor' admitted that she was unable to accept the fact that things would end that way and that she would always try for a happy ending. This difficulty had caused serious complications in her relationships and explained her constant 'happy ending' attitude in the group's previous sessions. The group accused her of depriving them of the relief given by the mother's death, and the dreamer and protagonist confessed that, in reality, she thought of what a relief it would be for her if her mother had died.

New members in the group usually try to follow only the exact instructions and do not rely on their own feelings; so during the first sessions they feel quite confused when they are playing a role; frequently, they turn to the audience asking what to do next. They try to interpret their own or others' dreams, according to previous knowledge, or stereotypes derived from books on psychology, psychoanalysis, etc. However the non-interpreting culture of the group, combined with the revelation of one's own feelings, provides a hard but also fascinating experience, since the enactment is usually connected with personal reactions and attitudes, and provides unexpected insights into one's own behaviour.

Though each dream appears initially as a property of the dreamer, through the group's free imaginative and physical participation, it is converted into a property of the group. The interweaving of feelings, problems, conflicts, projections, aspirations, attitudes and so on in the short period of the performance constitutes an exclusive 'dream book' for each member and for the group. This 'book' will be expanded and revised in the following sessions.

The idiosyncracies of the supervising group

Supervision of any group work in the OPC is conducted according to a model developed in the Institute of Group Analysis (IGA) Athens, quite satisfactorily since 1983 (a full description of the model is published in Tsegos 1995). The supervision of the oneirodrama group sessions follows these procedures and it includes a description of the enactment and also the discussion before and after. The supervision procedure can be divided into three stages: the Presentation, the Analysis and the Synthesis (Figure 2).

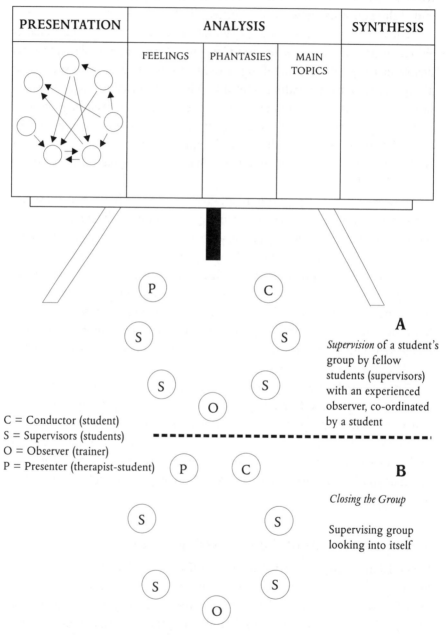

PRESENTATION	ANALYSIS			SYNTHESIS
	FEELINGS	PHANTASIES	MAIN TOPICS	

C = Conductor (student)
S = Supervisors (students)
O = Observer (trainer)
P = Presenter (therapist-student)

A

Supervision of a student's group by fellow students (supervisors) with an experienced observer, co-ordinated by a student

B

Closing the Group

Supervising group looking into itself

Figure 2: Two phases of peer supervision²

During the Presentation stage, an oneirodrama group session is presented in the usual way with the student-therapist reading out his or her notes while marking the group exchanges on the blackboard.

According to this model the supervisory procedure is now undertaken by the whole supervising group which is a group in its own right, with a fixed time and place of meeting, conducted by one of the students, while the trainer (or supervisor in the old sense) is present only as an experienced observer.

The supervising group sits in a semicircle in front of the blackboard and is expected to take an active part in the second stage of supervision. This is the Analysis, which follows the Presentation stage. During the Analysis each of the supervisor-students follows the presentation procedure and records in a special format (the supervision protocol, see below) his or her feelings during or after the presentation, and fantasies (images that passed through the mind during the presentation). Whatever is perceived as impressive or important or strange is regarded as suitable for the column of the main themes or topics of the oneirodrama group.

After the presentation, when all the students have written down their fantasies, feelings and main topics, the conductor-student asks each member of the supervising group to read out their notes which the presenter records on the blackboard.

The final stage is the Synthesis of all this material, in which the whole group takes part, including the experienced observer, and they try to connect the material that has been presented with that produced in the supervising group as it is recorded on the blackboard. Finally, there may be some suggestions concerning practicalities of conducting or the way that the conductors have handled the dream material, the cast's enactment or any other thoughts or comments.

At times the supervising group may give evidence that it is blocked within itself or that it is not productive, or that there is something going on in relation to the material offered by the supervising group during the Analysis stage. Such occurrences usually arise as a repercussion of mirroring or resonance phenomena coming from the presented group, or indeed because something is going on in the supervising group.

If this is not noticed by the supervising group, or if it is avoided or denied, then, and only then, is it time for the experienced observer to ask if there is something missing or going on and to suggest that there may be a need for the group to 'close the circle' and look at itself (Figure 2B). In this case the presenting student sits down, the circle is closed and the whole group is involved in a 'here and now' situation.

The whole procedure can be clarified further by examining the supervision protocol itself (Figure 3).

A SUPERVISION PROTOCOL

1. Supervisory session of the . . year students
2. Present members of the supervisory group:

3. Absences :
4. Conductor's Name:

	Presented Group	Supervisory Group
P R E S E N T A T I O N	5. *Type of Group* Group analytic ☐ Experiential ☐ Sociotherapeutic ☐ Psychodrama ☐ Oneirodrama Group ☐ 6. *Therapist* (Presenter): Co-therapist (Presenter): 7. *Date of Session:* 8. *Location:* 9. *Time:* 10. *Frequency:* 11. *Absences:*	13. *Conductor* (student) 14. *Observer:* (trainer) 15. *Location:* 16. *Date:* 17. *Time:* 18. *Additional Information*

	19. FEELINGS	20. FANTASIES	21. THEMES-TOPICS
A N A L Y S I S			

| S Y N T H E S I S | 21. Comments and Conclusions:

22. Was there any need to «close the circle»?   YES ☐   NO ☐

23. Who intervened ?   Conductor ☐   Observer ☐   Supervisor-students ☐ |

Figure 3 The Supervision Protocol [3]

A sample oneirodrama group session

The atmosphere in the group is quite tense as it is the first session with a new therapist, Claudia,[4] who until now was the co-therapist; the old therapist (Larisa) left the group at this session, after a period of two months. Shortly before the beginning of this session, one of the members of the group, who was very dependent on the previous therapist, left a phone message saying she was quitting the group.

The session starts with three empty chairs. The discussion refers to the missing members as well as to the missing conductor. Some members express their feeling of security in the presence of the new conductor.

All the members present are females and they wonder about the delay of the only two males. The therapist makes no comment and instead asks if anybody had a dream. Two members narrate their dreams:

1. A quarrel in a shop for a T-shirt

Phaedra, in her dream, went shopping with Andromache, another member of the group. In a shop she picked out a very nice T-shirt, but Andromache liked it too. They began to quarrel about it, because it was the only one left in that colour.

2. Fear of flying

Electra, who is known to be afraid of flying, dreamed – but she remembers her dream only vaguely – that she was traveling on an aeroplane.

A FLIGHT TO PARIS FOR SHOPPING

A member suggests, and the group decides, to combine the two dreams: the 'fashion-victim' women would go shopping to Paris on a plane accompanied by Electra and other members as passengers. Just before the enactment, one of the male members (Hermes) enters the room; he apologises and explains that he has been at a job interview. The group repeats to him briefly the scenario and he comes forward to play the role of the pilot.

During the enactment the other male member (Diogenes) enters the room. The therapist (Claudia) nods to him to remain in the audience, but after a while Diogenes decides to join the action, and goes to the stage proclaiming himself as the second pilot. The passengers explain that they already have one, but he insists and takes the role of the captain. In a while he announces that one of the engines is broken. Claudia (who is Italian) asks him to try to land the aeroplane in Milan, so they can do their shopping there. He pays no attention to her, and announces that the second engine is also broken and they are going to crash. Hermes, the other pilot brings parachutes and Penelope, one of the passengers, organises their jumping off the plane, though Diogenes, the intruder captain, disagrees; eventually they all jump and they arrive safely in Milan where they finally go shopping. During shopping Diogenes continues his provocative manner towards the women of the group, but despite his behaviour the others enjoy their visit and shopping in Milan.

In the discussion following the enactment, Electra confesses that she was really afraid on the plane for some time but Andromache helped her to overcome her fear by holding her hand. Diogenes recommends Claudia to try conducting the group like Larisa (the old therapist). The group disagrees with him by saying that they like the way Claudia is conducting the group and besides they do not expect anyone to behave as somebody else. Then they talked about Larisa who they are going to miss, and after that the group talked about the approaching Christmas holiday, on which the session ended.

The supervision of the session

Claudia recorded the session and in January she presents it to the supervision group. It is her first session in the role of conductor and apart from her reasonable anxiety, she has not yet been given a co-conductor, Greek is not her native language, and last but not least in the above session three patients were absent (Antigone, Athena and Hera) and one, Cassandra, dropped out.

It is evident that the account of the group's session consists of some vignettes and snapshots taken from the group's discussion before and after the acting and also from the performance. As for the supervision session, Figure 4 shows an almost exact translated copy of the original supervision protocol.

As 'Comments and Conclusions' (number 21 of the supervision protocol, Figure 4) show, the supervising group focuses on the important event of the group's conductor change which was expressed by Diogenes's anger towards Claudia. There is no further commentary by the supervising group (correlating Diogenes's motive to be a co-pilot with that of being a co-therapist), most probably because the supervising group was more concerned about their own colleague's new role as a conductor.

As the authors, we do not participate in the oneirodrama or the supervision group. We discussed this session with the group's conductor who, taking into consideration the pathology of Diogenes, said her impression was that his behaviour was most probably motivated by a camouflaged murderous-suicidal intent.

A SUPERVISION PROTOCOL

1. Supervisory session of the 4th year students   3. Absences: no one
2. Present members of the supervisory group : 3   4. Conductor's Name: Ariadne

P R E S E N T A T I O N	**Presented Group**
	5. *Type of Group*
	   Group analytic ☐
	   Experiential ☐
	   Sociotherapeutic ☐
	   Psychodrama ☐
	   Oneirodrama Group ☒
	6. *Therapist*
	   (Presenter): Claudia
	   Co-therapist
	   (Presenter):
	7. *Date of Session*: 15.12.00
	8. *Location*: B 2 (O.P.C.)
	9. *Time*: 2.45 - 4.00
	10. *Frequency*: Once fortnightly
	11. *Absences*: Hera, Athena,
	   Antigone, Cassandra
		Electra
		Andromache Diogenes
		Phaedra Hermes
		Penelope Claudia
		12.
		
		Supervisory Group
		13. *Conductor*: Ariadne (student)
		14. *Observer*: Aspasia (trainer):
		15. *Location*: D 3 (O.P.C.)
		16. *Date*: 11.01.2001
		17. *Time*: 12.30 - 14.30
		
		18. *Additional Information*

19. FEELINGS	20. FANTASIES	21. THEMES-TOPICS
A N A L Y S I S Interest, surprise, pleasure , amusement, annoyance, strength *Observer* comfort, relief, familiarity, an interesting group	- An expedition to a jungle - A maestro who gives the signal to his orchestra to start playing with the note «do» - Penelope as a Snow White - A football team which sits on the grass and waits for instructions from the coach for the limber up	- A hen party - Cassandra's drop out - «I like you with serious look» - «Did anyone had a dream?» - The «pilot» Diogenes - Diogenes comment: «I would recommended you to be like Larisa» - «The group is not only Larisa»

S Y N T H E S I S

21. Comments and Conclusions: A change in the climate of the group is noted since Larisa's departure. The anger against the new conductor (Claudia) is directed now towards the old one. Claudia appears to be accepted and secured her new role.

22. Was there any need to «close the circle»?   YES ☐   NO ☒

23. Who intervened ?   Conductor ☐   Observer ☐   Supervisor - students ☐

Figure 4 The Supervision Protocol of the above mentioned session

The vicissitudes of dreams and dreaming

The nature and content of dreams

In the following pages a short account is provided of our theoretical psychotherapeutic attitude in general and most particularly as regards the use of the dream material for any kind of psychotherapeutic purpose. It should be noted that this approach, which is mainly a derivative of the group analytic and the therapeutic community approach, is applied flexibly and undogmatily.

The nature and the content of dreams has preoccupied thinkers and laymen since ancient times in ways directly related to the prevailing intellectual fashion of the period, to the extent that the study and utilisation of the dream appears to be also a cultural matter. In the old days the nature of dreams was regarded, according to their content, as deriving from gods or from the dead and dreamers were treated by self-appointed experts (priests, healers, oneiromantists, monarchs, politicians, etc.) according to their skill, or to the dreamer's anxiety or naivety. As for the modern psychodynamic approaches this attributes the dream's origin to another obscure area, the unconscious.

The other quite old way of studying the dream tries to shed light on this enigmatic human experience through focusing on the process and the origin of the dream while ignoring the content. The modern neurophysiological approach again studies the origin and the process and ignores the content, while the psychotherapeutic approach deals with both but using the content to explain its origin.

The first who dealt with the dream's nature is Heraclitus (sixth century BC) who said: 'For those who are awake there is one and a common world, while those who are asleep each one withdraws to his own private world' (Heraclitus, fragment 89, p.171). Aristotle in his two short dissertations 'On Dreams' and 'On Prophecy in Sleep' holds similar views. Aristotle's approach is regarded as quite serious to the extent that some scholars (Dodds 1951) believe that even contemporary research has not added very much to this topic. 'What a dream is and how it originates we can best study from the cir-cumstances which attend sleep' he wrote (Aristotle, 'On Dreams', 459, a24, p.352), and 'it is absurd to hold that it is God who sends dreams' (Aristotle, 'On Prophecy in Sleep', 462, b22, p.375); and also 'since some of the lower animals also dream' (Aristotle 'On Prophecy in Sleep', 463, b12, p.379). This last has been proved through the modern study of REM sleep. It is worth noting here that Freud is rather cautious with the work of Aristotle (in the first edition of his book he appears ignorant of the second work of Aristotle 'On Prophecy in Sleep', as he writes in a note in subsequent editions), while he appears much more in favour of 'On Oneirocrisia' by Artemidorus, an author of the second century AD of a dubious reputation today (Papamichael and Marketos 1995). It is interesting to note that while Heraclitus and Aristotle refer to the dream process and set aside the dream's content as not important, Artemidorus deals almost exclusively with the latter. Freud in his celebrated work, which takes up two out of the 23 volumes of his writing, manifests with successive modifications of the previous editions a retreat from his initial 'revolutionary pride' (Roazen 1976, p.114), and by changing among others his first view of the dream's nature from egoistic to altruistic (Freud 1900, p.270).

Pines's important review paper (1999) focuses on the dream content, referring to the distinction of dreams into personal or individual and social ones and concluding that a dream is of a double nature, i.e. individual and social. We prefer the word 'individual' to 'personal' as we are of the opinion that 'personal' and 'social' are almost identical in meaning, as person is formed through a socialising process. In this manner we would call an individual dream one that has never been communicated; of course such dreams exist but are unknown to anyone. For example Freud's dreams, since they had been published, could not be called individual (or egoistic as he calls them) any more, but social dreams. Therefore we view the dream process as an important and continual product of the person's relationships (with other people and with parts of the dreamer's body[5]) elaborated in the mind. This constant mutual influence between internal and external worlds is portrayed by artists more elegantly than by scientists.

The poet Odysseas Elytis (1911, Nobel Laureate 1979) approaches his dreams as follows:

> I have a feeling of a mutual penetration of life inside the dream and of the dream into life; as we could say, bays and capes composing a landscape, here, probable and improbable actions composing a human being... The nearest [to dreaming] that comes to my mind comes from music...all that I was doing in my dreams I understood them to deviate very much from the line of my life, but always in agreement with it. I want to say that they reach with phantasmagoric meanders to the four extremities of the improbable and again, in the end, revert and unite with the main part that I continue to play awake. Precisely as in concert for a violin and orchestra; awake, I was the violin; in my sleep, all the other instruments followed their own flow in order to return harmoniously and to sail together with the primary melody; and this, until a unique and consistent whole is finally composed, I should say, from the lyric aspect, beneficial. (Elytis 1974, pp.168–169)

Another Greek poet, Yorgos Seferis (1900, Nobel Laureate 1963), writes on his own dreams:[6] 'such is our life; an island into sleep: rounded with a sleep' (Seferis 1981, p.238). Similar is the approach of Samuel Johnson (1709–84): 'In solitude we have our dreams to ourselves and in company we agree to dream in concert' (quoted by Pines, this volume).

The ownership of dreams: use and misuse

Studying the dream from the group's point of view we come to another issue: that of the possession of a dream, which, we feel, leads to an unproductive and sterile discussion as it brings again through the back door the preoccupation with the content.

Dreams, to start with, derive from the dreamer's life, internal or external (from his relationships), past or present, and therefore belong to the dreamer; the important question is to whom they are addressed, what for, and most particularly what kind of use is made of them. For a dream after it has been narrated belongs neither to the dreamer any more nor to some invented conjectures, but to the relationship developed between the narrator and the listener, even though the dream has been narrated with a purpose of being decoded or interpreted. This applies also in a group setting where again a dream, after narration, belongs neither to the dreamer, nor to the group as an audience but to the network of communication, i.e. the matrix of the particular group.

This approach can become more explicit and perhaps useful if it is extended to the issue of the use and occasional abuse of dreams. For example the dream that is used by an interpreter for whatever purpose, after narration, is the property of the interpreter (individual or group) and its use could be called an advantageous one. While the dream which has been used to serve the dreamer's personal purposes (e.g. to support a decision, a dream which leads to a discovery, or a dream used as an inspiration for scientific or artistic purposes), while initially an individual dream, becomes social and could be called a creative dream. The same applies when the content of a dream is used in any way either by the dreamer alone, or with the participation or assistance of another, or a group, to create something. On the contrary, if the culture of a group is orientated towards the interpreting process according to a preconstructed theory then this use can become an advantageous one for the group and rather disadvantageous for the narrator.

The abuse of dreams

> [with] the depth psychologies…the concept of the unconscious acquired a mystical halo and a clinical odour.
>
> *Koestler (1964, p.147)*

Some dreams provoke a considerable emotional tension, mainly fear, constituting an attractive target for interpretation, and the dreamer, ardently desiring an explanation, is at the mercy of the interpreter.

As dreams have always challenged people's attention (we meet written evidence in the Bible, in Homeric epics, etc.), dreamers and 'experts' try to decode their secret meaning; it is interesting however that when the dreamer is a powerful person (e.g. a king) he explains the dream's meaning by himself and acts accordingly. History and literature are full of successful (confirmatory) dream interpretations, while there is no recording of the unsuccessful ones!

Inevitably dreams have also been utilised this way by religions; however Saint Basil the Great (330–79 AD) advised Christians not to believe in the divine or the devilish origin of dreams and also not to take refuge in oneirocritics (see Migne p.467).

The old belief that dreams come from gods or from the dead convinced the laity that their dreams could be used for anticipatory or therapeutic purposes. Nowadays such beliefs and practices are not rare though a more sophisticated view is that dreams constitute coded messages broadcast by the unconscious,[7] a concept of the Enlightenment period which concept Freud decided to illuminate through reason. He regarded the unconscious as being full of suppressed sexual and other unspeakable desires all hidden there and as such constituting neuroses. Freud thought that dreams could help him to descend into the unconscious area by explaining their meaning through reasonable interpretations following his assumption that if the unconscious material (e.g. a dream, or slip of the tongue, or a free association) is interpreted then it will become conscious and as a result would stop causing an undesirable behaviour. Freud did this with an unusual boldness, and as regards his own dreams with merciless self-revelation written with a remarkable elegance. However the fact remains open that introspection is not a widely accepted way to construct an objective method for research or therapy.

The spontaneous creative use of dreams

> In a creative state a man is taken out of himself. He lets down as it were a bucket into his subconscious, and draws up something which is normally beyond his reach.
>
> *E. M. Forster* (Dodds 1951)

According to use of their content, cited in Dodds (1951, p.64) dreams appeared to fall into three categories: those of the future (prophetic), those of the past (psychoanalytic), and creative ones. F. A. Kekule von Stradonitz (a German chemist 1829) striving to form the structure of benzene, conceived it's ring structure after a dream he had of a serpent catching its tail. This is a good example of a creative use of dreams in science.

The conditions under which a creative act occurs have been studied extensively by Koestler who, besides dreaming, includes into the creative process the reverie, manic flight of thought etc., stating that the creative condition occurs 'when the stream of ideation is free to drift'. 'The creative act, in so far as it depends on the unconscious presupposes a relaxing of the controls and a regression to modes of ideation which are indifferent to the rules of verbal logic, unperturbed by contradiction, untouched by the dogmas and taboos of so-called common sense' (Koestler 1964, p.178).

The same applies to poets who use dreams as an inspirational starting point for the composition of a poem or a play. It is interesting to note that in ancient Greek tragedy (e.g. *Iphigenia in Tauris*) the importance of a dream has nothing to do with the specific dream; it has only to do with the way Euripides uses it, to serve the plot of his play.

Another example of an initially creative use of dreams is that of Freud who by studying his own dreams searched for hidden material in the abyss of the unconscious. The problem with Freud arises from his trying to construct a theory of the unconscious out of this and particularly a universal one. Freud's dream book may be entirely correct as far as he dealt with his own dreams, which he interpreted exclusively by himself. However since then, in psycho-therapy practically no one has been allowed to interpret his own dreams. Nonetheless this is still regarded as the scientific approach of our time, and dream content is used as the 'royal road to the unconscious' by some psycho-analysts who exhibit their ability for interpreting, though we never know if an interpretation of a dream is deriving from transference or from counter-transference.

Although Freud was aware of the difficulty of constructing a universal dream language for illuminating the darkness of the unconscious, neverthe-less he pursued it, using mainly visual forms despite the obvious impossibility of creating a universal key of dreams, either with words or with forms and symbols, regardless of cultural differences. Dream words and dream dialogues as well as forms and symbols carry different weight and meaning in certain languages and also in certain cultures. Metaphors, neologisms, proverbs and puns are difficult to translate as they derive from particular cultures and situations.[8]

An Intentional Creative Use; The Actualisation of Dreams A Therapeutic
Hypothesis

Man is completely human only when he is at play

Schiller (1759–1805) [cited in Jung 1954, p.46]

The centuries-old human habit of identifying whatever is beautiful and unattainable with the dream can somehow become reality by acting it; as again through acting we can dissipate the fear and the terror of a nightmare or the possible guilt or shame of an unacceptable dream. This can be easily achieved through the group's agreed constructive reality. There is a statement by Anzieu (1984, p.129) which, to some extent, I like: 'Human beings go into groups as they go into dreams. Our thesis is that in terms of psychological dynamics, the group is a dream.' To this we would like to add some of my reservations; the group may appear, and to some extent should be, free and non-obstructing as regards a disciplinary reasoning; in other words the group is like dreaming in spite of the presence of others and particularly of an expert; however with a slight alteration of the metaphor the group is not exactly a 'dream' but is a kind of sleeping in 'concert' where some dream phenomena come true. This is more evident in the oneirodrama group where the dream is taken as a potentially creative raw material which is treated in a recreational way in order to cultivate what is needed to encourage and facilitate the process of relating, which yields maturity and possibly cure.

The oneirodrama group's approach to dream is to use the dream for the group, and consequently for the dreamer, and not with the purpose of verifying a theory or boosting the confidence of the interpreter with the pretext of rendering unconscious material into conscious in order to provide insights. Injected interpretations or pretentious silences do not produce insight; they rather teach the interpreter's theory and subordinate the patient. What we actually try to do is to use the dream, which we view as an originally relational material, in order to promote further, through a recreational process, the faculty of relating. In other words our intention is rather humble in comparison to that of Freud who regarded himself as one of those who have 'disturbed the sleep of the world' (Roazen 1976, p.114) and whose motto in *The Interpretation of Dreams* (1900) was 'if I cannot end the higher powers, I will move the infernal regions'.[9]

The oneirodrama group's aim is to use every member's dream (including the conductor's) in a group 'analytic way' i.e. 'to use a group's dream by the group, for the group, the entire group including the conductor', to paraphrase Foulkes's definition (1975, p.3).

Instead of making a game of somebody's dream we play the game of several imaginative worlds or fantasies which we mutually interweave with several concrete, real, actual and rational interventions. To be more specific, we can focus on a group's perspective narrator in order to sort out the following experiences into which every other member participates: the dreaming – the awakening condition under the influence of the dream – the interval before arriving at the group – the discussion of group matters – the decision to reveal the dream – the narration or hearing of the dream – the selection of the cast – taking part in or watching the performance – the return to the group – the discussion and exchange of feelings – and finally the end of the session. This is a multitransitional process between imaginative and actual situations with several intervals in between them which all take place within a boundaried space; it is a kind of 'sauna' process which we count as an integrated form of the ego training in action process.

The prevailing climate in the group is like that of the entire therapeutic community, which intentionally is rather light, quite playful and occasionally cheerful, because the general attitude is that pleasure is reality too, therefore cannot act as an obstacle to the acquisition of some insight even in the absence of interpretation; particularly when we consider the concept of actuality as additional to that of common sense which usually is not so common. As for unpleasant aspects, which are not so rare in any place of therapy, these are not ignored, but neither pursued by all means, as an ingredient of a more effective psychotherapy. Similarly with transferential material which, is not ignored but is not hunted for either. The same applies to the excessive use of interpretation which usually underestimates our patients' quickness and quite often exposes the therapists to the wit of everyone; instead facilitating interventions are useful, particularly at the beginning. Within such a procedure we pursue familiarisation with the absurd and the irrational and also with madness, which is important for the patients but equally profitable for therapists.

Guilt is also reduced by impersonating wicked characters or by getting involved through acting in unacceptable events; as for shame, acting makes it acceptable and proves that bashfulness can become creation when shameful materials are communicated to others or when they are acted by them.

All the various conditions mentioned above, and also the sudden 'external' modifications during the performance (which actually as regards the group matrix are internal modifications), we believe strengthen the ego, because they constitute a continuous alternating process between perceptive and apperceptive experience (Winnicott 1971, p.132) and also between reality and actuality (Winnicott 1965, p.21) which is a very succinct distinction quite demonstrable in the oneirodrama group and which we reckon applicable for adults too.

It appears that this recreational procedure further promotes the maturational process by providing a quite suitable facilitating environment, because the dream becomes a constant impregnator for the group's creativity and a first-class nourishment for the matrix. On the whole we believe that the oneirodrama group provides quite a lot of the requirements for becoming a good enough group particularly useful for ego training in action.

As for the supervision, after the group the student conductor records the session in order to present it in the supervision group. He or she presents it on the blackboard and the supervision group's members 'supervise' this material not from above but from inside as, in this procedure, they use first not their reason and their pre-existing knowledge but their feelings and fantasies, and then note the topics of the session that each one regards as important. The supervision group, as has been mentioned, is conducted by a peer in order to emphasise and secure the horizontal character of communication and to allow all the aspects of the session which may have not been included in the recording but which nevertheless unavoidably accompany the presentation like an invisible haze which is of paramount importance for a complete conveyance of the momentous and special event of the session. At the same time the presenting student acquires knowledge through first-hand experience of the multidimensional nature of the group's potentials and also learns the lesson that the best way of conducting is not to lead the group but to trust the group in doing the job, while he/she keeps quiet in order to hear some of the whispering.

Through these two procedures, the oneirodrama group and the supervision by peers, the trainee can be convinced that knowledge, and the enterprise of transforming unconscious material into conscious, can be better achieved through relating. After all, the concept 'con-scious' in its Latin source meant 'to know with' (to share knowledge with another) and not to 'know in oneself alone' (Whyte 1962, p.43).

References

Anzieu, D. (1984) *The Group and the Unconscious.* Translated by Benjamin Kilborn. London: Routledge and Kegan Paul.

Aristotle, 'On Dreams' and 'On Prophecy in Sleep'. Loeb Classical Library, Volume 288.

Dodds, E.R. (1951) *The Greeks and the Irrational.* New York: University of California Press, 1973.

Elytis, O. (1974) *Anoikta Hartia.* Athens: Asterias.

Foulkes, S.H. (1975) *Group-Analytic Psychotherapy: Methods and Principles. London: Gordon and Breach. London: Karnac Books, 1986.*

Freud, S. (1900) *The Interpretation of Dreams. Standard Edition 4/5.* London: Hogarth Press.

Heraclitus, 'On the Nature.' In Diels and Kranz (1996) *Fragmente der Vorsokratiker, Vol. 1, Fragment 89, 171.* Zurich: Weidmann, 1996.

Jung, C.G. (1954) 'The Practice of Psychotherapy.' *Collected Works, Volume 16.*

Lec, S.J. (1957) *More Unkempt Thought.* Translated by Jacek Galazka. New York: Funk & Wagnalls, 1968.

Koestler, A. (1964, 1969) *The Art of Creation.* London: Hutchinson.

Migne, J.P. (ed) *Patrologiae Cursus Completus; Series Graeca 4. (1857–1887), Volume 29.* Paris.

Papadakis, T. (1984) *The Group-Analytic Psychodrama: The Enactment of Matrix.* Athens: Institute of Group Analysis.

Papamichael, E. and Marketos, S.G. (1995) 'Artemidorian oneirocrisia.' *History of Psychiatry VI,* 125–31.

Pines, M. (1999) 'Dreams: are they personal or social?' Open lecture at the introductory course on group Psychotherapy and Psychodrama. Athens: OPC.

Roazen, P. (1976) *Freud and his Followers.* London: Penguin Books.

Seferis, Y. (1981) *In Dokimes B.* Athens: Ikaros.

Tsegos, I.K. (1995) 'A Greek model of supervision. The matrix as supervisor – a version of peer supervision developed at I.G.A. (Athens).' In M. Sharpe (ed) *The Third Eye: Supervision of Analytic Groups.* London: Routledge.

Whyte, L.L. (1962) *The Unconscious Before Freud.* London: Tavistock Publications.

Winnicott, D.W. (1965) *The Family and Individual Development.* Tavistock Publications.

Winnicott, D.W. (1971) *Playing and Reality.* London: Penguin Books.

Endnotes

1.   OPC is a 21-year-old private non-profit organisation working to provide psychotherapy for patients and training for people interested in becoming psychotherapists. For this second activity four institutes are in operation (Institute of Group Analysis, Institute for Psychological Testing, Institute of Psychodrama-Sociotherapy and Institute of Family Therapy). For students of these institutes clinical experience is obtained by active participation in the place's psychotherapeutic activity.

2.   Figure 2 'Two phases of peer supervision' is reproduced by kind permission of Routledge and is taken from *The Third Eye: Supervision of Analytical Groups* edited by M. Sharpe. London: Routledge, 1995.

3. Figure 3 'The Supervision Protocol' is reproduced by kind permission of Routledge and is taken from *The Third Eye: Supervision of Analytical Groups* edited by M. Sharpe. London: Routledge, 1995.

4. For people participating in the oneirodrama group we have provided false names for both patients and therapist, and also avoided giving specific diagnoses in order not only to protect the patients from identification, but mainly by prevent the reader's possible misorientation.

5. Embryos' dreams, which have been proved through REM sleep, derive from bodily stimuli.

6. In 1970 Seferis, who was also a distinguished diplomat, dreamed that he went up to the Acropolis and found it being auctioned and eventually knocked down Americans.

7. Or 'subconscious' as it was known before Freud's time since 1770 (Whyte 1962, p.160–1). Freud disliked the term 'subconscious' because it was used by Pierre Janet (Roazen 1976, p.92).

8. Searching in the records of the group's sessions we came across expressions which would become incomprehensible if translated into another language. For example the Greek expression 'Whoever has the fly he is flied' corresponds to the English 'If the cap fits, wear it.' The zip or buttons of a pair of trousers is called a 'fly' in English; the corresponding colloquial Greek word is 'shops'.

9. Originally written in Latin: *Flectere si nequeo superos, Acheronta movebo.*

Acknowledgements

We are indebted to Francesca Bassiala, Stela Lamprouli and Anna-Maria Kyriakopoulou for providing records and elucidations of the oneirodrama group's material, and we are particularly grateful to Youla Pantou for her extensive rewriting of the manuscript and for her vigilant eye during the long writing process.

CHAPTER 17

The Dream and the Large Group

PAN(all)DORA(giving)

Anna Maria Traveni and Monica Manfredi

A salon, many guests, who we are receiving…

Sigmund Freud

Why have we decided to take the first words of Freud's 'Irma's dream' as our starting point for a work on the interactions between the Large Group and the dream?

Because this was the founding dream of the Traumdeutung and the psychoanalytical building, the starting point of a new way of accessing unconscious mental life and a major, highly significant turning point in our culture, not only psychoanalytical but also political, social and intellectual.

Because a Large Group is present in a conformation that characterises it as a group and not as a crowd; all together at the same moment, with a common purpose and with a person (in the dream, the host; in the group, the leader) who assumes the task of ensuring that the conversation, and therefore communication, flows smoothly from one guest to another, without any weighty silences, without excluding this or that person in an impotent isolation. In other words, in both realities, there is a person who performs the function of welcoming without giving priority to anyone.

Because it is a dream; and very often, when participating in a Large Group, one has the confusing sensation of being immersed in a dreamlike atmosphere, in which there is a feeling of having lost one's own boundaries, in which one feels invaded by other people's thoughts.

As in the dream, in which the mind of each personage continually becomes that of the dreamer, the reality of a Large Group is often perceived as extraneous to the will and responsibility of the person. As in the dream, in the Large Group also, awareness of what is happening can be perceived as cancelled, with the feeling of a momentary loss of one's own feeling of identity (Turquet 1978).

Because Freud's dream is a dream that oversteps the personal dimension of the dreamer. It is also a social dream, an oneiric vision that permits access, not only by the author, to the typical dynamics and realities of daily life at the end of the century that was to be such a fertile breeding ground for psychoanalytical theory.

The Large Group is often a good 'spinner' of dreams, with contents that overstep the dimension of the individual, permitting access to a more collective level, represented by icons that reproduce realities drawn from the external collective, in the current social and intrapsychic fragmentation. Threads are interwoven between the inside and outside which, by establishing a connection between the echoes of the story of the individuals, also promote a clearer vision of what is happening in the reality of everyday life. In this way, it is possible to find a modern trace of ancient primitive beliefs according to which the dream was often a message that affected the entire community.

As permitted by the dream in relation to the real life of the person, the Large Group can therefore also allow access to an interpretation of cross-sections of contemporary reality, interweaving the external collective dimensions, the social unconscious, with that of the individual participants in the experience. Interpretation of the oneiric images that emerged in a wide range of Large Group sessions (all with teaching and training purposes in a public and private ambient and consisting of more than 100 participants) has therefore permitted a new interpretation of the characteristic dynamics of the Large Group set-up, enriched with the typical freshness of the practical vision of the theories drawn up.

In this work, in view of this dreamlike atmosphere, as already mentioned, we will use reports of dreams that emerged during the group experience and images that came to light spontaneously during these experiences in order to use a 'life line', which is indispensable to avoid getting lost in the confused and confusing labyrinth of observation of what happens in a Large Group dimension.

New thoughts emerge only at moments of reduced understanding and of inadequacy. The Large Group often causes long moments of apparent reduction in understanding and strong feelings of inadequacy in the participants, identical to those experienced in many situations of social life and which can be clearly identified through the images of the dream recalled: 'I was in the middle of a lake, on a very small boat. The water was black and all around me was dark. I felt very bad, lonely and the lake was becoming larger and larger.'

As Bion asserts in *Learning from Experience*: 'The intolerance of frustration can attain such a high level that it is possible to have, by an immediate evacuation of beta elements, an exclusion of alpha function.' The group, by the deep participant's depersonalization, by the activation of the protomental level (in which physical and psychical activities are in an undifferentiated state), permits the birth, of an embryonic new thought. It's a sort of 'membrane's passage' from one condition to another, where apparent caesuras are, in reality, links and synapsis.

It is now clear that the Large Group and the social dimension are characterised by far-reaching similarities and this makes it possible to assert that the Large Group dimension is that which, more than any other, permits a vision of the founding action of collective myths and their significance in the determination of the social life of the individual. The Large Group therefore makes it possible to see in action those social processes that are deeply rooted in man (and now considered as ascertained by social biology) and it does this in such an evident manner as to force us to reinterpret the 'theory of instinct' so as to also include the so-called 'social instincts'.

In the structural theory of the id, the ego and the superego, already extensively revised, inclusion of a structural part that highlights the social functions of personality, the intracollective, which Tom Omay defines as 'NOS', becomes ever more important.

In-depth reading (Foulkes, Bion, Lewin, Anzieu, Jung, Yalom, Kaës, Le Bon, Kreeger, Galzigna, Kurosawa) and direct work with Pines, Pat de Marè, de Innocentio, Earl Hopper, Knauss and Kreger are important stages in carrying out a permanent experience on the Large Group, considered to be a basic matrix to which we can refer the dilemma existing between the personal and collective unconscious, because the Large Group makes it possible to represent the activation of social conflicts in a dimension of circularity with individual conflicts.

As the 'single individual consists of many masses and through identifica-tion is subject to multi-lateral links, a participant in many collective souls' (Freud), the symptoms of social conflicts are activated, in the dimension of the Large Group, in a manner that transit through and continually with the conflict of the individual. Therefore, mindless aggression, so dominant in contemporary culture, can be seen and focused on, highlighting through the group dynamics that emerge, the possibility of a process of learning, of inter-preting the inhibitions and limitations of the ego and superego, of an intracollective political movement. The Large Group dimension (and this is a point on which the various authors fully agree) not only facilitates but often activates expression of the psychotic mechanisms of the individual partici-pants (Kreeger).

PAN(all)DORA(giving): in Greek mythology, the first woman fashioned by Hephaestus, on whom the gods bestowed their choicest gifts, wife of Epimetheus, brother of Prometheus, who spurred by curiosity opened the jar entrusted to her from which all the evils flew out all over the Earth. Hope alone remained inside.

By highlighting basic assumptions, interpreted as defences against the occurrence of primordial psychotic anxieties, each individual participant can succeed, during the Large Group experience, in identifying and defining some of the phenomena unknown until that moment which often block thought and action in the outside world. The following is taken from a dream of a participant of a Large Group.

> When I was a child I often dreamt I was trapped between my bedroom's wall and my parents' wardrobe. It was completely dark outside, I was alone and I felt more and more compressed, just like a big mass star turning in a black hole. It was a very painful situation because I knew there was no way out of this.

It therefore becomes easier to observe oneself in the often rigid situations assumed in the social dimension and because these are seen as reproduced in a more protected environment, this may pave the way towards reflecting on the various unconscious processes involved in many unconsciously stereo-typed attitudes.

Also, in groups where the psychopathological element has been mainly excluded (through screening of the participants), the very dimension of the experience can trigger paranoid anxieties with massive projections right from the first phases of formation of the group. The very action of preparing the room for the experience, according to the instructions of the leader who asks for the chairs to be arranged in a circle – a distribution in space that considerably facilitates communication and reduces persecution anxieties of being seen without being able to see – may create resistance and intense mistrust in some participants. This can be perceived for example by observing the boycotting attitudes expressed through the difficulty of forming a perfect circle in which the chairs are continually moved a little forward or back in relation to neighbours or by the refusal, expressed very forcibly, of excessively close physical contact with the other person. Phrases that bring into play the concept of the 'impenetrability of physical bodies' are accompanied by others that propose an even more intimate physical closeness.

Therefore everything and the contrary of everything take possession of the group scene, strong powers that oppose and confront each other. Each member of the group studies the other, trying to assess his/her threat or harmlessness. This is the moment of very tense or very evasive looks, of bodies that have difficulty in keeping still, of apparent acts of misbehaviour or acting-out (such as leaving the room with the group almost completely formed), only superficially incomprehensible for professionals aware of the importance of the first phases of constructing the experience.

Trust is a very difficult feeling to perceive (and maintain), especially in the initial phases, and tension and anxiety facilitate the formation of subgroups in which the members find again, for previous belongings (or assumed such), that more familiar, reassuring dimension which, at the beginning, seems to be completely absent in a Large Group dimension. Rapport, relationship, the process of reciprocal influence between the individual and the group, thus become an expression in miniature of those existing between other groups and institutions, between the individual and society.

In the Large Group the mental fields within the environment of the individual, of the family, of society, lose that assumed, discontinuous diversity of founding structure to rediscover a deep connection in the unconscious of the collective, an expression of the real tie that exists between the individual and the group. The first moments of the experience, often characterised by long, heavy silences, experienced in a persecuted or anguished manner, with eyes lowered, breathing fast, arms tightly wound around the stomach, legs tightly crossed, are a tangible expression of the tense atmosphere, the air of a danger that threatens the individual.

All this is confirmed by the first images that emerge which often relate to difficulty in 'diving into a sea' (frequently identified with the empty space that separates the chairs) experienced as threatening, dangerous or simply too cold; dreams in which large ribbon-tied boxes may be both a pleasant, expected gift and a letter-bomb ready to explode, or which speak of the danger of contamination with some fatal disease (an expression of the explosion of beta elements).

Almost always the person who breaks the silence looks with deference, almost childish dependence, at the leader and very often a sign of approval (or presumed such) provides that trusting impetus that makes it possible to continue with subsequent associations. In these initial phases, the images (oneiric or imagined) often refer to primitive and archetypal themes; scenes of great mothers appear, of initiation rites, of journeys in unknown lands, with difficult paths or with dark horizons, real pictograms.

For each change, man is equipped to act according to knowledge he has acquired and which has settled in him over time. The natural constitution of the human being permits continuous recombinations of the mnesic material, with the possibility of modifying personal schemes according to the inputs provided by the movement of the group. The Large Group is characterised by movements of a highly specialised structure which operates at a high level of complexity and differentiation, oscillating between the more primitive roots and more contemporary possibilities. In the Large Group, the dream therefore brings together highly undifferentiated elements with others with a high level of specialisation, acting as a border line for highly selective enrichment of the basic memory of the individual.

Primary links and transgenerational belongings provide the background for the appearance of the oneiric figures of members of the family, of ancestors, of 'monuments' to the memories of entire generations, of guardians of unmentionable and never mentioned secrets. It is as if a strenuous effort is made to hold on to a reassuring, ancient, already known member of the family, in opposition to a too uncertain present and future.

Once communication has started, very often the group splits into sides: on the one hand there is the subgroup that has already demonstrated trust and is sharing even very personal spaces of intimacy with each other, and on the other there is a second grouping characterised by deep, stubborn silences or in some cases by shouting, speaking very quickly, often with very domineering attitudes which reveal an absolute inability to listen to other people, and compulsive repetition of the same point of view, also in an openly aggressive manner.

Observation of the subgroups in relation to each other makes it possible to highlight the borders that are forming; in fact, the various stereotypes in action and in relation with each other permit founding of common thought through activation of the transpersonal dimension.

Aggressiveness with an underlying fear of being invaded – often expressed in the form of images or oneiric associations in which dreams of air-raids, attacks on defenceless people, destruction of family homes, plane crashes or memories of abortions or miscarriages may appear – is an obligatory passage in various phases of the Large Group experience. Fear and the feeling of overload, of a lack of a personal inviolable and inviolate space are expressed with public announcements of feelings of claustrophobia, of suffocating, of intense distress attributed for example to the outside noises perceived as too 'inside'.

In these phases of confusion, sea-related images may return (such as gigantic abnormal waves that threaten to sweep everything away, to destroy firmly established values and stable certainties) or images of the land (a huge mountain to be climbed, the top of which is invisible), expressions on the one hand of the paralysing feeling of powerlessness that the individual often feels in a Large Group dimension and on the other hand of rock-like stiffness, perceived when faced with an obstacle that reminds each individual of the smallness of the human being (only the gods can dwell on the summits of the highest mountains). In a Large Group, the individual often has a feeling of being isolated, of losing his/her personality, of blocking of thought and all this is expressed also by images of mist, shadows, of tangles and of tangled skeins (Turquet).

The feeling (and for some the desire) of anonymity that the Large Group dimension always seems to promote can be readily understood when images appear such as the battery breeding of animals – all the same, manipulated – or dreams in which the person is in a strange place where he/she does not understand the language. The aim of creating a language common to all the participants in the Large Group experience is achieved only slowly and with great difficulty.

The leader is in fact located in a borderline position between the *domi* and the *foris*, upon waves of probability of new activations that must be collected taking into account not only psychological and individual factors but also the impact of the social dimension in the processes of cohesion and disintegration of mental life of each person. (In a few papers of his *Vocabulaire des Institutions Indo-europèenes*, Emile Beenveniste outlines the history of a conceptual couple, meaning the opposition and the complementarity between two parts of space: *Domi-Foris*, the inside and the outside, elements placed in two distinct territories: *Domi* in home, *Foris* in relationship with who is in home.)

It is in the Large Group that the leader is able to really perform his/her function of 'social engineer' (Battegay), collecting what everyone has to say with equal value in order to achieve freedom of communication. Listening to the various interventions proceeds therefore not only in a horizontal direction of the here and now but also vertically with the introduction of the time perspective on what is happening.

And it is when the time variable appears (represented first of all by clocks with hands blocked, mechanism broken, stopped in a fixed and unchangeable place and time, always identical to itself) that, from chaos, from the loss of easily violated or violable borders, the group may very, very slowly discover that a new language has been created which is now mastered in a more aware manner by all the participants.

The chorus of voices perceived by most initially as a harsh-sounding babble now starts to be understood like a language and in some cases compared to a Greek chorus which observes, facilitates and amplifies communication.

The recombinations of the mnesic material, tied initially to personal schemes, are gradually modified according to the structures that operate in the group. In this way, in the first phases of the group experience, the word of the individual, often in contrast with and contradicted by subsequent interventions, is now resumed and rewoven with the experiences of others. The silences which so far have been experienced as defences thrown up as a protection against criticising looks can slowly dissolve, and this is the moment in the life of the group when the participants seek each other's looks, looking for confirmation and reassurance other than from the leader (who in this phase of the group may even appear, to a superficial observer, to be the only member in a more background, peripheral position).

In this phase, the individuals feel that the group is a container able to provide a reassuring holding, and images of death (both personal and collective) often appear in this phase shared by the entire group. It is as if the presence of the others, no longer contaminated by paranoid and persecutory experiences, permits contact with personal suffering without now the perception of the risk of devastation. It is at this moment that the second meaning attributed to Pandora is perceived: the Earth, goddess who gives everything to everybody.

The mind of man is structured to maintain information and to use it to plan both the present and the future. In the dimension of the Large Group, the place of memory, a prospective memory, a 'working memory' makes it possible to listen to many points of view and to use these as links to formulate more collective personal thoughts. This gives practical expression to the double root of the word 'group': the Germanic matrix means gullet and mixture of substances swallowed. The Latin etymology on the other hand stresses the concept of grouping, of everything in a relationship, paving the way to the concept of 'com-plexus' interpreted as intermingling.

Very often, the final images precede the appearance of a subsequent over-turning of the situation. The appearance of the limitation often generates the thrust required to explore new opportunities, to find new directions. It is perhaps for this reason that dreams which frequently relate to death are followed by images of births (even those that have occurred beyond any expectations) or possibilities of new conceptions of family (mostly broadened), symbolic expressions of the effective creative expressiveness of group power.

It is however important to always take into account the fact that, in a Large Group, each level reached can (and in most cases this is what effectively occurs) be challenged and overturned immediately afterwards, with therefore a continuous fluctuation between levels of greater primitiveness and deeper levels of awareness and constructiveness, without it being possible to establish a scale that can be standardised for all the groups or for different moments in the same group.

This is perhaps also the reason why it is so difficult to write about Large Groups in a systematic manner; it's as if there is a continuous contamination between the typical atmosphere of the Large Group and the rational planning structure of the mind of the researcher. Chaos (the main element in any Large Group experience) is lying in ambush – and, paraphrasing the birth of the universe, the Large Group can be seen as that huge crucible in which primordial matter is blended and then reseparates without ever obtaining a definite substance, always only starting points for other compounds, often very unstable.

Briefly, the Large Group fully complies with its function when it makes it possible to express 'mosaic-like' aspects of self; deep, regressive, organised sides are activated in almost concurrent manners, permitting a view of reality and of oneself in relation from a wider viewpoint, like a photograph taken with a fish-eye lens. The Large Group can therefore truly become the place where one learns each time from the experience, once one accepts working in groups inside and outside oneself.

I have left a part of me amongst
a hundred souls, I have left my dream, a thought
in a hundred minds,
I have let my ideas disappear
in a collective idea,
I have let the thought of my thoughts be cradled by
other minds!
I have let myself be transported
by a hundred arms
adrift of my dreams!
Now I am no longer a lonely soul
And I know that those
hundred souls
No longer feel lonely,
because we have given one to the other,
we have donated other minds
to our mind.

(Anon, after a Large Group experience)

References

Autori, V. *The dream Discourse today*. London: The Institute of Psycho-Analysis.

Anzieu, D. (1979) *Il gruppo e l'inconscio*. Rome: Borla.

Anzieu, D. (1987) *L'Io folle*. Rome: Borla.

Artemidoro (1975) *Il libro dei sogni*. Milan: Adelphi.

Bateson, G. (1976) *Verso un'ecologia della mente*. Milan: Adelphi.

Bion, W.R. (1971) *Esperiense nei gruppi*. Rome: Armando.

Bion, W.R. (1971) *Apprendere dall'esperienza*. Rome: Armando.

Bion, W.R. (1973) *Attenzione e interpretazione*. Rome: Armando.

Bion, W.R. (1993) *Memoria del futuro – Il sogno*. Milan: Cortina.

Borges, J.L. (1986) *Tutte le opere*. Milan: Mondadori.

Bosinelli, M. and Cicogna, P.C. (1991) *Sogni: figli di un cervello ozioso*. Torino: Boringhieri.

Bowlby, J. (1989) *Una base sicura. Applicazioni cliniche della teoria dell'attaccamento*. Milan: Cortina.

Canetti, E. (1981) *Massa e Potere*. Milan Adelphi.

Cardomo, G. (1993) *Sogni*. Marsilio.

Caruso 'Germania senza colpa'. (Manoscritto inedito.)

Chevalier, J. and Gheerbrant, A. (1986) *Dizionario dei simboli.* BUR Dizionari Rizzoli.

Corrao, F. (1998) 'Il concetto di campo come modello teorico.' In *Gruppo e funzione analitica.* Milan: Cortina.

De Marè, P. (1991) *Koinonia.* London: Karnac Books.

Dentone, A. (1996) 'Agonia dei significati.' In *Vocazione dell'analogo,* Italy: Bastogi.

Dentone, A. (2000) *Dialogo-Silenzio-Empatia.* Italy: Bastogi.

Derisio, S. 'Dinamiche individuo gruppo.' Rivista Italiana di Gruppoanalisi II.

Facchinelli, E. (1975) *Claustrofobia.* Milan: Feltrinelli.

Fornari, F. (1987) 'Gruppo e codici affettivi.' In F. Angeli (ed) *Il cerchio magico.*

Foulkes, S.H. (1967) *Psicoterapia a Analisi di gruppo.* Torino: Boringhieri.

Foulkes, S.H. (1976) *La psicoterapia gruppoanalitica.* Astrolabio.

Foulkes, S.H. (1998) *L'approccio psicoanalitico alla psicoterapia di gruppo.* Rome: ed. Un. Romane

Freud, S. (1971) *Psicologia delle masse ed analisi dell'Io.* Torino: Boringhieri.

Freud, S. (1971) *L'interpretazione dei sogni.* Torino: Boringhieri.

Freud, S. (1971) *Pulsioni e loro destini.* Torino:Boringhieri.

Freud, S. (1971) *Il disagio della civiltà'.* Torino: Boringhieri.

Grinstein, A. (1990) *Le regole di Freud per l'interpretazione dei sogni.* Torino: Boringhieri.

Hadfield, J.A. (1968) *Sogni e incubi in psicologia.* Giunti.

Hopper, E. 'The social unconscious in clinical work.' *Group Analysis 20,* 7–42

Hopper, E. 'L'esperienza traumatica della vita inconscia dei gruppi. Un quarto assunto di base.' In F. Angeli (ed) *Rivista Italiana di gruppoanalisi. Volume 24.*

Jung, C.G. (1975) *La libido. Simboli e trasformazione.* Rome: Newton Compton.

Jouvet, M. and Galzigna, L. (1997) *I paradossi della notte.* London.

Kreeger, L. (1978) *Il gruppo allargato.* Rome: Armando Armando Editore.

Kurosawa (1992) *Volare.* Gruppo Abele.

Langs, R. (1988) *Decodificare i propri sogni.* De Agostini.

Lewin, K. (1965) *Teoria dinamica della personalità.* Firenze: Giunti-Barbera

Mancia, M. (1987) *Il sogno come religione della Mente.* Rome: Laterza.

Napolitani, D. (1987) *Individualità e gruppalità.* Torino: Boringhieri.

Neri, C. (1995) *Gruppo.* Rome: Borla.

Pines, M. (1990) *Bion e la psicoterapia di gruppo.* Rome: Borla.

Resnik, S. (1982) *Il teatro del sogno.* Torino: Boringhieri.

Segal, H. (1991) *Sogno, fantasia e arte.* Miln: Cortina.

Tabucchi, A. (1992) *Sogni di sogni.* Sellerio.

Turquet, P. (1978) 'Minacce all'identità in gruppo allargato.' In Kreeger (ed) *Gruppo allargato.* Rome: Armando.

Van Gennep, A. (1981) *I riti di passaggio.* Torino: Boringhieri.

Winnicot, D.W. (1974) *Gioco e realtà.* Rome: Armando.

CHAPTER 18

Dreams as Stimulators
of Group Processes

Ophélia Avron[*]

What can it mean when a participant in a psychotherapy group reports a dream? How can we develop our understanding and make it part of the ongoing group dynamics?

Before I examine these issues in detail, I should make it clear that during the many years I have practised psychodrama and expression therapy in groups, only rarely have participants spoken of their dreams. Does this mean that the group situation and the implicit task of adapting to and maintaining the immediate continuity and multiplicity of communication within the group tend to push these 'children of the night' into the background?

There is, however, one exception to this general statement. Last November, I began a psychodrama group in which, contrary to the other two groups that have been operating now for several years (one of which is a psychodrama group, the other an expressive therapy group), from about the sixth session on, the participants have frequently reported their dreams. I shall take advantage of my own surprise at this situation in order to make a more detailed analysis of this dream material and the role it plays in the group.

---

[*] English translation by David Alcorn ('Le Rêve, Stimulateur des Processus Groupaux').

The psychodrama setting

Let me first of all give some background information about the context in which this work takes place.

Each weekly psychodrama session lasts two hours. The aim of the group is therapeutic, and there are seven patients. The group is not quite an 'open' one, in that participants are required to agree to an initial commitment of one year's attendance before deciding when to leave the group once they feel they have done enough work in it. Average length of participation is in fact three years. I am the sole psychodrama therapist.

Patients are referred by other psychoanalysts and belong to the convenient but poorly defined category of 'borderline cases'. It happens more and more frequently that patients come to me after having had some experience of individual psychotherapy. This is an important point, for it implies that they are already familiar with the idea of free association and of teasing out the meaning of their dreams.

Each session is divided into three parts:

- open-ended discussion among patients, which gives them the opportunity to get back in touch with their problems, their free associations and the continuity of the sessions;

- the play itself. The theme is suggested by one of the participants, who chooses whatever partners he or she wants to have take part in the play;

- general discussion in which all participants can respond to what they have just seen and what it evokes for them.

It is almost always in the initial open-ended discussion – when patients talk over their difficulties and experiences in the interval since the previous session – that any dreams are reported; only on two occasions have dreams been proposed directly as play themes.

What exactly are we doing when we communicate to a group our nocturnal images, the weird and ingenious structure of which is beyond our understanding, though we know in some obscure way that they tell more about us than we can guess? This offering, with all its ambiguity, intrigues me just as much as the dream content itself and gives me much food for thought.

In the psychodrama group on which this chapter is based, I have counted, in the space of 28 sessions, some 35 dreams, 15 of which have been reported by the same person. The theme of my investigation could be formulated thus: in so far as a dream narrative is drafted in such a way as to be presented to a permanent group of people, its thematic content, structure and function may well be modified by that particular context. The point at issue involves relating a personalised thematic content to the modifications in meaning that the group situation entails, and exploring the influence of this nocturnal creation on certain group processes. This difficult task developed slowly over the 28 sessions I mentioned previously, and forced me to re-examine not only Freud's hypotheses on dreams but also my own thinking about how a group functions.

Dreams – the royal road to the unconscious

What makes dreams such intriguing material for thought is that their narration implies the quasi-experimental creation of something very personal that the dreamer constructs in the solitude of his or her sleep without the participation of consciousness. Dreamers are asleep and they think they are living out the scene; they are asleep and they think they can see, hear and experience.

Freud's use of this instrument of the mind – 'that most marvellous and most mysterious of all instruments' (Freud 1900a, p.608) – enabled him to emphasise in the fullest sense of the word his discoveries concerning the workings of the unconscious drives, for example the fact that they take no heed of day or night. He had already suggested that repressed drive representations are behind neurotic symptoms; he thought also that unconscious infantile desires lay behind dream imagery. Though apparently incomprehensible, dreams have meaning: they are the fulfilment of a desire. In 1900, when he published his major opus based on the analysis of his own dreams and those of his patients, he wrote:

> Dreams are psychical acts of as much significance as any others; their motive force is in every instance a wish seeking fulfilment; the fact of their not being recognizable as wishes [is] due to the influence of the psychical censorship to which they have been subjected during the process of their formation. (Freud 1900a, p.533)

Interpreting dreams, therefore, consists in decoding the mental work that led to their creation then their distortion, in uncovering the infantile wishes that are always eager to find some means of expression, and in identifying the censorship that is constantly attempting to make them unrecognizable. A strange kind of combat results in compromise images subjected to condensation, displacement and the beginnings of logical elaboration. In order to

catch a glimpse of these unconscious operations that resemble nocturnal hallucinations, Freud again made use of the technique of free association that
had enabled him to discover the 'pathogenic reminiscences' behind
psycho-neurotic symptoms. He suggested that the patient:

> divert his attention from the dream as a whole on to the separate portions of
> its content and to report to us in succession everything that occurs to him in
> relation to each of these portions – what associations present themselves to
> him if he focuses on each of them separately. (Freud 1933a [1932], p.11)

Though resistance can be loosened somewhat as a result of this technique, it
is still very much in operation. In fact the patient 'has only touched on in his
associations' (Freud 1933a [1932], p.12) the drive-impelled wish. It is up to
the psychoanalyst, wrote Freud, to bridge the wide gap between the manifest
content of the dream and the latent dream thoughts. Though 'the interpretation of dreams is the royal road to a knowledge of the unconscious activities
of the mind' (1900a, p.608), interpretations do not fall 'like manna from the
skies,' as Freud himself wryly pointed out (1900a, p.522). The patient's free
associations, the analyst's theoretical assumptions and their confirmation by
different kinds of mental phenomena are all indispensable parts of the
process. Freud himself had 'the justifiable expectation that in this as in other
respects dreams would behave as neurotic symptoms' (1900a, p.522). In
1932, in spite of the breakthrough that his second structural theory represented, when he undertook his 'revision of dream theory' (1933a [1932]),
his explanatory model of dreams being reactivated by infantile wishes
remained essentially unchanged: 'imperishable unfulfilled instinctual
wishes...throughout life provide the energy for the construction of
dreams... A dream is a fulfilment of a wish' (1933a [1932], p.29–30).

Group interlinking

How do this fundamental discovery and its concomitant methodological
approach operate when the psychoanalyst listens to the account of a dream in
a group context? In such a situation, the dreamer cannot ignore the fact that
other patients are present, nor can he or she remain isolated from the actual
dream presentation that is being offered. As dreamers remember and narrate
their dreams, they have to take into consideration their 'audience', the
reactions and responses the dream narrative may evoke, what they are communicating to the others, the point in group-time at which the narrative is
offered and, even more obscurely, the dynamic tension that always exists

between members of any group. This is a far cry from the classic analytical approach that tries to bring patients as closely as possible into touch with their free associations, images, affects, memories and transference dynamics; in order to do this, each dream fragment is considered separately in order to break up the apparent logic of the whole and to make contact with the unconscious drives condensed into a meaningless image or displaced onto strange replacement situations. When we encourage group communication, we deliberately expose our patients to the disturbing pressure of a real group situation. But what does this give rise to?

No process can be apprehended directly; we need to look at the ways in which it becomes manifest. In order to understand interpsychic functioning, we shall therefore have to combine hypotheses, observations and inferences, just as Freud had to do to understand the intrapsychic world. As for myself, Bion's work on groups made me more aware of how currents of tension are created and become organised as soon as several people come together. However, I avoid equating these with 'Basic Assumptions', because the latter cannot adequately further my understanding of how each individual is simultaneously yet unknowingly author and beneficiary of a shared creation. For a deeper understanding of what goes on at this level of interpsychic processes, we have to agree to suspend temporarily any interest in the content of the communication in order to concentrate on the *participant perception* of the currents of tension whose rhythm makes us alternate between reception and stimulation.

I have elsewhere called these fluctuating forms of tension/attention linked to the concrete, tangible existence of human beings the 'effects of presence'; this was an attempt to distinguish them from the effects of desire relating to sexual activity and structured around the absence of primary cathected objects. As we have noted, in this case it is the unconscious and indelible traces of these, imprinted on the unconscious, that form each individual's reservoir of primary affect representations concerning satisfying and unsatisfying experiences, the revival of which is ceaselessly sought after.

Individuals in groups still carry with them their past libidinal experiences and want, just as in other contexts, to re-establish situations of primary satisfaction. Dreams as hallucinatory representations are one of the ways in which the individual's desire is expressed. It is quite legitimate to try to identify the manifest elements in group life that awakened the dreamer's unconscious wishes, the indirect sexual enticement expressed through offering the dream to the group and the particular group members aimed at, given that transference displacement is another blind way of 'making the patient's hidden and forgotten erotic impulses immediate and manifest' (Freud 1912b, p.108).

These complex issues relating to the reactivation of infantile wishes in a group are difficult enough to deal with; we have, however, to complicate them even further if we suggest that in every human situation not only are unconscious repressed wishes undeniably in operation, but also the instantaneous interlinking of minds – and this activity is just as important and as continuous as the former. These two sources of non-conscious activity operate simultaneously, coming together and separating. The clinical and conceptual problem is how to identify them, deal with them, combine them and separate them out.

To my way of thinking, narrating a dream to a group forms part of this double activity.

Before analysing the dream, we have to have more details concerning the reciprocal and non-conscious activity of all the participants (Avron 1996). We shall have to put to one side, at least for the time being, the powerful category of representational and affect-laden traces capable of re-cathecting or hallucinating new substitutive objects; our focus must be on another category, just as powerful and original – that of the dynamic forces that enable specific systems of interpsychic linking and unlinking to be achieved directly. Three points must be emphasised here, even if only briefly:

1. Actualization of this type gives rise to an immediate collective organisation by means of a global energising process that does not have to take into account the multiple and diverse nature of individual representations and affects (hence its instantaneous quality). All participants unwittingly act as energy sources with a double polarity, switching over from stimulation to receptivity according to their reciprocal interplay. Collective circuits in constantly unstable equilibrium relative to the stimulation/ receptivity dimension are created. From time to time, when either collective manic overstimulation or passivity becomes dominant, this acts as an inducement to individualised reactions. A kind of energy interdependence is set up, not only between individual participants but also with respect to the shared creation. Without the non-conscious capacity for basic energy reciprocity, development towards more sophisticated structures involving dialogue and cooperation would be impossible.

2. It is extremely difficult to give a precise definition of the permanent and unstable creation of energy processes involving interlinking because we have no representative benchmarks available. But we remain sensitive towards these energy-driven relationships thanks to participant perception and assessment of the dynamic forcefield, on both inter-individual and group levels.

3. Repeated experiences of linking and unlinking within the human environment enable us to refine our basic participant perception and to develop a scenic or dramatic way of thinking that helps us to anticipate and to act in an ever more subtle way when it comes to setting up reciprocal interdependent relationships. Scenic thinking, a fundamental aspect of human relationship experience, gradually expands to include perception and the possible transformation of inter-causality processes that involve people, events and things.

It would take too long to analyse the circumstances in which this activity breaks down. Malfunctioning is often linked to innate or acquired defects in polarity and/or to concomitant environmental inadequacy. When break-down is temporary, we have a vague feeling of either belonging or not belonging to a whole, of being supported or oppressed, of having our inner strength reinforced or of wilting away. When malfunctioning becomes more endemic, defensive splitting between polarities either breaks off all links with the environment or hands the individual over to it in a systematically passive way. Psychotic anxieties emerge, involving collapse, asphyxia or emptiness in relation to excessive, defective or immobilised energy in the polarities required for keeping links alive; these links make us feel we exist with and through other people, since we are constantly acting on them and being acted upon in return.

The scenic model of dreams

My general idea is that the twofold intra- and interpsychic activity, corresponding respectively to the mental energy of sexual desires and to the energy dynamics of interlinking, creates *scenic organisations*. The scenic or dramatic nature of the activity arises when individual wishes are brought up against the energy circuits of reciprocity; conscious and unconscious compromises have then to be made between individual pleasure and the safeguarding of shared links. Fantasy could be regarded as the primary internalised form of this association, and in their own way dreams could also be seen as a transient manifestation of it. That is why, in real life, fantasies and dreams with their internalised scenic structure are continually stimulating representations of cathected imagos and the interlinking patterns that lie at the root of their creation.

This scenic model can be applied to all kinds of communication. When we use it in the analysis of dreams, it is no longer a case of following the meanderings of the dreamer's free associations as we do in individual analysis. Here, the analytical method must above all focus on the overall scenic dynamics present in individual narratives as well as in the communication that is taking place. The specific nature of group therapy lies in the fact that participants are required to maintain a transforming kind of attentiveness that involves issues relating both to personal desire and to the collective safe-guarding of interlinking.

The first dream

Beatrice reported a dream in the sixth session, and in the eighth Theresa began her series of 15 dreams. I shall not attempt to discuss all of these and the context in which they emerged; I shall deal with Beatrice's first dream in some detail, and its replica in the twenty-fourth session. As for Theresa's dreams, I shall simply give a brief outline of their overall scenic dynamics.

When this new group began in November, none of the patients knew any of the others. It is worthwhile emphasising again that this kind of situation is replete with curiosity, apprehension, traumatic prospects and innovative potentiality. Scenic mobilization of mental representations and of inter-linking stimulation is at a climax. Beatrice and Theresa, each in her own way, will demonstrate their sensitivity and their defensive attitudes with respect to the globality that is being created.

I began by giving the participants some indication of how the group would function; this was followed by a deep silence. People began giving one another sidelong glances. There was a period of anxious expectancy. Theresa, the oldest member of the group, broke the tension/attention by suggesting that they introduce themselves; she herself led the way, giving her name, age and profession. A period of somewhat formal presentations then ensued, which suddenly became alarming when Beatrice took the floor. With none of the usual verbal warnings people give, she spoke of her anxieties:

I have come here because from time to time I feel my mind is empty, I can't think, it's almost as though I didn't exist any more, it's worse than the dark thoughts I used to have some years ago. Emptiness. I can't talk about it to anybody, and certainly not to my partner, he wouldn't understand. At times like those, I'm worried I'm going mad.

This abrupt statement, in forcing all participants to face up to the mystery of the workings of their own mind, seemed to throw everybody into a panic. Those patients who had not yet said anything avoided going deeper into the question: they hurriedly gave their first name, then fell silent. The difficulty in combining a shared interlinking activity with personal issues that brought the individual members to the group in the first place was particularly obvious in those initial moments of our first meeting.

In subsequent sessions, Theresa and Beatrice were to remain faithful to these response patterns. Theresa was always ready to encourage intra-group communication and leave her own worries to one side, arguing that her age and the ten years she had spent in individual analysis enabled her to put her own problems into some perspective. It was only much later that we would learn of her phobic fear of illness and accidents.

Beatrice, on the other hand, did not seem to be particularly attentive towards the other participants; she was completely absorbed in her own anxieties and unable to associate freely about them. Her thinking was very concrete and factual in style, focusing on events in everyday reality that she was unable either to cope with or to put aside. Though she remained indifferent to the actual narratives of her fellow patients, she was extremely sensitive to change, absences, returns, attitudes and tones of voice. From time to time she would react abruptly as though she felt herself to be in an emergency situation. At such times, what she said was experienced as provocative by the others, given the sharpness of her tone of voice and the terse repetitiveness of what she had to say (which often had little to do with the topic then under discussion). As a result, there was either an increase in overall tension/attention, so as to get her more involved, or a sudden loss of interest on the part of the others if this failed.

My own understanding of group events is a function both of my participant perception and of my analytical training. I intervene whenever I feel that, in the energy dynamics of the situation, interlinking and expressions of individual desire are either too far apart or reduced to a standstill. We could say that I intervene whenever comments, images, reactions or thinking lose the energy that gives them their scenic structure and tend towards breakdown or devitalisation.

And so we come to the sixth session. Beatrice had a dream. She began by saying how surprised she was, because normally she never dreamed. She added that in fact it was more of a nightmare than a dream. She is in a shop with her three-year-old daughter beside her. Suddenly she realises the little girl is no longer by her side. She has been taken away. In a panic, Beatrice searches everywhere for her. The girl has been taken to China. Then the dream goes off on another tack: two years later, Beatrice finds her daughter again, but the girl doesn't speak French any more. Beatrice has to teach her daughter her mother tongue all over again, because she no longer remembers it.

The other participants, who were paying close attention to Beatrice's narrative, reminded her that in the previous session she had expressed the fear that her daughter's father, with whom Beatrice is not married, might want to keep the girl if they separated or she (Beatrice) fell ill. This obvious link to the previous session astonished her – as though each situation was encapsulated for all time.

Behind her dream, I could sense she was saying something about a traumatic experience. The way she seemed to paralyse her own thinking paralysed other people's responses towards her. Without mentioning what had just been said, two other patients abruptly intervened with their own personal matters, as though they had already forgotten Beatrice and her nightmare.

That, then, is the clinical context in which the first dream unfolds: content, reactions, linking and unlinking, and apparent forgetting occur in such rapid succession that they give us the feeling of being overwhelmed – hence the need both for models that help us understand and for intuitive empathy.

Let us return to Beatrice's dream. The actual content can be read, from a scenic point of view, in two ways: the underlying libidinal fantasy, and the interlinking that is set up between the characters in the dream. The group will be affected on both of these levels.

For purposes of clarity, I shall make a somewhat artificial distinction between these different aspects even though this does not correspond to the immediate synthetic apprehension of the clinical context.

1. THE SCENIC ELEMENTS OF THE DREAM

- Three characters: Beatrice, her daughter, a thief.

- One action: a sudden kidnapping.

- One initial response: panic searching for the missing child.

- Three items of information: her daughter has been taken to China – to the other side of the world; the separation lasted two years; then the girl came back, but could no longer speak her mother tongue.

- One final reaction: Beatrice again taught her daughter her native language (so that they were again able to communicate).

2. THE UNDERLYING FANTASY

In an identification relayed by the child, the dream both reveals and hides the (young girl's) desire to be kidnapped by the father and taken far away from the mother. Hence the feelings of guilt, the reparatory return and the submission to the mother's way of communicating.

This latent content was related to the actual manifest situation: Beatrice was afraid that her daughter might be taken from her and put in the father's care. From a transference point of view, there is an obvious need for removing guilt behind the constant quest for reassurance about being within her rights: she certainly would not be the one to abandon a little girl to the father! Though she received advice from some of the other group members, her mind was still not at rest. This Oedipal scenario could not be dealt with there and then, because of the important issues relating to interlinking. Once she felt a little more easy in this respect, later play sequences enabled Beatrice to make a new attempt at coping with her difficulty over getting in touch with her positive feelings for her father – a formidable but nonetheless admired figure, against whom she had always taken her mother's side in their many marital quarrels.

3. DRAMATISING INTERLINKING SCENARIOS

If we now consider the dream from the point of view of reciprocal linking dynamics, we see that a link between two persons is abruptly broken via a brutal attack coming from outside – the kidnapping. When the dreamer loses all ties, she gets into a panic. The switch that occurs in the second part of the dream implies that she finds the child again after two years of emptiness as far as the relationship is concerned – but the child has to be taught how to communicate. This is an example of traumatic unlinking, as well as of a defensive modality that takes the form of a closely attuned relationship between two people.

To some extent, the way the group functioned echoed this pattern. Beatrice tended to respond to variations in environmental tension/attention either by suddenly reacting or by just as suddenly withdrawing. In return, the others tried, first, to calm her down and think things through for her, but when she froze her responses, they reacted by ignoring her. It was as though the stimulation/receptivity polarities tended to split quickly down the middle, thereby blocking all possible development of communication. When the dynamic dramatisation of scenarios malfunctions, the therapist has to pay particular attention to the forces at play in the situation. No analysis of unconscious content can properly be undertaken if the group members are unable to maintain reciprocal functioning of interlinking.

My spontaneous comment on the situation would be to say that the effect of this narrative/nightmare on the group was a prime example of reciprocal circuit-breaking. The dream was offered up as an anxious appeal for communication, and the group immediately responded by globally focusing its attention on the issues raised. Beatrice was linked to the group through the connection made between her dream and the material in the previous session (about which she herself had forgotten). But she was unable to take in and expand on the group's stimulatory role towards her; consequently, the other participants began to lose interest, and two of them, no longer heeding what she had to say, talked of their own personal problems. Beatrice herself then fell into her usual state of aloofness. However, I was struck by the violence of the dramatised breakdowns indicated in these two new narratives – it was as though Beatrice's nightmare continued to manifest its unlinking force through this new material.

One of the patients spoke of his difficulty in telling a candidate that he had been eliminated, the other complained that he could not defend himself against people who acted in bad faith; the example he gave was his insurance company and the aftermath of a serious accident in which he had felt broken.

I then brought together the traumatic unlinking represented in the material of these two narratives, Beatrice's nightmare and what the group knew of her symptoms. I said that our fear of being 'eliminated', 'broken', or 'separated' may be so intense as to empty our minds of all thinking and desire for relationships. To some extent, I put into words the scenic dramatisation of unlinking. Surprise. Silence. They looked at her, looked at one another. The tension/attention circuits necessary for scenic dramatisation of linking were re-established. It was only later that I realised that Beatrice reported her dream in the session that preceded the Christmas holiday – separation was part of the group's experience of time at that particular moment.

A series of dreams

Developments of that initial dream were to come from Theresa. As I have mentioned, Theresa always took care to keep open the channels of communication between group members; she would make Oedipal-like interpretations that were often quite apposite, the fruits of her own personal analysis and her experience as a social worker. But she rarely spoke about herself, as though she had nothing more to discover. She was aware that she played a role in the group that set her up as a rival to me – she would express this with a knowing smile that sought to make me connive with her. She said that in her analysis she had gained insight mainly into her jealousy with respect to her mother. Her fear as regards me was that of appearing not to be up to what she supposed were my expectations. She would carefully scrutinise my reactions. I waited. The other members of the group kept at a respectful distance, afraid of her sometimes intrusive perceptiveness. One day, someone said she talked too much. That deeply affected her. She felt excluded, and wondered if she should stay on in the group. Her sensitivity to exclusion, with none of the usual parrying explanations, caught my attention.

When Beatrice reported her dream in the sixth session, Theresa made no immediate comment. However, nothing that occurs in a group is ever forgotten, whether it involves human relationships or the strategies of desire. During the initial discussion period of the eighth session, Theresa announced, as though it went without saying, that she had had a nightmare, of which only a single image remained: she is in the group; everybody – and me [OA] in particular – is giving her a disapproving look. When she wakes up she feels very upset. Theresa herself related this to the play sequence she had proposed in the previous session in which her husband, his usual careless self, had forgotten they had arranged to meet. As she played out that scenario, she had thought that I must have found her too demanding.

She went on talking about what she already knew concerning her jealous desire for sole possession. I, however, was much more interested in the fact that she made use of a dream in order to appeal for communication – and not just a dream but, as with Beatrice, a nightmare. It was as though the idea, contained in Beatrice's nightmare and the responses of the other two group members, of a relationship heading for trouble in an unthinkable way had awakened Theresa's own anxieties about this. Though she could not keep in her mind the scene as a whole, the association to the previous session gave her the impression of 'having once again been forgotten'.

I made no comment, but I thought of how over-zealous she was in her attempts to maintain links between us; I was thinking also about her idea of breaking off all contact with the group after what was really quite a simple remark – though she had taken it to be a total rejection.

The group listened carefully to what she had to say, without making any comment. To my surprise, in the following session, four other patients pursued the theme of attacks and violent breakdowns via four nightmarish images:

- Theresa is being attacked by wild animals.

- Beatrice is caught up in a hurricane. An enormous tidal wave is about to sweep her away.

- A woman lets go of her baby in order to save a little girl from drowning. The dreamer, a woman patient, sees herself catching the baby as it starts to fall.

- The fourth participant no longer remembered his dream when he woke up; but, though he never used to dream (he said), he knew it was full of anxiety-arousing images.

It was pointed out that once again the group was dealing with dream material, probably influenced by Beatrice and Theresa's first dreams. I emphasised the variations on the theme of fear of being attacked, of disappearing and of falling down, as well as the tendency to erase everything.

After the ninth session, the content of group discussion varied little, but the participants seemed to be more able to listen to one another and to associate more freely to what was being said; it was as though the reciprocal movements of stimulation and receptivity were being split off to a much lesser degree. Theresa, for example, became less inclined to interpret; she said that the problems brought up by other members of the group made her think more about her own.

In the fifteenth session, Beatrice, who went on telling us of her day-to-day relationship difficulties with her partner, gave the group an important item of information. Echoing what another female member had said about her memory of family relationships, Beatrice said that she was astonished by her mother's very unsympathetic attitude towards her granddaughter, all the more so since she had been very loving towards Beatrice herself. Then she suddenly fell silent.

> I was told – though I have no actual memory of this – that until I was three years old, my mother used to leave me all week at her parents', only taking me back at the weekend. She has never spoken to me about that; I heard it from my grandparents. It's surprising that one can leave one's child in the care of strangers.

As usual, there was very little affect in Beatrice's voice as she said this, as though she were flatly making a statement of fact. The group as a whole, however, was keenly interested in all of this. They asked her for more details, they linked her material to many other themes – I felt the group to be highly mobilised. They were speaking about her, about themselves. Communication was very much the order of the day.

Beatrice: But if you don't remember something, it's not important.

Me: So it's better just to have your mind go blank?

Immediately after this exchange, other participants reported nightmares that they had had in their childhood: ferocious beasts, aliens from outer space, witches – one female patient had even had a horrible vision of her own face falling to pieces.

Though apprehension about losing the vitality of reciprocal links or of losing one's identity were palpable in the session, it became much more possible to discuss these topics now that channels of communication within the group were open.

In the twenty-fourth session, Beatrice reported her third and final dream, which turned out to be a remake of the first. Beatrice is out walking with her daughter, whom she is holding by the hand. Suddenly someone comes up to them and tears her daughter away. Beatrice cries out, and at that point she wakes up.

This was the same kind of 'tearing apart' dream as the first one she had reported. This time, however, she herself made a link with her original nightmare and with her anxiety about parental rights. Somebody in the group reminded her of what she had told us about the week-long separations from her parents when she was a baby. Beatrice immediately said that all that was not really very important: 'I was too young. I don't remember anything about it.' Then she recalled a more recent traumatic event, which occurred when she was ten years old. Her parents had separated, and her mother had been 'locked up'. Beatrice could not understand what was going on, and nobody spoke about it. Again she had been put in the care of her grandparents. All of this was a tremendous shock to her. She was very shaken, and, as though she could hardly believe it herself, she said: 'Do you think all this is related?'

Theresa seemed to echo this when she spoke of her own family and the separations they had experienced: a country at war, continually moving house, changing schools, learning a new language. She went on: 'I managed to cope with all that by becoming nice and transparent, but deep down inside I was dead.' She was later to bring more dream material – but less nightmarish – to the sessions.

Group communication became more and more open. The memories the participants brought became much more Oedipal in quality. Theresa had one more dream. She is the adult woman she now is in real life. She meets the English pen pal she had when she was an adolescent. They flirt tenderly. She says to herself: 'If his parents knew how old I am, they would not be pleased!'

For further reflection...

The unusual amount of dream material in this group – stimulated no doubt both by the traumatic impact that always occurs when strangers meet for the first time, and by the presence of two members who were particularly sensitive to issues involving unlinking and defusion – encouraged me to think more not only about the unconscious meaning of dreams but also about their scenic or dramatic structure. Dreams mobilise both the sexual energy that pushes individuals towards the object of their desires and the interlinking forces that oblige human beings to be constantly in some kind of relationship with one another. The scenic expression of this double constraint is an unstable equilibrium, given that it is never easy to adapt the search for pleasure to the requirements of communication (and vice versa). From this point of view, narrating a dream in a group context becomes an invitation to and an encouragement of dramatic expression, which in turn gives an impetus to new organisations of transference dynamics and interlinking processes.

As for nightmares, I would suggest that they have mainly to do with anxieties about unlinking or defusion and loss of identity. When they become repetitive, nightmares no doubt indicate the existence of early traumatic experiences; however, as with Beatrice, such events become all the more meaningful when they occur in a context in which the reciprocal and continuous activity of interlinking processes is already both threatened and threatening.

On the methodological level, though Freud felt it important to 'divert [one's] attention from the dream as a whole [and] to analyze the separate portions of it', the reader will have noticed that in a group situation I prefer to take the opposite approach and consider scenic structure and function as an active whole. This approach enables us to refine our reciprocal participant perception of the dynamics of linking and unlinking as regards communication within the group. Each of us becomes directly involved in whatever the others arouse in us and in what we arouse in them. I shall leave the last word to Beatrice, who expressed this point in her own way: 'Now I feel a bit less disconnected.'

References

Avron, O. (1996) *La Pensée Scénique*. Toulouse: Erès Éditions.

Freud, S. (1900a) *The Interpretation of Dreams. Standard Edition 4/5*. London: Hogarth Press.

Freud, S. (1912b) *The Dynamics of Transference. Standard Edition 12*. London: Hogarth Press.

Freud, S. (1933a [1932]) *New Introductory Lectures on Psycho-Analysis (Lecture 29). Standard Edition 22*. London: Hogarth Press.

Glossary

Paolo Cruciani, Rafaella Girelli and Claudio Neri

Our aim is to offer the reader a useful device. This glossary is made up of entries concerning psychoanalytic theory, group psychotherapy and group psychology. Every entry includes theoretical content and a specific presentation by an author whose name appears in brackets next to the entry heading. We list here the key material to elucidate the concepts. We have also attached an 'Essential bibliography' to each entry.

acting (Marinelli)

The term 'acting' means sudden and impulsive behaviour, a deviation from the usual behaviour patterns and a break in its phenomenological continuity. Psychoanalytic literature distinguishes between 'acting out' (behaviour acted outside the therapeutic setting) and 'acting in' (that acted within the therapeutic setting). The main characteristic of these actions is the unconscious expression of:

- repressed unconscious contents;
- contents of which the subject is not able to build a mental representation or, in other words, to think of them (he therefore 'acts' them).

Marinelli, in her contribution to this work, examines acting in the context of group dreaming, stressing its communication and transformation significance. The author illustrates how determinate group dreams, the 'dual-faced dreams', distinguish themselves as being less symbolic than others, full of corporeity and concrete elements. They are comparable to a collective rite, especially in the sharing process within the group. These characteristics, according to the author, make them a valid therapeutic instrument for groups of patients with somatic and psychosomatic disorders. They lead the group to mental states wherein it becomes

282

possible to deal with the primitive dynamics related to a sense of identity and self-coherence. In order to elaborate these areas, it is necessary, in fact, to go back to their matrix, namely a mental condition in which the physical and the psychic are confused: the protomental state.

See also protomental state

Essential bibliography

Langs, R. (1973–4) *The Technique of Psychoanalytic Psychotherapy*. New York: Aronson.

Laplanche, J. and Pontalis, J.B. (1973) *The Language of Psychoanalysis*. New York: Aronson.

alpha function (Grotstein)

One of the fundamental concepts of Bion's model of mind is that 'the alpha function acts on all sensorial impressions, whatever they might be, and on emotions of every kind that come into the patient's consciousness. If the alpha function's activity has been carried out, alpha-elements are produced. They are stored and answer to the meanings asked by dream thoughts.' The alpha function elaborates all content of both internal and external emotive experience, transforming them into sensorial impressions that, after being placed in the memory, can be useful in building dreams. 'The alpha elements, digested by the alpha function, become suitable to thought operations.'

In his work, Grotstein extensively discusses the importance of dreams in establishing the workings of the psychic life. 'The dream – together with the alpha function that makes it possible – is in the centre of conscious and unconscious operations, on which the orderly thought depends...the dream...is a combination in narrative form of oneiric thoughts, deriving from alpha-element combinations.'

According to Bion's conception, the acting of the alpha function determines the existence itself of an equilibrate mental life, in which the emotive experience enables contact with the external reality.

See also dream-work alpha, contact barrier

Essential bibliography

Bion, W.R. (1961) 'A psycho-analytic theory of thinking.' *International Journal of Psychoanalysis 43*, 306–10.

Bion, W.R. (1963) *Learning from Experience*. London: Heinemann.

collective subject (Neri)

Neri (1998) conceptualises the group, once it has achieved a specific developmental phase, as a collective subject. The group achieves consciousness of itself as a thinking unity, capable of emotional elaboration. This is made possible by repeated affective investment on the part of the members in the process and experiences undergone together. The group thus acquires a shared affective patrimony, a deeply significant story in which every member can identify and recognise him- or herself as part of a whole. This is the moment, moreover, in which the group, acting as a unity, can reveal all its therapeutic potentiality.

Essential bibliography

Neri, C. (1998) *Group*. London: Jessica Kingsley Publishers.

contact barrier (Grotstein)

As Bion (1963) reminds us, Freud, 'to indicate a physiological entity, today known as a synapse' used the expression 'contact barrier'. In this sense he directly refers to a separation between two elements or groups of phenomena that can be consistently impermeable to an exchange or reciprocal influence between them. Bion defines the contact barrier in this same text, referring to the acting of the alpha function, he specifies how the expression 'contact barrier' defines 'the existence of contact between the conscious and unconscious, and the passage of selected elements from one to the other'. Dreams 'that allow us direct access to the study' of the contact barrier 'maintain the privileged position in psychoanalysis assigned them by Freud'.

Grotstein's reading of Bion emphasises the coincidence between the creation of a contact barrier and dream activity that, considering the way the barrier acts, becomes a condition for the separation between the conscious and unconscious, and the subsequent possibility of thinking.

See also alpha function

Essential bibliography

Bion, W.R. (1961) 'A psycho-analytic theory of thinking.' *International Journal of Psychoanalysis 43*, 306–10.
Bion, W.R. (1963) *Learning from Experience*. London: Heinemann.

day's residues (Kaës)

Freud stated that 'the wish represented in dreams is necessarily an infantile wish'. If we consider that dreams are caused by the subject's wishes, and his aim is to fulfill these wishes, even if in a hallucinatory form, and that, moreover, the day's residues (consisting of situations belonging to the state of wake) appear in the manifest dream, we can assert that even if the residues are not enough to form a dream, they become enough the moment they, as recent events, are given meaning by unfulfilled wishes, and activate related unconscious wishes.

Some types of dreams by children, or infantile dreams during adult life are an exception. In these cases, censorship does not intervene because the unconscious wishes are so strong and primary (hunger, thirst) that they don't clash with the subject's defence. Here, manifest content and latent content coincide.

The intervention of the day's residues is simply necessary in all other types of dreams (which make up the majority) in which wishes, searching for fulfilment in the manifest content, undergo the intervention of censorship and have recourse to the day's residues for representation in the consciousness.

The above helps explain how some day's residues (that cannot be properly defined as unfulfilled wishes) finally serve to realise a wish, which is, after all, the aim of dreaming. In fact, every type of daytime thought, even if negative, enters into a relationship with an unconscious infantile wish, which can then be 'transformed' and brought back to consciousness.

See also manifest/latent content

Essential bibliography

Freud, S. (1900) *The Interpretation of Dreams. Standard Edition 4/5*. London: Hogarth Press.

Kaës, R. (1993) *Le groupe et le sujet du groupe. Eléments pour une théorie psychanalytique du groupe*. Paris: Dunod.

Kaës, R. (1994) *La parole et le lien. Processus associatif dans les groupes*. Paris: Dunod.

dream projective identification (Friedman)

The process of integrating split-off emotions may be accomplished through 'dream projective identification'. The dream 'stage director' (Grotstein 1979), an unconscious inner-self agency, can choose the 'right' character to process during the dream hitherto uncontained elements. No dream figure is considered to be an arbitrary choice. He is estimated as being able to contain and work through unbearable emotions. It is as if every dreamer enlists from a collection of 'containers' in his emotional timeless memory one fit to unconsciously cope with difficulties. A similar working-through mechanism is suggested by Palombo (1992). The process of splitting off intolerable dreadful and exciting feelings during the dream and projecting them into a 'not me' dream object in order to be coped with is the dream projective identification.

Essential bibliography

Friedman, R. (1999) 'Dreamtelling as a request for containment in group therapy.' *Funzione Gamma*: www.funzionegamma.edu

Friedman, R. (2000) 'The interpersonal containment of dreams in group psychotherapy: a contribution to the work with dreams in a group.' *Group Analysis 33*, 2, 221–34.

Grotstein, J.S. (1979) 'Who is the dreamer who dreams the dream and who is the dreamer who understands it.' *Contemporary Psychoanalysis 15*, 1.

Palombo, S.R. (1992) 'The eros of dreaming.' *International Journal of Psychoanalysis 73*, 637–46.

dream-work alpha (Grotstein)

Grotstein reminds us that Bion (in a work still unpublished) has also used the expression 'dream-work alpha' to indicate a similar operation, though not identical to what Freud called 'dream-work'.

Grotstein, in the work included in this volume, summarises some essential elements in an attempt to define this concept. 'Dream-work alpha constitutes a mythification of beta elements (evolving 'O') into myth-themes or dream-fantasy narratives utilising a dialectical interchange in the 'position' (P-S←D). Emotional experience must be worked on by alpha function in order to produce dream thoughts for memory and unconscious reflection. Dreams represent the introjection of emotional reality.'

See also alpha function, contact barrier

Essential bibliography

Bion, W.R. (1961) 'A psycho-analytic theory of thinking.' *International Journal of Psychoanalysis 43*, 306–10.

Bion, W.R. (1963) *Learning from Experience.* London: Heinemann.

dual-faced dream (Marinelli)

Marinelli, in her contribution to this book, describes a particular type of dream, the 'dual-faced dream', observed in groups of patients with psychosomatic symptoms. The distinctive characteristic of these dreams is the complete absence of symbolic contents. They represent, however, crucial moments of passage in group life. In fact, they express primitive themes, for example, the dreamer's basic sense of identity. These themes are often at the root of psychosomatic patients' diseases in homogeneous groups. The expression 'dual-faced' refers to their double function: 'On one hand, the function of the dream is the representation that is directed towards the body of the group and its most profound state... On the other hand, we have a situation where the dream's function is to portray and communicate with the outside. Both sides possess an active quality to them that more symbolic dreams do not have.'

empathic closeness (Livingston)

By 'empathic closeness', Livingston, in his chapter, means the attitude the analyst and the group members must maintain towards each other to facilitate the therapeutic progress of each group member and of the group as a whole.

It is very important to approach the subjective experience of each group member emotionally and to be able to return what is felt, so that the subject feels accepted and included in the group.

More specifically, according to Bacal (1998), Livingston thinks that empathic closeness can be obtained through an equilibrate dosage of attitudes of reactivity and responsibility on the part of the group members towards one another, and on the part of the therapist. The first reaction modality supposes a personal reading key of events; the second one comes from the recognition of one's self in relation to the group.

Essential bibliography

Bacal, H.O. (1998) 'Notes on optimal responsiveness in the group process.' In I.N.H. Harwood and M. Pines (ed) *Self Experiences in Group*. London: Jessica Kingsley Publishers.

group as a whole (Schlachet)

The expression 'group as a whole' indicates a particular approach to the group as a unitary aggregate. Bion, Ezriel and Foulkes – each with his own specificity – described this model, focusing on the group as a self-governing entity, irreducible to the sum of its members, with its own phenomenology, and hence a specific object of analysis and treatment.

Neri (1998) explored the peculiarities of the 'active capacities' of the 'group as a whole', speaking about a 'collective subject capable of thinking and emotive elaboration'.

Schlachet seems to be close to this perspective when he considers dreams reported in a group to be a product of the whole group. Here the 'group as a whole' will engage in the associative and/or elaborative analytic work.

See also collective subject

Essential bibliography

Neri, C. (1998) *Group*. London: Jessica Kingsley Publishers.

group culture of embeddedness, group culture of enquiry (Pines)

Pines (1996) pointed out two aspects/typologies of group culture: the culture of embeddedness, and the culture of enquiry. As Pines explains, the first one 'enables each person to develop a strong attachment to the group situation, to the other group members and to the group conductor'; the second 'offers group members the opportunity to investigate the nature of one's own self and those of their group neighbours'.

Essential bibliography

Pfeiffer, G. (1992) 'Complementary cultures in children's psychotherapy groups: conflict, coexistence, and convergence in group development.' *International Journal of Group Psychotherapy 42*, 3, 357–68.

Pines, M. (1996) 'The self as a group. The group as a self.' In I.N.H. Harwood and M. Pines (ed) *Self Experiences in Group*. London: Jessica Kingsley Publishers.

group social matrix (Foulkes)

The concept of 'matrix' is attributed to Foulkes (1964): 'Matrix is the supposed communication and relation texture in a given group. It is the shared common background that ultimately determines the meaning and importance of all events and on which all communications and interpretations, both verbal and non-verbal, are based.' It is important to underline that the global effect of the group social matrix cannot be reduced to the sum of the properties of links among its individuals.

Essential bibliography

Foulkes, S.H. (1964) *Therapeutic Group Analysis*. London: Karnac Books.

Foulkes, S.H. (1973) 'The group as matrix of the individual's mental life.' In L.R. Wolberg and E.K. Schwarz (ed) *Group Therapy 1973: An Overview*. New York: Intercontinental Medical Book Corp.

hallucinatory representations (Avron)

The hallucinatory character of the representations constituting the manifest content of the dream is a central element of the classic theory of dreams.

The dream appears to the dreamer with the same realistic character of external sensorial perceptions as found in hallucinatory phenomena. To explain this, Freud (1900) assumed that, while during the state of wake excitation follows a path across the psychic apparatus from the structures involved in perception to those controlling motility, in the state of sleep, excitation coming from desires which stem from the unconscious proceeds backwards. Using the mnesic traces reprocessed by the dream-work, excitation activates the perceptual system in which the representative content of the dream appears with the vividness of a real perception or of a hallucination. Scenes representing the compromise between desire and censorship (and in the case of the group, the reciprocal bonds among participants) function, in this way, as 'desire hallucinatory fulfilment'.

Essential bibliography

Freud, S. (1900) *The Interpretation of Dreams. Standard Edition 4/5*. London: Hogarth Press.

indigenous peer culture, therapeutic group culture (Pfeifer)

Pfeifer took an interest in the communication system of symbols and meanings constructed spontaneously by every group in its internal interactions, and he deduced important implications for group psychotherapy. He asserted that it is possible in the first phases of a therapeutic group of children and pre-adolescents to distinguish two cultures which become gradually more integrated: first an 'indigenous peer culture', or the system of meanings coming from the children's daily interactive experiences. This system is 'idiomatic' because it is relative to each group member and his/her story. The second is a 'therapeutic group culture', or the system of meanings created by the group in collaboration with the therapist. This system of meanings is relative to the group and points to the group's specific therapeutic objectives. The function of the 'indigenous culture' is to keep the children in the group from the outset of therapy, engaging them in regular activities and a modality of relations, calming down the anxieties common to the treatment situation. The approach Pfeifer recommended to the therapist is to observe and learn that culture so as to facilitate communication with group members and make the therapeutic process as natural and collaborative as possible, accompanied by the gradual construction of the 'therapeutic group culture'.

See also group culture of embeddedness, group culture of enquiry

Essential bibliography

Pfeifer, G. (1992) 'Complementary cultures in children's psychotherapy groups: conflict, coexistence, and convergence, in group development.' *International Journal of Group Psychotherapy 42*, 3, 357–68.

Pines, M. (1996) 'The self as a group. The group as a self.' In I.N.H. Harwood and M. Pines (ed) *Self Experiences in Group*. London: Jessica Kingsley Publishers.

intersubjective bonds (Kaës)

Kaës maintains that the interest in intersubjective bonds arises from the acknowledgement that they are necessary in building our subjectivity.

While in object relations the ego binds itself to an internalised object, in intersubjective bonds the 'other' cannot be considered simply a representation of the subject, but an external 'other' as well, existing apart from what it represents for us.

In an intersubjective bond, we clash with the other who cannot be just a representation or figuration of myself. Object relations can be included in intersubjective bonds but they do not define them.

Essential bibliography

Kaës, R. (1993) *Le groupe et le sujet du groupe. Eléments pour une théorie psychanalytique du groupe.* Paris: Dunod.

Kaës, R. (1994) *La parole et le lien. Processus associatif dans les groupes.* Paris: Dunod.

Large Group (Traveni and Manfredi)

Large Groups are analytically-oriented and formative groups, conducted in both a public and a private context, comprising more than one hundred participants, including the facilitator.

Traveni and Manfredi affirm that the Large Group can be a more suitable context than others for the dream dimension due to its 'destructuring' properties in relation to the thoughts of the individual: 'when participating in a Large Group, one has the confusing sensation of being immersed in a dreamlike atmosphere, in which there is a feeling of having lost one's own boundaries, in which one feels invaded by other people's thoughts'. It is just this loss of boundaries that permits an enlargement of perspective and a different, wider comprehension of reality:

> The Large Group is often a good 'spinner' of dreams, with contents that overstep the dimension of the individual, permitting access to a more collective level, represented by icons that reproduce realities drawn from the external collective, in the current social and intrapsychic fragmentation. Threads are interwoven between the inside and outside which, by establishing a connection between the echoes of the story of the individuals, also promote a clearer vision of what is happening in the reality of everyday life.

Essential bibliography

Kreeger, L. (ed) (1975) *The Large Group: Dynamics and Therapy.* London: Constable.

loss of identity (Traveni and Manfredi)

Traveni and Manfredi in their contribution mention a (temporary) loss of identity. The expression 'loss of identity' means a state of loss of boundaries of the self, a sensation of feeling extraneous regarding oneself and one's own body.

In cases of decidedly pathological manifestations (for example in psychosis and/or in splitting disorders) the phenomenon manifests itself with a degree of persistence and seriousness, negatively influencing social/working functions.

Traveni and Manfredi emphasise how the condition of temporary loss of identity in the Large Group facilitates the activation of a less structured thought form, permitting a vision of reality enriched by new perspectives: 'The Large Group can therefore really become the place where one learns each time from experience, on condition of acceptance of working by groups inside and outside oneself.'

Essential bibliography

Gaburri, E. (1986) 'Disturbi del pensiero e identità tra l'individuo e il gruppo.' *Gruppo e Funzione Analitica* 7, 2, 111–21.

Neri, C. (1998) *Group.* London: Jessica Kingsley Publishers.

manifest/latent dream (Resnik)

In *The Interpretation of Dreams,* Freud introduces the distinction between the manifest and latent content of dreams. The first corresponds to the dream report made by the dreamer; the second corresponds to the one reconstructed through the work of psychoanalytic interpretation. The content reported by the subject results from what Freud defines as 'dream-work', consisting of two blocks of psychic operations:

1. production of dream thoughts;

2. their transformation into 'acceptable' (then 'referable') contents by the consciousness.

All this is based on dream theory: the meaning of every dream is the fulfilment of a repressed infantile desire.

Essential bibliography

Freud, S. (1900) *The Interpretation of Dreams. Standard Edition 4/5*. London: Hogarth Press.
Laplanche, J. and Pontalis, J.B. (1973) *The Language of Psychoanalysis*. New York: Aronson.

metaphor (Schlachet)

The term derives from Greek and literally means 'transfer'. Actually, the use of metaphor permits the expression of potential meanings through an image connected to a certain concept, but neither directly nor usually explicitly.

From a clinical point of view, the metaphor can be an effective means of communication between analyst and patient about certain contents, temporarily inexpressible in explicit terms.

Schlachet, in his contribution to this work, underlines the metaphoric character of dream group language, emphasising, in particular, the variety of meanings that can be explored starting from the association made by the group on one member's dream when it becomes a metaphor for the whole group.

oneiromancy (Resnik)

The term, as commonly used, indicates divination through dreams.

According to Freud, some dreams can contain a diagnosis of some unhealthy processes that cannot be noticed during wakefulness. In addition, some tendencies or deep personality conflicts are revealed by dreams. During sleep, because interest is totally addressed to one's own person, some premonitory signs (unobservable during the state of wake) are introduced in dreams.

playspace (Livingston)

Livingston uses the term 'playspace' in self psychology-oriented group psychotherapy, a translation of the German *Spielraum*. This term indicates an atmosphere that facilitates the therapeutic progress of both the members and the group as a whole.

The relational attitude promoting this atmosphere is similar to the attitude between mother and child described by Winnicott, referring to 'transitional phenomena'. The child can experience a neutral space (the first separation between self and not-self) where he/she will neither experience the clearly 'external' nor 'internal' origins of the object (transitional object).

In our case, the 'playspace' atmosphere relates to the analyst's attitude in listening to the dreams within the group: he will not search for symbols to interpret, but will find an 'empathic closeness' in accordance with the subjective experience of each group member. This concept is in line with the self psychology approach to group dreams: they contain relational conflicts between self and self-object. Relationships within the group can represent a useful opportunity for each member to 'restore self-object relations'.

See also empathic closeness, self-object

Essential bibliography

Laplanche, J. and Pontalis, J.B. (1973) *The Language of Psychoanalysis.* New York: Aronson.

Winnicott, D.W. (1965) *The Maturational Processes and the Facilitating Environment.* London: Hogarth Press.

primal scene (Marinelli)

Freud initially introduced the expression 'primal scene' in his work as a generic term to indicate fantasies connectable to infantile traumas. It assumes the specific meaning of the image of parental coitus in the Wolf-man case.

Marinelli emphasises that a characteristic of the 'primal scene', a 'strong emotional impression', starting from the subjective experience of the members, is present during the establishment of the group. The author further describes how the 'dual-faced dreams' will later recall that atmosphere typical of the group's origins more than other group dreams.

See also acting, dual-faced dreams

Essential bibliography

Laplanche, J. and Pontalis, J.B. (1973) *The Language of Psychoanalysis.* New York: Aronson.

protomental state (Marinelli)

The protomental state, as described by Bion, is characterised by a lack of distinction between the psychic and the somatic.

Marinelli mentions the protomental state to designate that particular condition of non-differentiation within the group that enables the initial circulation and subsequent elaboration of emotions connected to the primitive dynamics at the root of psychosomatic disorders in group patients.

Essential bibliography

Bion, W.R. (1961) *Experiences in Groups and other Papers.* London: Tavistock Publications.

scenic exposition of the dream (Avron)

As in the classic conception, the dreamer is concomitantly the creator and the spectator of the scenic exposition of the dream. However, in the model proposed by Avron this condition is shared with other members of the group.

The scenic organisations are created by the contemporaneous action of an intrapsychic activity determined by the mental energy of sexual desires occurring in the individual mind, and an interpsychic activity going on between the participants. The dynamic energy involved in the bonding process or in the process of breaking bonds starts this interpsychic activity. In the group, the nature of the 'scenic' or 'dramatic' expression assumed by these activities springs from the conflict between individual desires and the energy involved in the bonds established among participants.

This conflict creates a type of compromise, both conscious and unconscious, adding to the conflict considered in the classic theory of individual dreaming between present desires in the latent content and censorship. This compromise takes place, however, between the search for the fulfilment of individual desires and the maintenance in the group of shared affective bonds.

Essential bibliography
Avron, O. (1966) *La Pensée Scénique*. Toulouse: Erès Éditions.

self-object (Kohut)

In self psychology-oriented literature, the term 'self-object' refers not to an object, a differentiated 'other', but to the function other individuals can take on in relation to the subject (his/her self).

The self-object is deputed to fulfil the fundamental developmental needs in growing a sane and integrated self. Kohut (1971, 1984) defines three types of self-objects: namely mirror self-object, ideal self-object, and twin (or alter-ego) self-object. According to self psychology, self-object needs last throughout life.

Essential bibliography
Kohut, H. (1971) *The Analysis of the Self*. London: Hogarth Press.
Kohut, H. (1984) *How Does Analysis Cure?* Chicago: Chicago University Press.
Neri, C. (1998) *Group*. London: Jessica Kingsley Publishers.

self-object restoring relations (Livingston)

From a self psychology perspective, the self grows in a pathologic way (fragmented and not coherent) in the case of failed fulfilment of self-object needs (mirror, ideal and twin) during the evolutive age. However, later experience of relationships with adequate self-objects is possible.

In the group setting, it is possible to experience new self-object relationships either among members, or between each member and the group as a whole. These relationships take on a therapeutic function, enabling the individual to experience and internalise a more responsive relational attitude.

See also self-object

Essential bibliography

Harwood, I.N.H. (1992) 'Advances in group psychotherapy and self-psychology: an intersubjective approach.' In I.N.H. Harwood and M. Pines (eds) *Self Experiences in Group.* London: Jessica Kingsley Publishers.

Neri, C. (1998) *Group.* London: Jessica Kingsley Publishers.

Segalla, R.A. (1998) 'Motivational systems and group object theory: implications for group therapy.' In I.N.H. Harwood and M. Pines (eds) *Self Experiences in Group.* London: Jessica Kingsley Publishers.

self-state dreams (Livingston)

Livingston employs the term 'self-state dream' to explain the self psychology approach to group dreams derived from this concept.

This term implies a dream typology not characterised by latent contents (to be revealed), but a kind of dream that represents a dreamer's fragmented self-state.

The self psychology approach to dreams is characterised by two features:

1. The analyst's task is not to reveal repressed contents/desires (through dream symbols interpretation), but to enlarge the possibility of expressing and thinking manifest dream contents (also rich in significance).

2. In addition, when the dream topic is conflictual, and therefore in need of interpretative work, the interpretation focus is still the whole of conflicts between self and self-objects.

Essential bibliography

Kohut, H. (1977) *The Restoration of the Self.* New York: International University Press.

social dreaming matrix (Lawrence and Biran)

Lawrence and Biran propose an innovative approach in this book to group work on dreams. They highlight the social character and content of the dream, rather than the individual one (evidenced by Freud's classical approach to dream). The specific setting of which a social interpretation key to dream is offered is the social dreaming matrix (SDM). SDM can include about 40 people and have from one to four conductors.

The psychoanalytic-oriented therapeutic group (TG) can include a maximum of ten people and be conducted by one or two therapists.

The aim of this contribution is to propose an integration between the two approaches, starting from the differences clearly expressed by the respective settings.

The therapeutic dream (TG)	The social dream (SDM)
Thr dreamer is central	The dream is central
The individual aspect	The social aspect
Profound exploration of the past	Looking to the future
Dramatising the personal biography	Facing life as a tragedy
Oedipus	Sphinx
Egocentric	Sociocentric
Finite	Infinite

sphinx (Lawrence and Biran)

As a proper noun, 'Sphinx' in the ancient mythology of the Middle-Eastern Mediterranean Sea indicates a monstrous creature with the body of a lion and a human head. The Greek myth tells us that near Thebes the Sphinx, from atop a cliff, posed a very difficult enigma to every approaching wayfarer, and killed those who did not solve it. Oedipus, according to the myth, was the only one who succeeded in this undertaking.

Lawrence and Biran, discussing their (social) approach to group dreams, utilise the Sphinx myth to describe the most appropriate mental attitude with which to approach them: opening up towards the unknown and the possible, towards listening to what the dream can reveal about every individual's fears about the future.

Francesco Corrao (1971) explained Bion's attribution of the Sphinx myth to the mental attitude towards knowledge typical of the group: 'Recalling a powerful mythological suggestion, Bion indicates the Oedipus symbol for individual analysis, and the Sphinx symbol for group therapy, a figure still deeply 'enigmatic' proposing *ab aeterno* the challenge to knowledge and death' (p.10).

See also social group matrix

Essential bibliography

Bion, W.R. (1961) *Experiences in Groups and other Papers.* London: Tavistock Publications.

Corrao, F. and Muscetta, S. (1971) 'Introduction to the Italian edition.' In W.R. Bion, *Esperienze nei gruppi.* Rome: Armando.

stimulation and receptivity (Avron)

As Avron specifies in her paper included in this work: 'All the participants [in a group] involuntarily work as sources of energy with a double polarity swinging from stimulation to receptivity, according to their reciprocal relations. Collective circuits are created in a constantly unstable balance relative to the produced stimulus/receptivity dimensions… Every time either manic overstimulation or passivity becomes dominant, it inspires some reactions at the individual level.' The activation of this double polarity constitutes some energy interdependencies among the group members, which also involve the investment of shared creations, like dreams and fantasies. The forms of collective communication and cooperation are made possible only by the unconscious energetic exchanges.

Essential bibliography

Avron, O. (1966) *La Pensée Scénique.* Toulouse: Erès Éditions.

unconscious alliances (Kaës)

Kaës underlines the existence of 'defensive organisations' inside group functions, supporting the defence mechanisms of individual group members when determinate anxieties arise.

When a group psychic reality is achieved within a group, the processes involved (like repression, rejection, shared ideals, leadership attribution etc.) also benefit the single member.

These processes form unconscious alliances. An unconscious alliance is an 'intersubjective psychic formation', aimed at benefiting every individual and the psychic life of every member included in this intersubjective reality.

See also intersubjective bonds, collective subject

Essential bibliography

Kaës, R. (1993) *Le groupe et le sujet du groupe. Eléments pour une théorie psychanalytique du groupe.* Paris: Dunod.

Kaës, R. (1994) *La parole et le lien. Processus associatif dans les groupes.* Paris: Dunod.

The Contributors

Ophélia Avron is a practising psychoanalyst and Member of the Paris Psycho-Analytical Society (SPP). A former President of the French Society for Group Psycho-Analytical Psychotherapy, she is also a Senior Lecturer in the University of Paris-VII. From 1980 to 1988 she was Director of the Institute for Clinical Psychopathology, which forms part of the University of Paris-VII and provides ongoing training for clinical psychologists.

Hanna Biran is a clinical psychologist and organisational consultant. She is a Lecturer on group psychotherapy at the Tel-Aviv University, School of Medicine. She is a Founding Member of the Innovation and Change in Society (ICS) foundation (founded in 1987). Hanna Biran is also a Member of Tel-Aviv Institute of Contemporary Psychoanalysis and a Member of The Israeli Institute of Group Analysis.

Paolo Cruciani is an Associate Member of the Italian Psychoanalytic Association and International Psychoanalytical Association. He teaches theory and techniques of group dynamics at the Faculty of Psychology, University of Rome 'La Sapienza' and tutors at the Specialization School in Clinical Psychology, University of Rome 'La Sapienza'. Paolo Cruciani is also a professional conductor of therapeutic groups and trains groups in various public and private institutions.

Robi Friedman is a senior clinical psychologist in private practice, teaches individual and group psychotherapy at Haifa University (Israel) and Technion, and supervises in the Carmel Institute for Groups. He is co-Founder of the Israel Institute for Group Analysis and former Head of Technion's Psychological Services. His special interest lies in groups centred in dreams and supervision.

Raffaella Girelli holds a degree in psychology from the University of Rome 'La Sapienza' with a focus in the area of theory and techniques of group dynamics and is currently specialising in clinical psychology. She also serves as a consultant for corporate and institutional organisations in projects focused on the analysis of group dynamics. She is co-author of articles on group dynamics.

James S. Grotstein is Clinical Professor of Psychiatry at the UCLA School of Medicine and a training and supervising analyst at the Los Angeles Psychoanalytic Institute and the Psychoanalytic Center of California, Los Angeles. He is the author of over two hundred published articles and eight books. His most recently published book is *Who Is the Dreamer Who Dreams the Dream?: A Study of Psychic Presences* (Analytic Press, 2000).

Irene Harwood is a psychoanalyst at the Southern California Psychoanalytic Institute where she teaches self psychology and group analysis from an intersubjective perspective. She is the co-Founder of the Society for the Study of the Self and consults and practices cross-culturally in English, Spanish and Russian. She is the co-Editor of *Self-Experiences in Group: Intersubjective and Self Psychological Pathways to Human Understanding.*

René Kaës, psychoanalyst, is an Associate Member of the Psychoanalytical Organisation Quatrième Groupe, Professor Emèritus at the University Lumière Lyon 2, Member of the International Association of Group Psychotherapy and of the French Society of Group Psychoanalytical Psychotherapy, he is also a Founding Member of the European Association of Group Transcultural Analyse and Past President of the French Studies Circle for the Formation and Active Research in Psychology (CEFFRAP). His special research interests lie in psychoanalytical group, in relation to analytical cure, institutions, transmission of psychic life and traumatism.

Peretz Lavie graduated from the Department of Psychology and Neurosciences at the University of Florida in 1973. After completing postgraduate training at the University of California, San Diego, he joined the Faculty of Medicine in the Technion where he established the Technion Sleep Laboratory. From 1993 to 1999 he served as the Dean of the Faculty of Medicine and he is currently the Technion Vice President for Resource Development. He has published over three hundred papers and five books on sleep and sleep disorders. His book *The Enchanted World of Sleep*, originally published in Hebrew, was translated into sixteen languages.

W. Gordon Lawrence discovered the Social Dreaming Matrix in 1982 while on the staff of the Tavistock Institute. He is now a visiting Professor at Cranfield University and The New Bulgarian University. His most recent books are *Social Dreaming @ Work* and *Tongued With Fire* (Karnac Books).

Martin S. Livingston is the Director of the Group Therapy Department at the Postgraduate Center for Mental Health and the author of *Vulnerable Moments: Deepening the Therapeutic Process*, published by Jason Aronson. He is also part of the faculty of the Training and Research Institute for Self Psychology and the Training Institute for Mental Health and is the Editor of *GROUP*.

Monica Manfredi, M.D., is a specialist in obstetrics and gynaecology. She is a Member of the Association for Research and Training in Individual and Group Psychotherapy and Institutional Analysis and of the IAGP and is attached to the University of Psychology, Turin, as a member of a group for Clinical Applied Research.

Stefania Marinelli is an Associate Professor in clinical psychology and Founder and President of the Association for Research on Homogeneous Groups (ARGO). She is a training analyst at the Italian Institute for Group Psychoanalysis (IIGP) and works in private practice both as a psychoanalyst and group psychoanalyst. Consultant to the National Health System and to several hospitals for the training of health professionals, she is also Editor-in-Chief of the electronic journal *Funzione Gamma*, published in both Italian and English.

Claudio Neri, M.D., has been deeply involved in group psychotherapy from the beginning of his career. His meeting with Wilfred R. Bion and contacts with his work have been of paramount importance for him in the development of personal ideas which are synthesised in the book *Group*, published by Jessica Kingsley Publishers, 1998.

Malcolm Pines is a Founder Member of the Institute of Group Analysis, London, Past President of the International Association of Group Psychotherapy and former consultant at Cassel, St George's and Maudsley Hospitals and the Tavistock Clinic. He is the Past President of the Group-Analytic Society and is the Editor of the *International Library of Group Analysis* series and author of *Circular Reflections: Selected Papers on Group Analysis and Psychoanalysis*, published by Jessica Kingsley Publishers.

Janine Puget, M.D., is a Full Member of the Asociación Psicolanalítica de Buenos Aires (APdeBA) and AAPPdeG and teaches in both institutions. She is the author of *Psychoanalysis and State Violence, El grupo y sus configuraciones, Psicoanálisis de la Pareja Matrimonial, Lo Vincular*, and has written extensively in Argentina, France and Italy, and has participated in several national and international conferences.

Salomon Resnik is a Member of the International Psychoanalytic Association. After his psychiatric training in Argentina, he left for London in 1958 and worked with Melanie Klein, underwent analysis with Herbert Rosenfeld and was supervised by Bion and Esther Bick. Visiting Professor at the Medical School of the Catholic University of Rome, he practises psychoanalysis in Paris and Venice and has worked with groups of chronic psychotic patients for several years. He is the author of *The Theatre of the Dream*, Tavistock Publications, 1987; *Mental Space*, Karnac Books, 1990; *The Delusional Person*, Karnac Books, 2001; and many other publications in Italian and French.

Cecil A. Rice, Ph.D., is President and co-Founder of the Boston Institute for Psychotherapy, Associate Editor of the *International Journal for Group Psychotherapy*, co-Founder of the Boston-Threshold Group (Northern Ireland Group Psychotherapy Conference), co-investigator The Troubled Mind Project Northern Ireland, Past President of the Northeastern Society for Group Psychotherapy. Recent publications include 'Group Therapists, Poets and Other Artists: Reflections on God, the Devil and Projective Identification.' (*International Journal of Group Psychotherapy 48*, 1); with J. Scott Rutan 'Personality disorders: Group psychotherapy as a treatment of choice' (*Journal of Psychotherapy in Independent Practice 1*, 2); and with R. Kapur (in press) 'The Impact of the 'Troubles' on Therapy Groups in Northern Ireland' (*Group*).

J. Scott Rutan, Ph.D., is Past President and a Distinguished Fellow of the American Group Psychotherapy Association. He is senior faculty and co-Founder of the Boston Institute for Psychotherapy, as well as Founder of the Center for Group Psychotherapy at the Massachusetts General Hospital in Boston. He has authored and co-authored a great many articles and books on various aspects of group psychotherapy.

Peter J. Schlachet (deceased) was a clinical psychologist, psychoanalytic psychotherapist, editor and teacher. He trained in analytical group therapy at the Postgraduate Center for Mental Health (New York), where later he was a senior supervisor and valued teacher. He was Editor of *Group* for ten years and President of the Eastern Group Psychotherapy Society. A prolific author of many papers on theory and practice, a passionate thinker in the field of group analysis, his untimely death is a loss to our discipline.

Marion Solomon, Ph.D., is a research analyst at the American Academy of Psychoanalysis. She is a Fellow of the American Group Psychotherapy Association and a Member of the American Psychological Association, Division of Psychoanalysis. She is a Professor at the American Behavioral Studies Institute and is senior faculty at UCLA, Department of Humanities, Sciences and Social Sciences, Extension Division. She is Founder of the Lifespan Learning Institute, dedicated to advanced training and application of research in individual, group and family therapy and is author of *Narcissism and Intimacy: Love and Marriage in an Age of Confusion* (WW Norton), *Lean on Me: The Power of Positive Dependency in Intimate Relationships* (Simon and Schuster); co-author of *Short Term Therapy For Long Term Change* (WW Norton); co-editor of *The Borderline Patient* (Analytic Press) and *Countertransference in Couples Therapy* (WW Norton).

Anna Maria Traveni is a psychotherapist, group analyst and long-standing co-Director of the Italian NHS Mental Health Services. She is a Founding Member, previous Chairman and current Cultural Director of the APRAGI and of the Accademia Sogno; she lectures at the COIRAG Training Institute, is co-Director of the Italian Group Analysis magazine and is a full member of the GAS and member of the IAGP.

Marianna Tseberlidou is a natural scientist, a psychodramatist sociotherapist and a family therapist. At present she works as an environmental education supervisor.

Ioannis K. Tsegos is a psychiatrist, group analyst and Director of the Training and Research Department of the Open Psychotherapy Centre, Athens. He is a graduate and a Member of the Institute of Group Analysis (London), Founder of the Institute of Group Analysis (Athens) and the European Group-Analytic Training Institutions Network and is the President of the Group Analytic Society of Greece.

Subject Index

Author Index